DEDICATION

For those who are committed to the power of art.
They make us think, feel, and change us.
They help us imagine a better world.

Dutch Golden Age

It is a time when economics, culture, and artistic prosperity in the 17th-century Dutch Republic history. This period was when it continued to influence Dutch society and the world, achieving significant achievements and development in various fields. At this time, the Netherlands formed the state's identity and left traces that could not be erased in art, trade, science, and social values. During the Dutch golden age, the Dutch Republic has become the world's most powerful country thanks to its economically very successful and extensive trade network. Dutch merchants dominated the international trade routes to build colonies and accumulate enormous wealth. This economic success led to the emergence of prosperous middle-class injuries and the emergence of high-quality consumer culture.

There was also a remarkable achievement in art, literature, science, and philosophy. Among them, famous artists such as Rembrandt Van Rijn, Johannes Vermeer, and France Hals have flourished in the art field. In this era, scientifically advanced progress was made, including optics, map production, and innovative development of natural philosophy.

Socially, religious freedom was relatively guaranteed, and intellectuals, artists, and merchants with various backgrounds gathered. The Dutch Republic became the center of intellectual and cultural exchanges, creating an atmosphere where innovation and creativity were recognized. Political change continued. The Dutch people established democratic governments and believed that state leaders should be determined by the choice of the people. This democratic tradition has made the Netherlands a stable and prosperous society. The Dutch golden age also left a continuous archi-tectural heritage along with symbolic canal houses, magnificent public buildings, and urban planning projects that changed the city landscape. Amsterdam's canals, which are listed as UNESCO World Heritage Sites, are typical examples.

Still Life of the Dutch Golden Age

During the 17th-century Dutch golden age, the Netherlands experienced an unprecedented economic and cultural boom. In this era, prosperity, trade, and the middle class increased, resulting in great changes in art, including still life. Still life, which emerged with a clear genre, gained tremendous popularity in the Dutch golden age. Still life was evidence of the wealth, beauty and sophistication of the time. Still life often depicted various objects such as flowers, fruits, food, dishes, and luxury goods as carefully arranged compositions. The still life of the Dutch golden age, featuring meticulous details, vivid colors, and amazing realism, commemorated the wealth and prosperity of the times. Still life created a deep and vivid presence by using the colorful expressions of things, the meticulous details of the texture, and the light and shadow.

The work of the early Dutch golden age plays an important role in symbolism symbolizing wealth. Fruits and flowers symbolize wealth and fertility, and luxurious objects such as silver products and glass products represent rich and refinement. These motifs captivate the viewer's attention and argue with longing for the material abundance and aesthetic pleasures of the time. The still life of the Dutch golden age is often realistic and characterized by attentive observation of nature. Artists used precise techniques to describe texture, reflection, and subtle details to express them almost real.

This feature of the Dutch golden age still life commemorated the wealth, prosperity, and aesthetics of Dutch society, reflecting the cultural, economic, and artistic atmosphere of the time.

Artists & Paintings

Jan Davidsz. de Heem

1606 - 1684

Jan Davidsz. de Heem is a Dutch painter famous for his exquisite still life works such as flower arrangements, fruits and banquet scenes. Born in Utrecht, the Netherlands, it is one of the most famous still life of the Dutch golden age. de Heem began to build his career as an artist under his father, David de Heem. He then moved to Leiden and became a member of the Guild of Saint Luke*. In the early works of de Heem, the influence of his father's style, which features precise details and understated colors, is revealed.

In the 1630s, de Heem moved to Antwerp, Belgium, the center of art activities at the time. There he had great success and developed his unique mature style. The painting of de Heem of this period shows the use of rich colors, highly stylish techniques, and meticulous details.

In the still life of de Heem, works that have been elaborately arranged with flowers, fruits, insects and other objects have appeared. He was good at expressing depth and realism by using light, shadow, and meticulously rendered texture. His work showed an excellent ability to capture the delicate transparency of the petals, the shiny surface of the fruit, and the glitter of light in the glass bowl. The work of de Heem was highly appreciated for his technical skills, sophisticated aesthetics, and symbolic characteristics. His painting often delivers wealth and vanitas* messages.

As a still life painter, the legacy of Jan Davidsz. de Heem is continuously commemorated. His work can be found in famous museums and collections around the world, including the Louvre Museum in Paris, the National Museum of the Netherlands in Amsterdam, and the National Gallery in London.

Guild of Saint Luke
Professional organizations or guilds in cities in the lowlands such as Antwerp, Amsterdam, and Haarlem In the Renaissance and Baroque eras. As a professional and regulatory organization, it established quality standards, protects members' interests, maintained monopoly rights for specific art activities, and played an important role in the development and promotion of the Dutch golden age.

Vanitas
A word derived from Latin, which means 'vanity'. In art, in general, it implies that human life is fleeting. In relevant works, symbolic objects such as skulls, watches, flowers, and fruits appear.

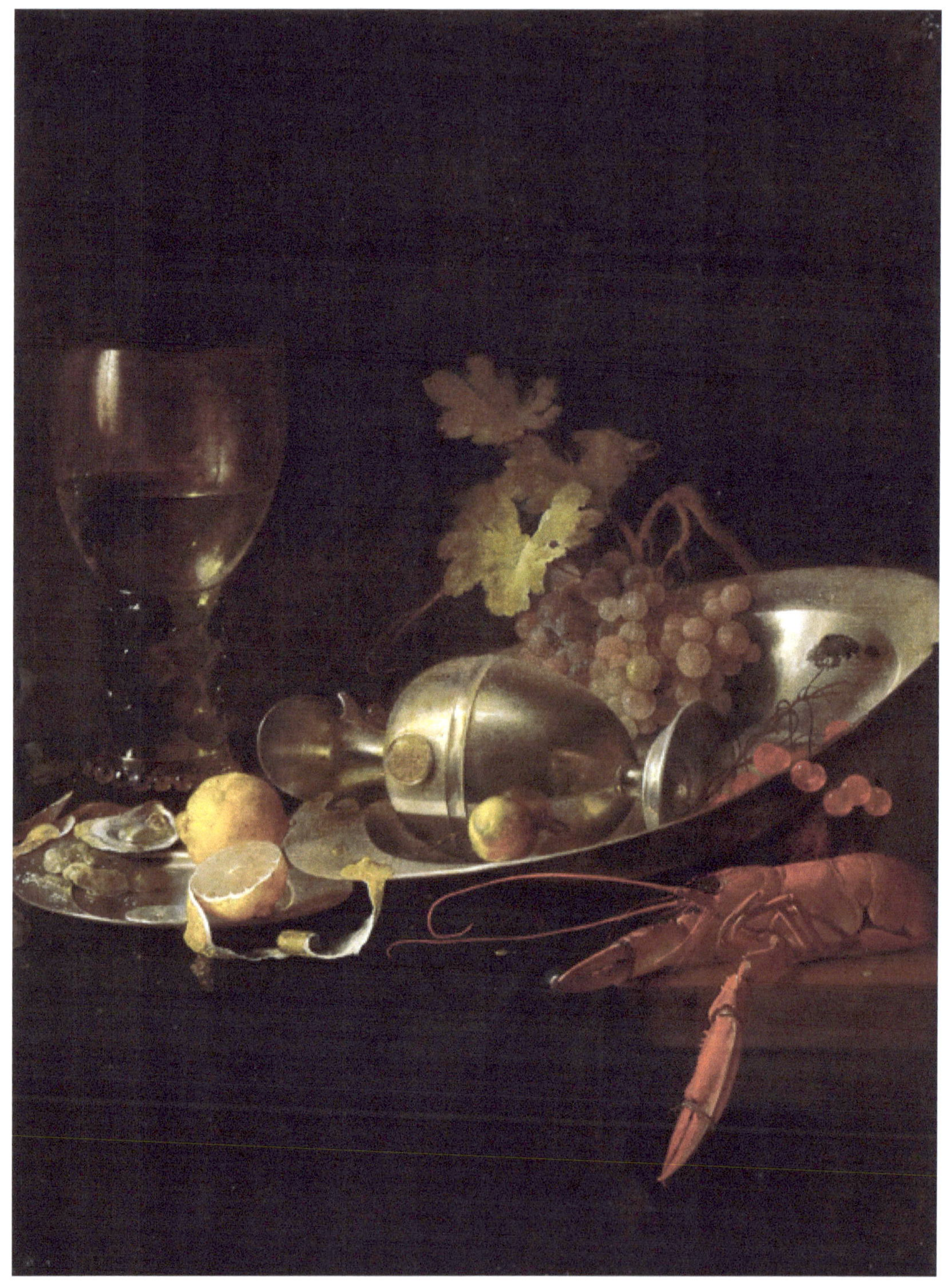

Breakfast with a Lobster, c.1630

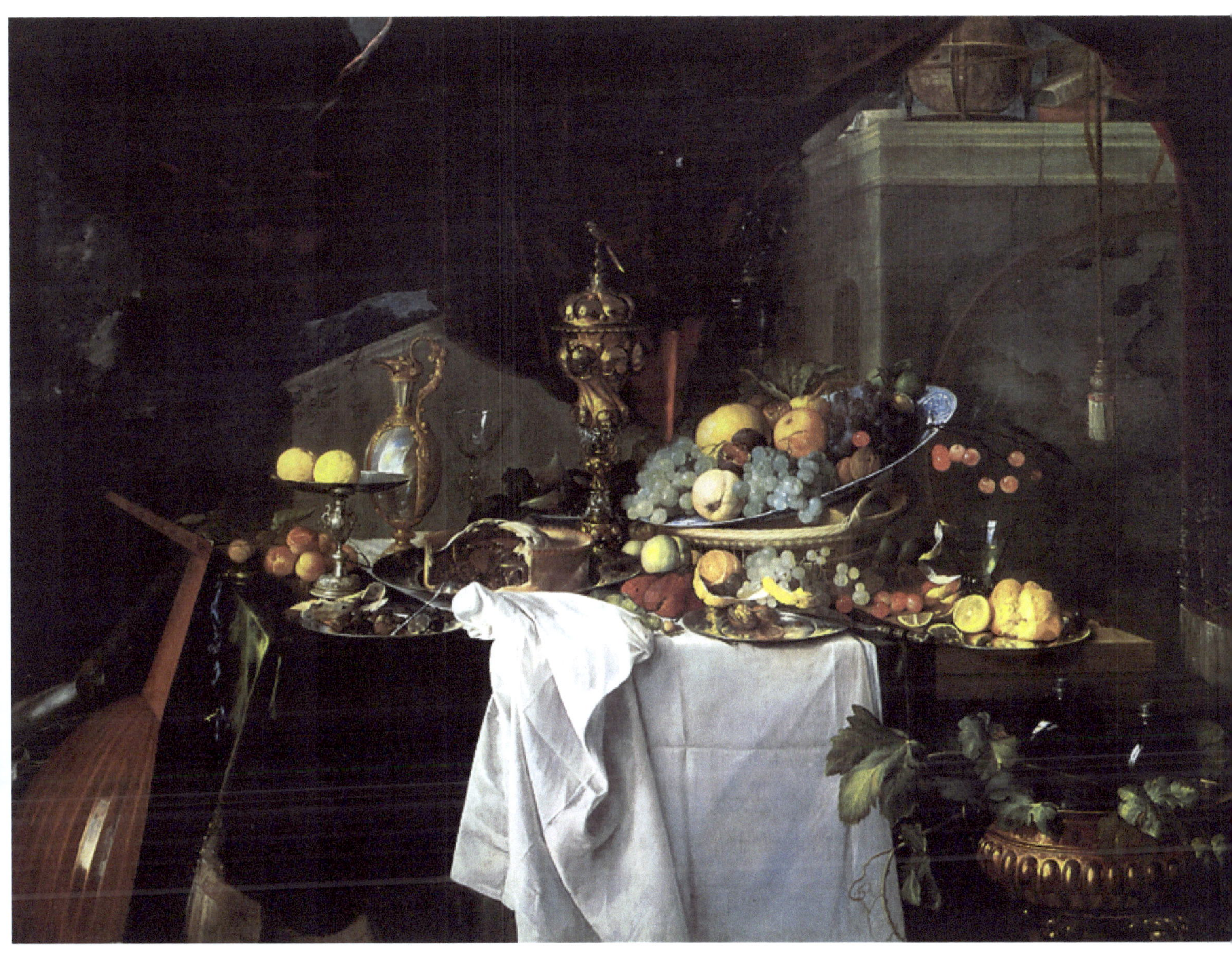

Dessert, 1640   149 x 203 cm

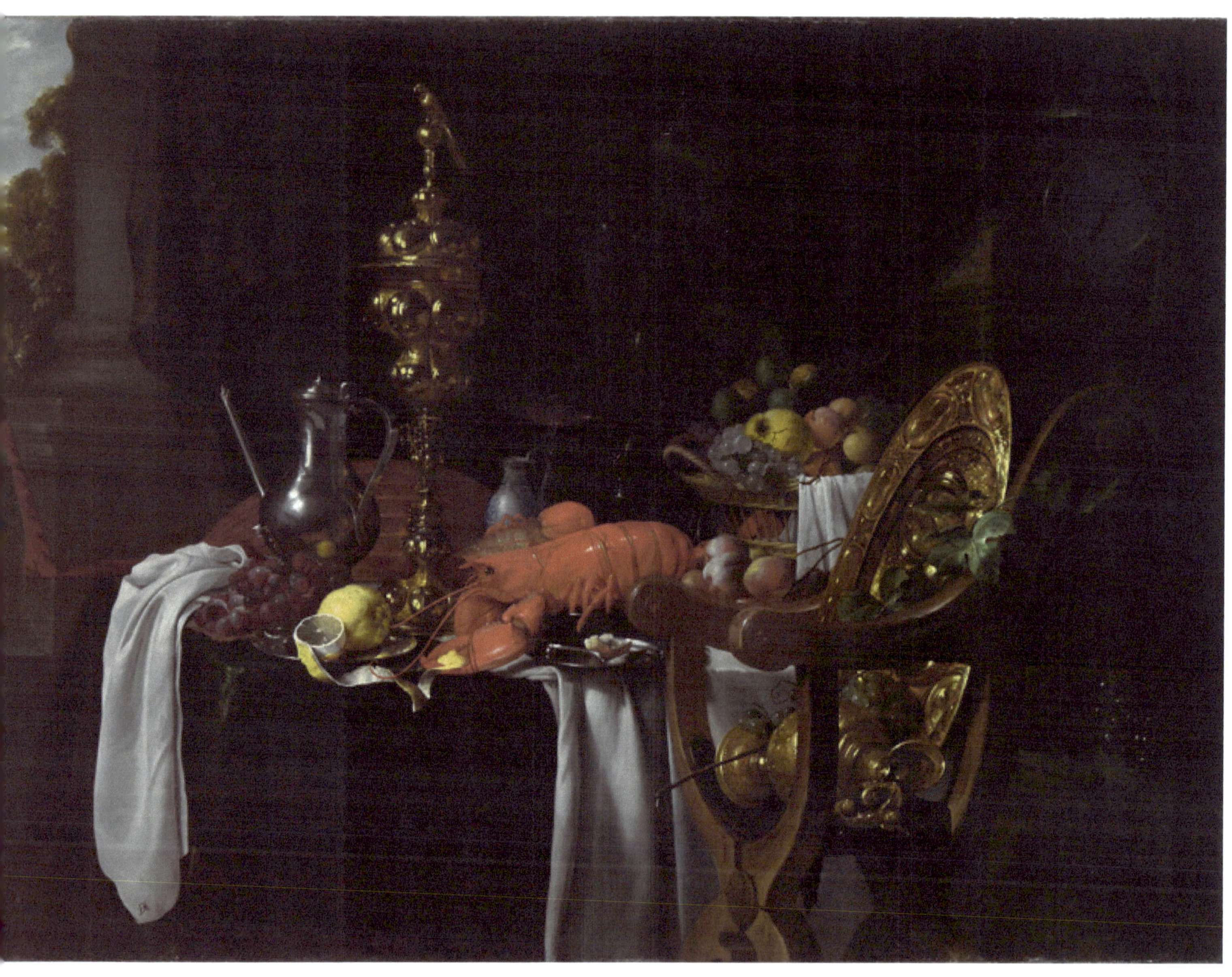

Feast, 17th century   135.3 x 185.4 cm

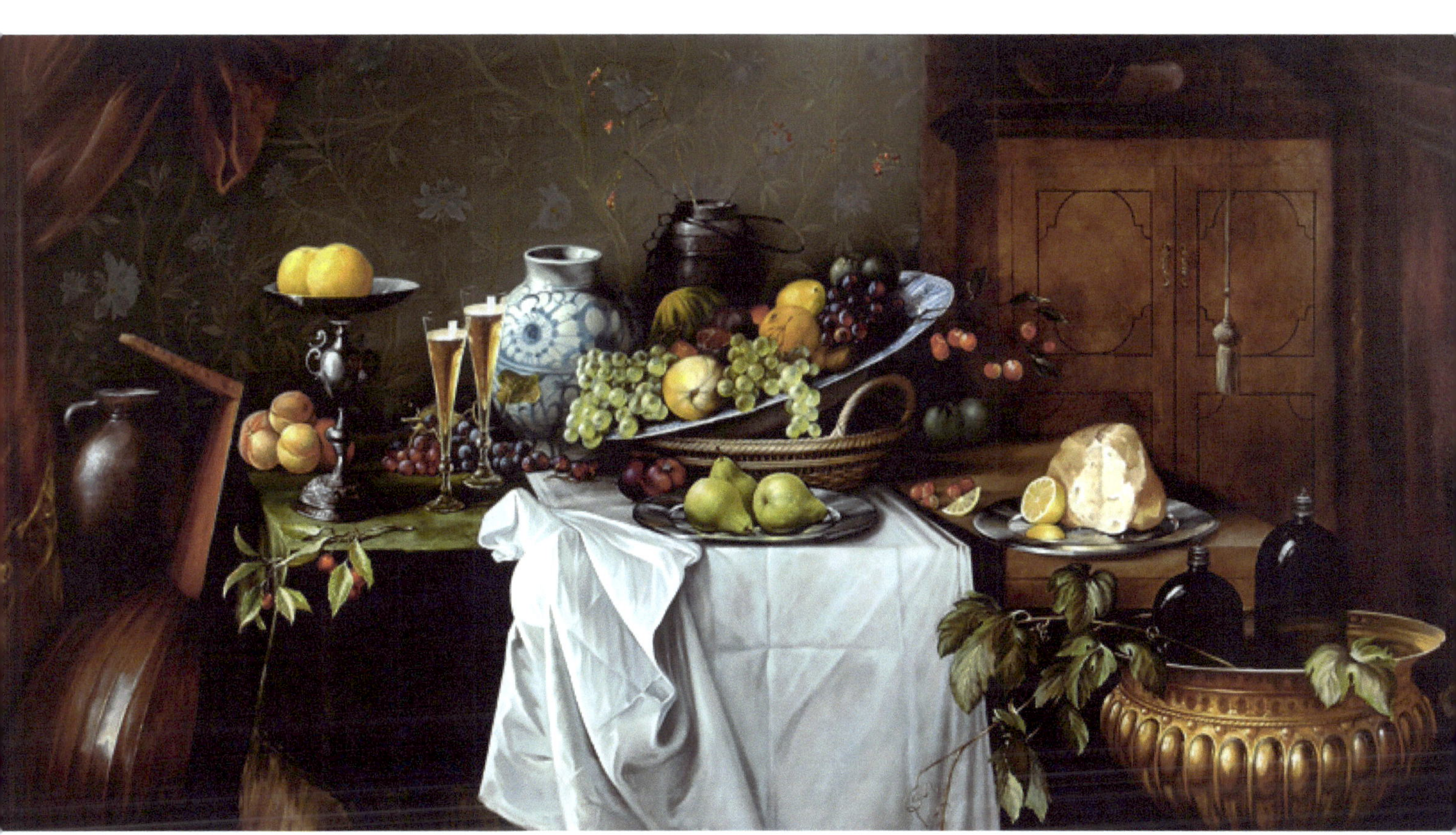

Still life with dessert

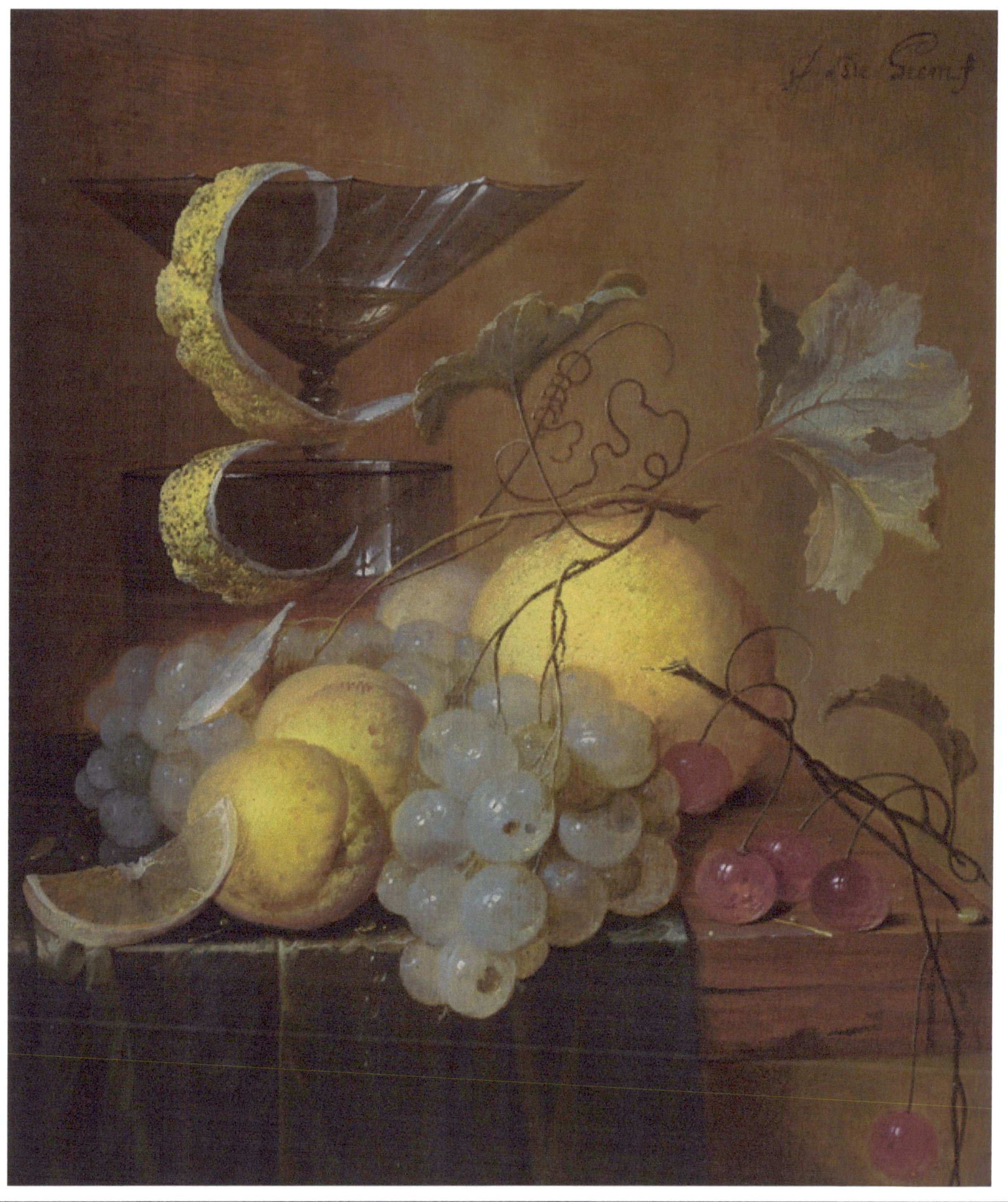

Still life with fruit and a jug of Wine

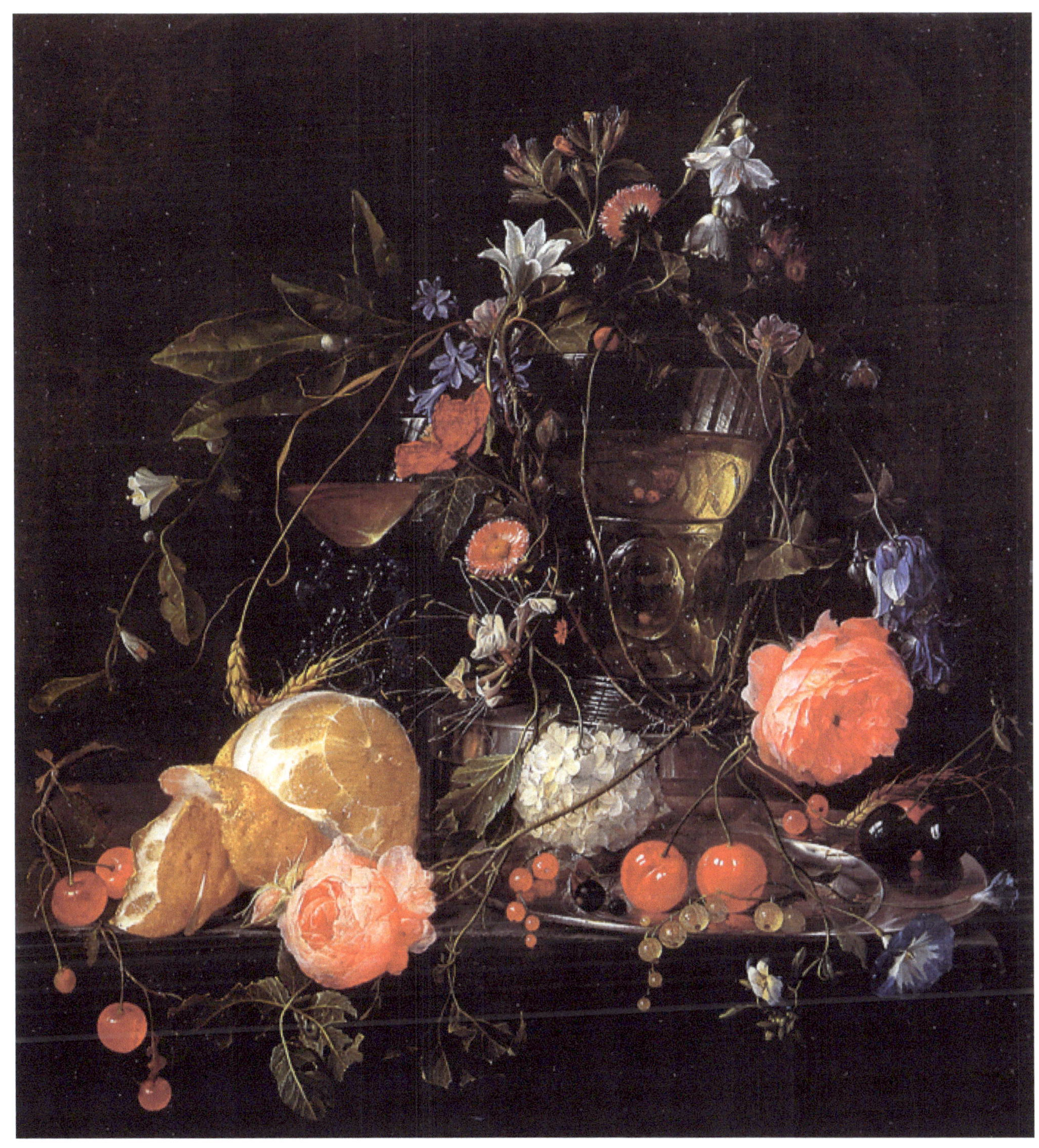

Still life with fruit and a jug of Wine 2

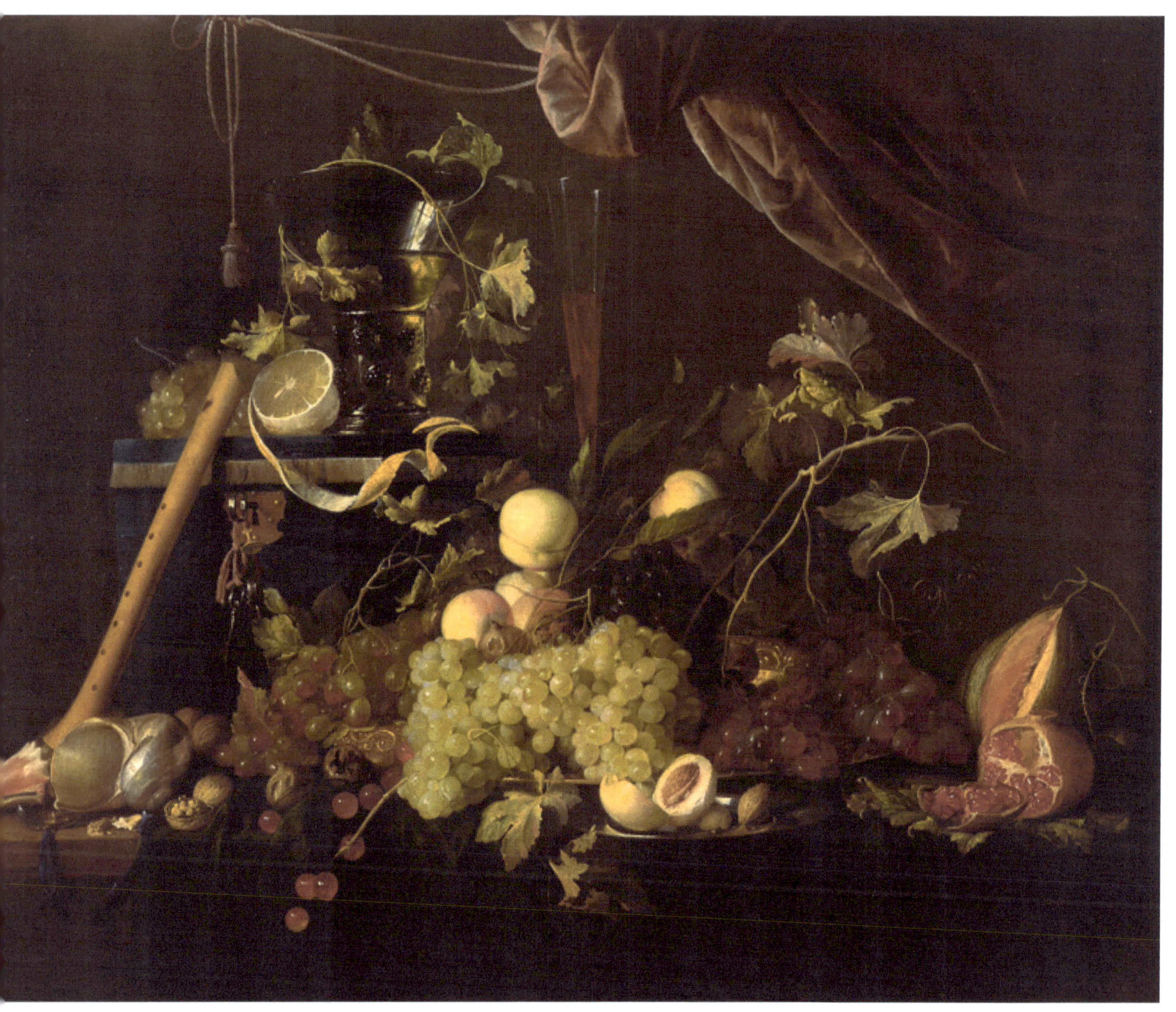

Still Life with Fruit and a Pipe, c.1650-55   94.7 x 120.5 cm

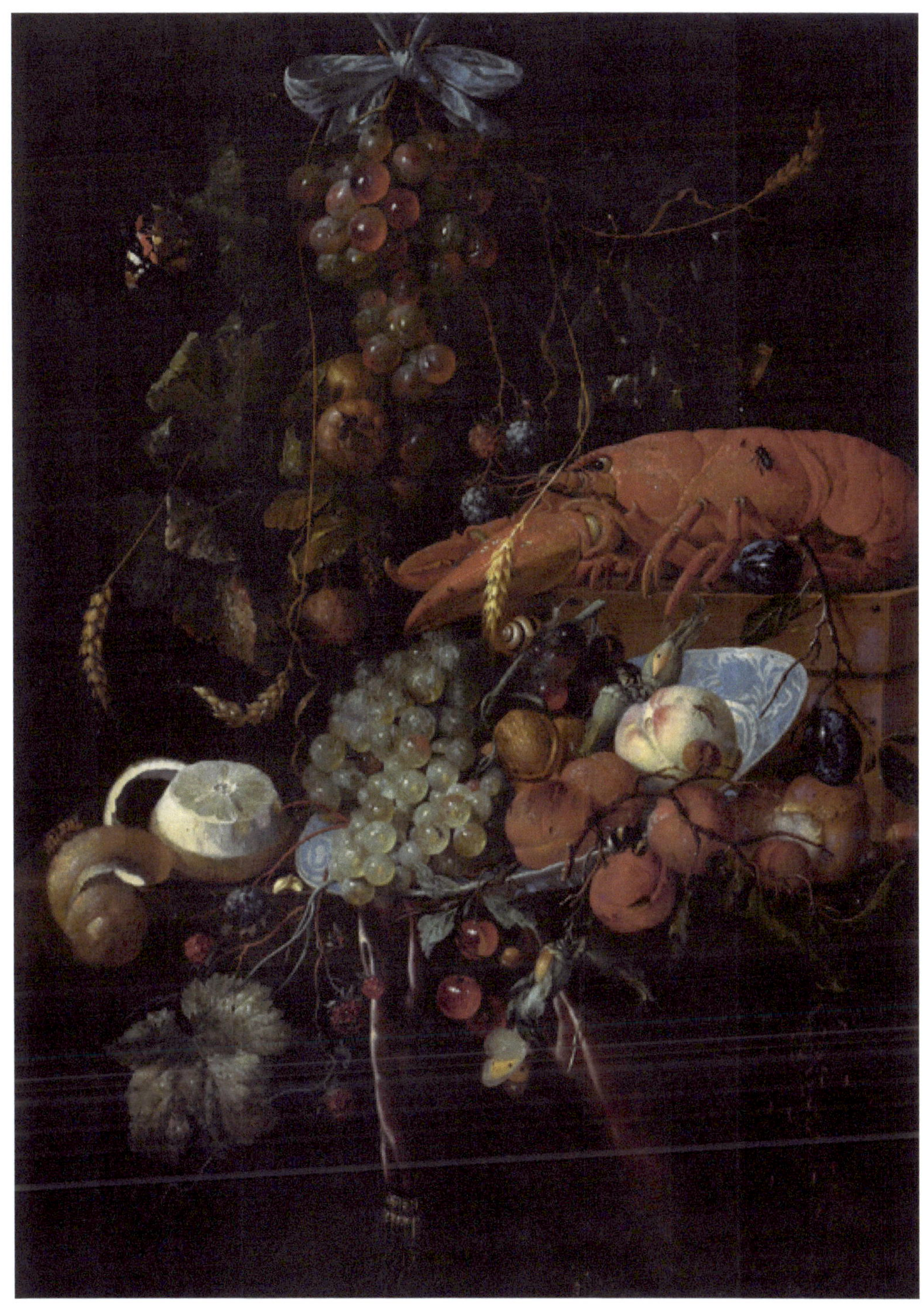

Still Life with Fruit and Lobster

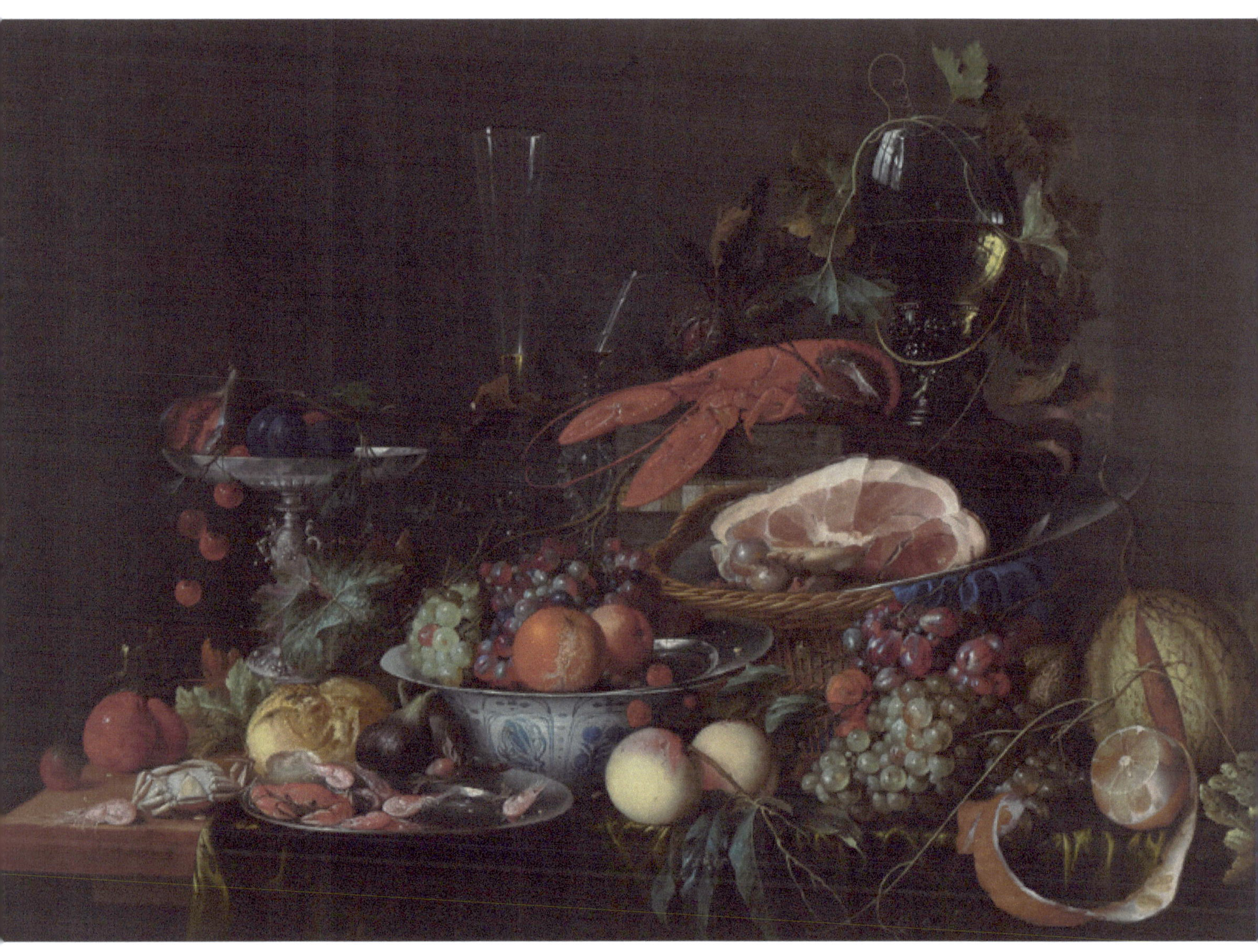

Still life with ham, lobster and fruit, c.1653   75 x 105 cm

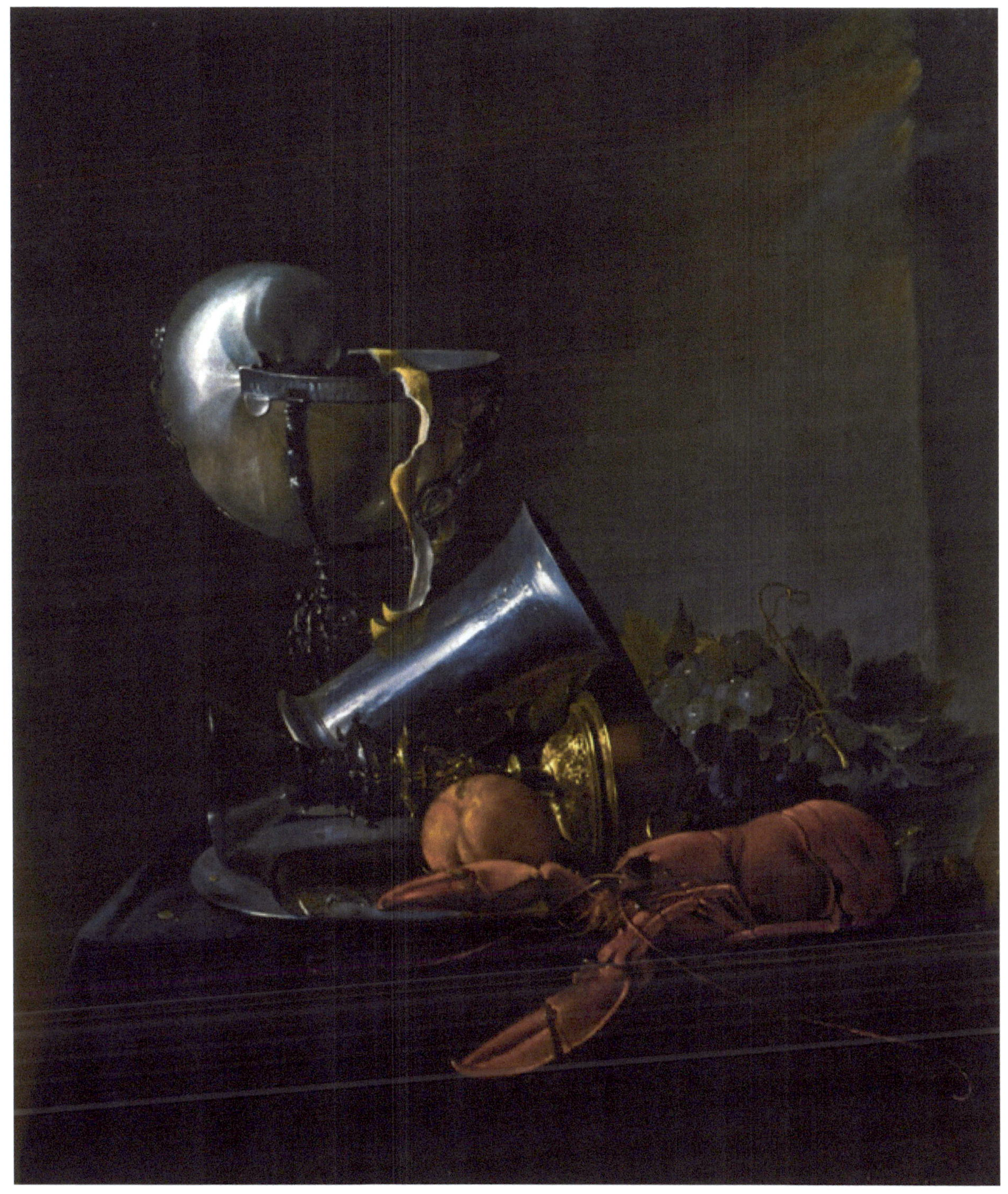

Still Life with Lobster and Nautilus, 1634   61x 55 cm

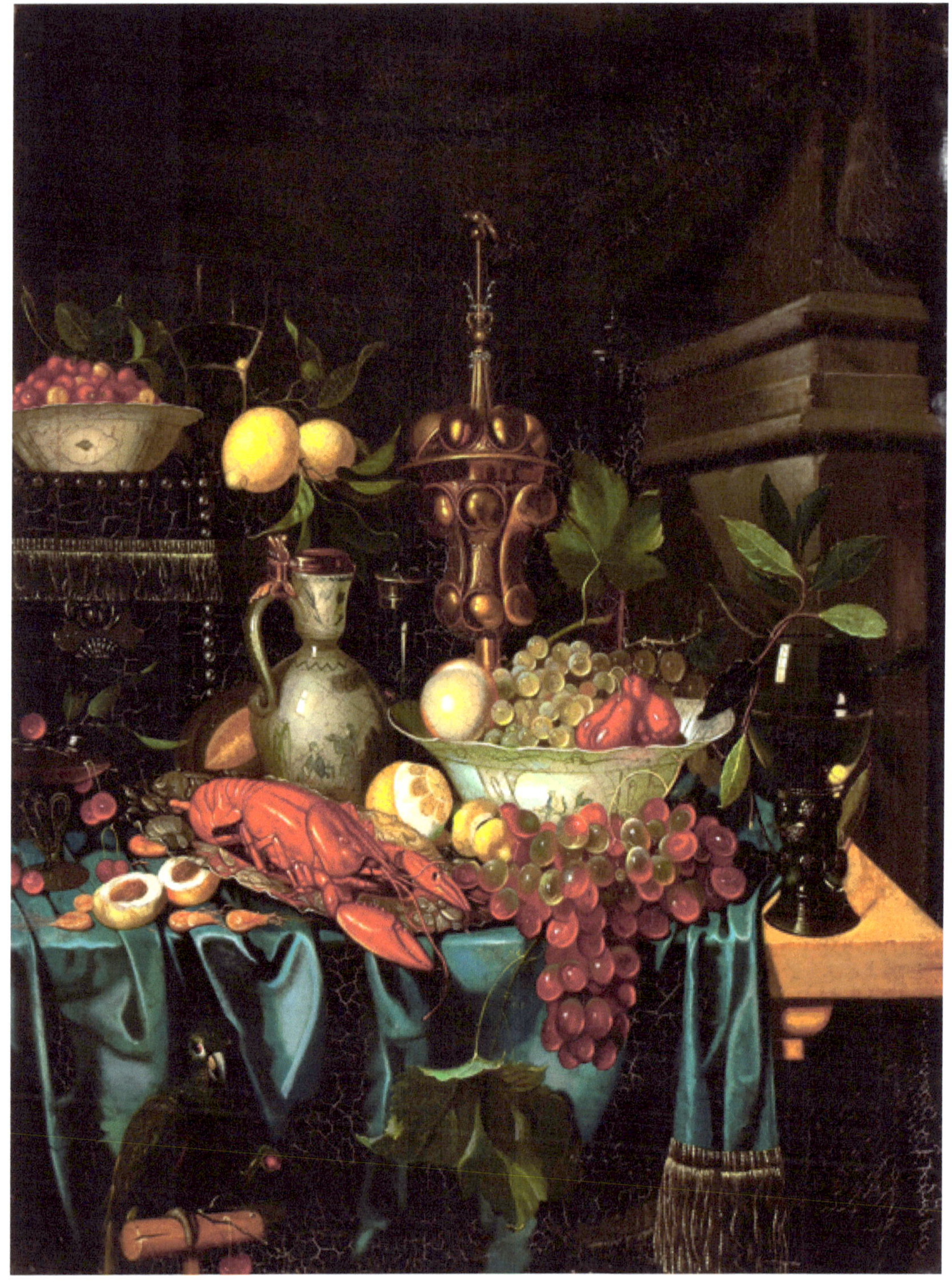

Still life with dishes, fruits and lobster

79.4 x 60.3 cm

Cornelis de Heem

1631 - 1695

Cornelis de Heem is a Dutch still life painter who specializes in flowers and fruits. He was born in a famous artist family in Leiden Leiden, the Netherlands, and his father is the famous painter Jan Davidsz. de Heem. Cornelis de Heem was educated under his father's guidance and improved his skills as a still life painter. He adopts a style similar to his father's to integrate careful attention and a vivid color palette about the details. Both artists specialize in still life, incwluding flower arrangements, fruits, and other objects, but there is a distinct difference between their lives and painting skills.

In the painting of Cornelis de Heem, visually and harmoniously arranged lush arrangements with flowers, fruits and other objects often appeared. His work is famous for creating depth and richness with a balanced composition and meticulous arrangement of each element. Jan Davidsz. De Heem is a famous still life painter famous for his complex composition, rich symbolism, and mastery of light and texture. The painting of Cornelis de Heem is often restrained and calm than the father's gorgeous. He preferred calm colors and focused on creating harmonious arrangements with balance and calm. His work has a stylish detail that captures the texture and subtle nuances of things, but more restrained and meditative aesthetics stand out. Also, Jan Davidsz. Deheem's works often feature abundant objects and overflowing with color and texture, while the work of Cornelis de Heem contains simplicity and elegance. He focused on the individual beauty of each element in the still life so that the audience can enjoy the delicate nuances of each object.

Jan Davidsz. de Heem was greatly reputed and recognized, but Cornelis de Heem's career was not very noticeable. He had a small number of works and did not have as much reputation as his father. Nevertheless, it should not be overlooked Cornelis' works which he developed his unique artistic style and contributed significantly to the genre of still life. Cornelis de Heem's life and painting skills compared to Jan Davidsz. de Heem, it can be seen that it has a personal touch and a distinct artistic vision while continuing the family tradition of still life. Cornelis's work creates calm and refined elegance, showing his unique artistic sensibilities and contributing to the extensive heritage of de Heem family in the Dutch still life.

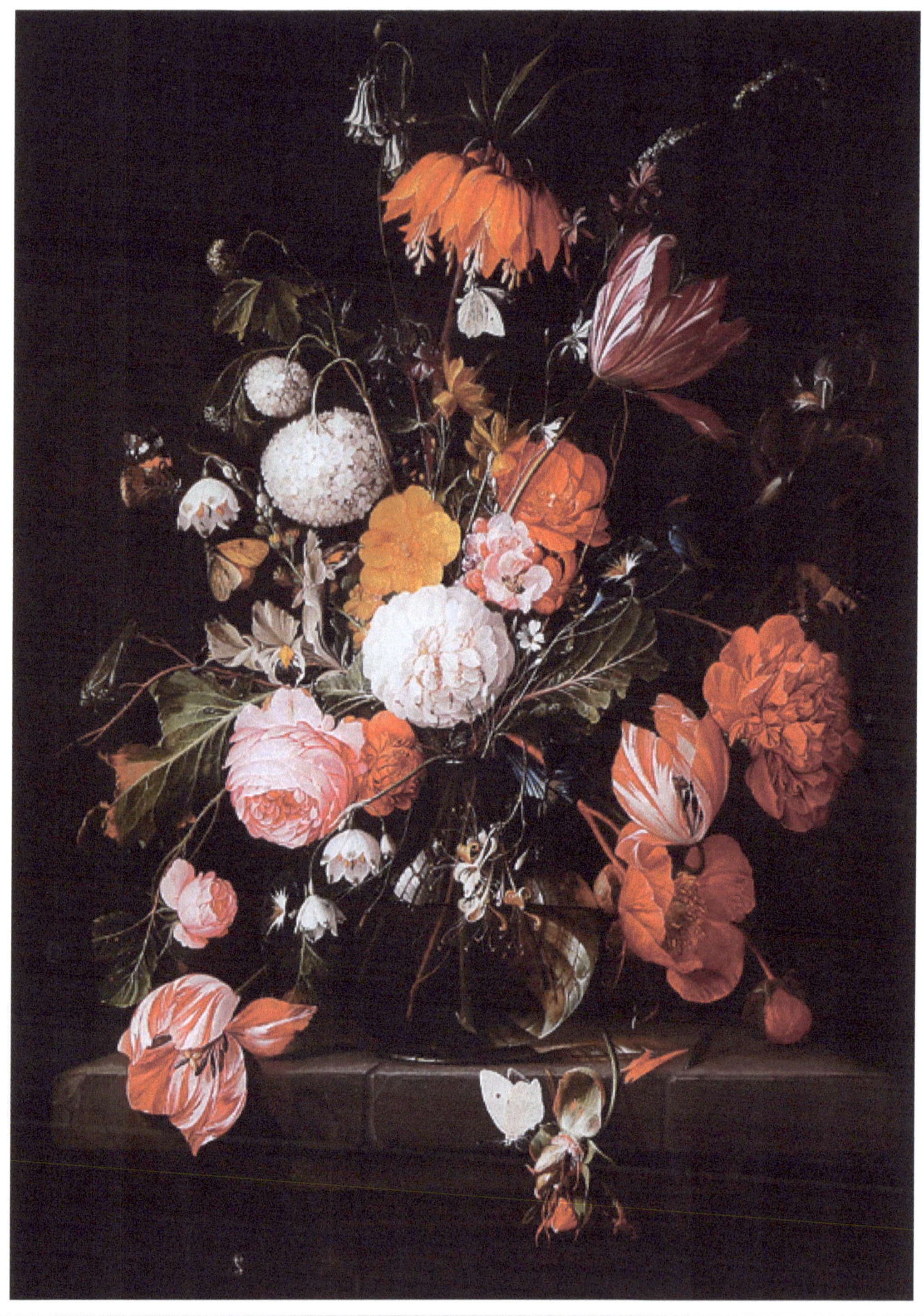

Bouquet of flowers in a glass vase

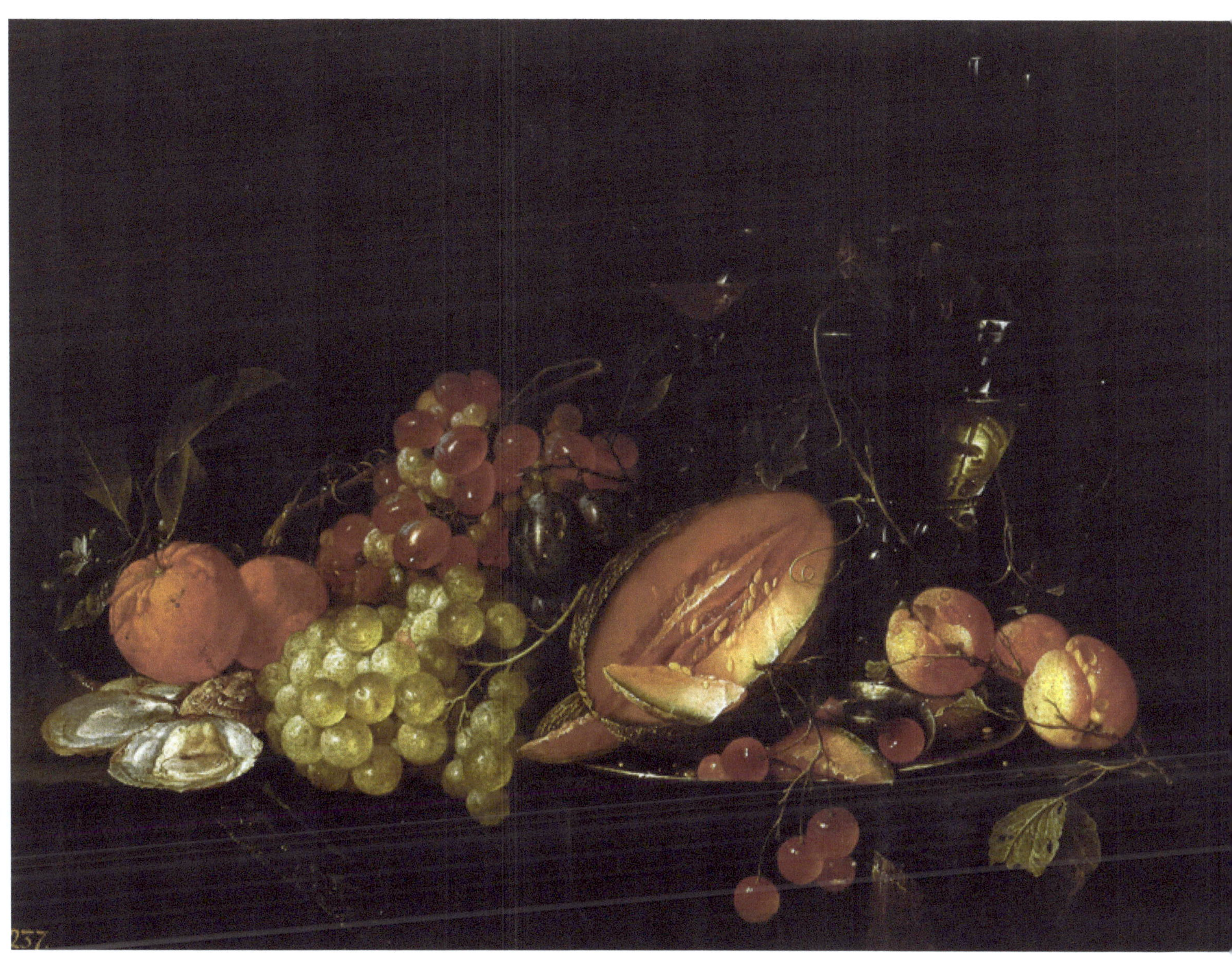

Still Life, 1670   43 x 60 cm

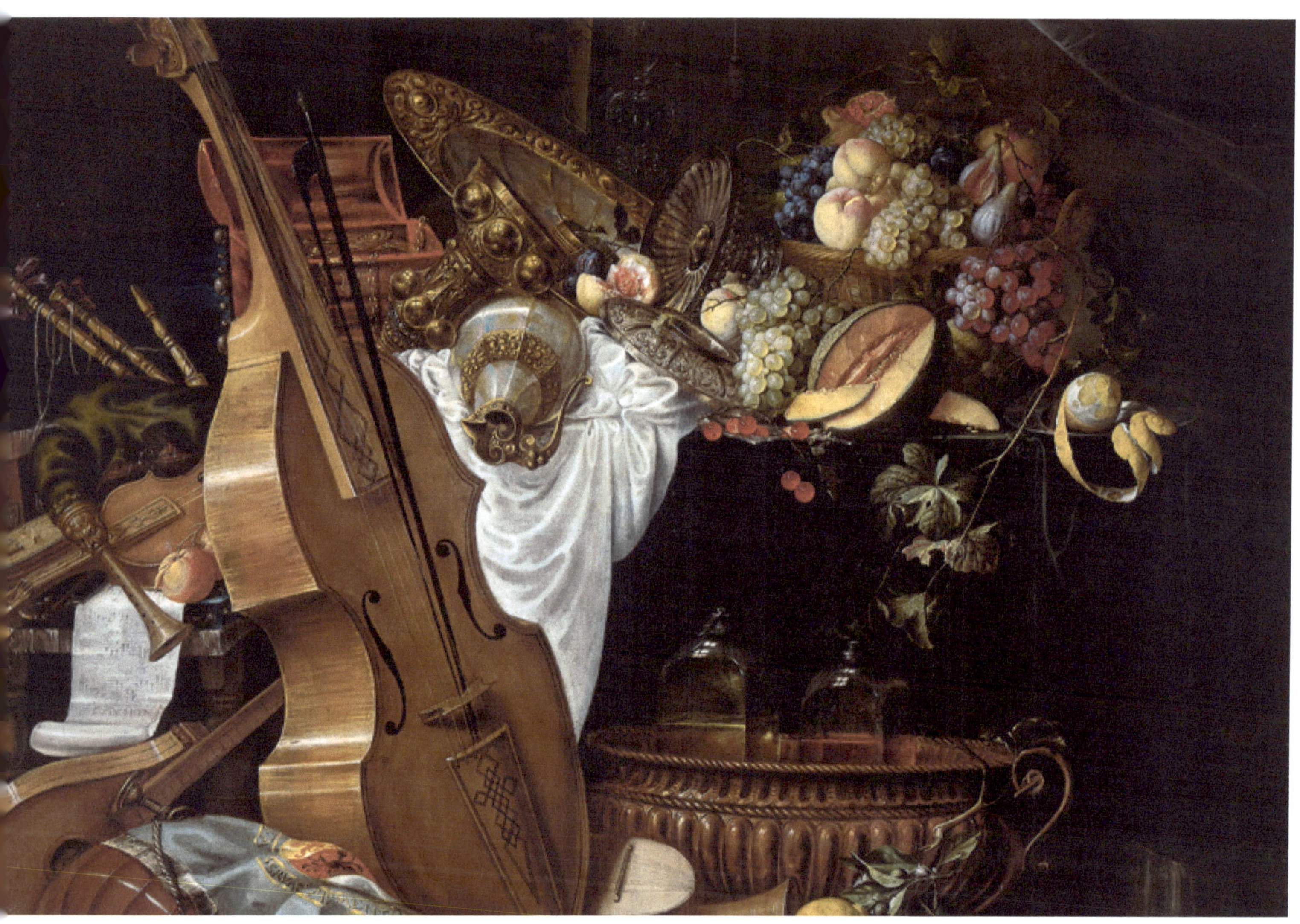

Still Life, 1681

153 x 166 cm

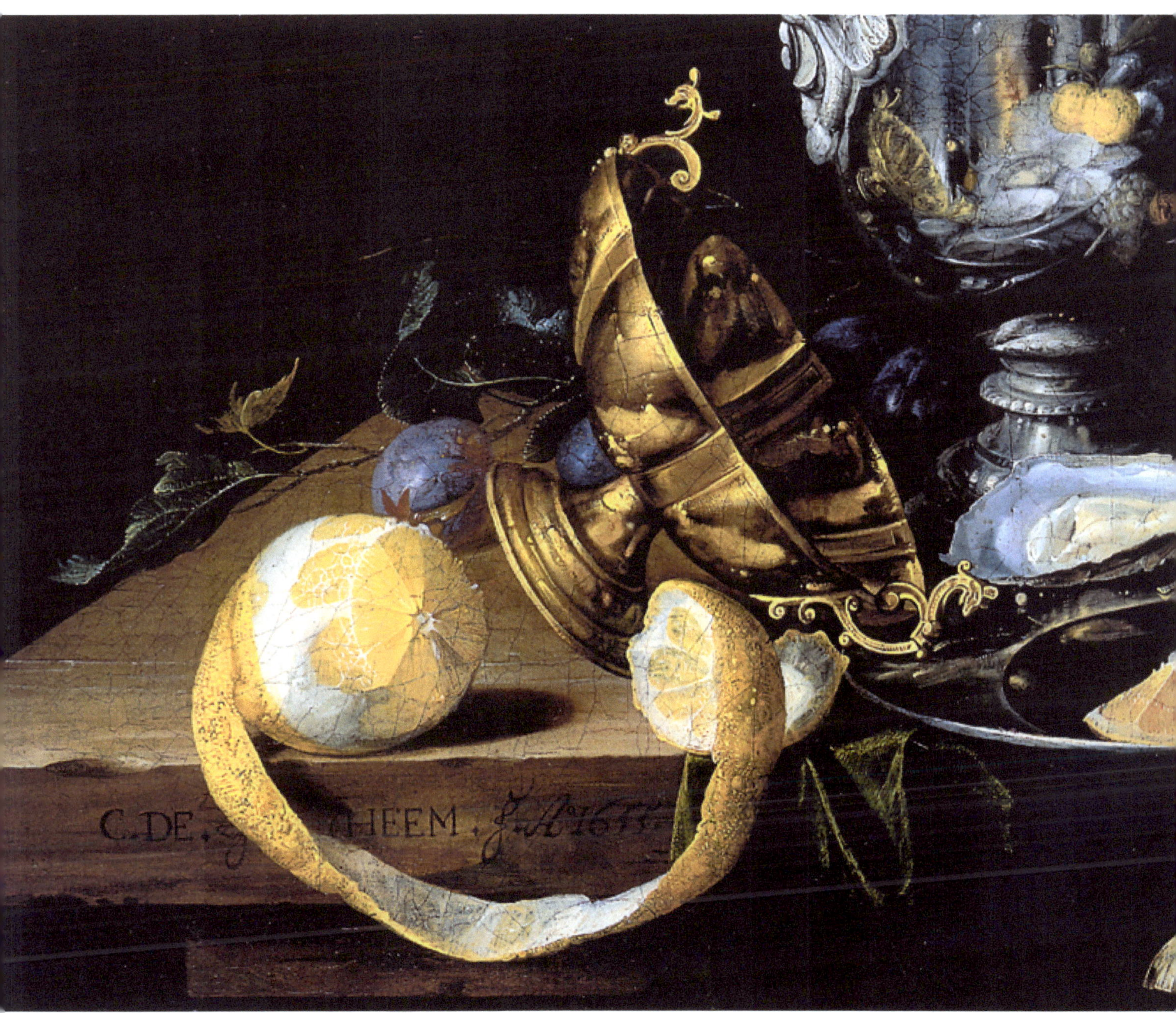

Still life detail

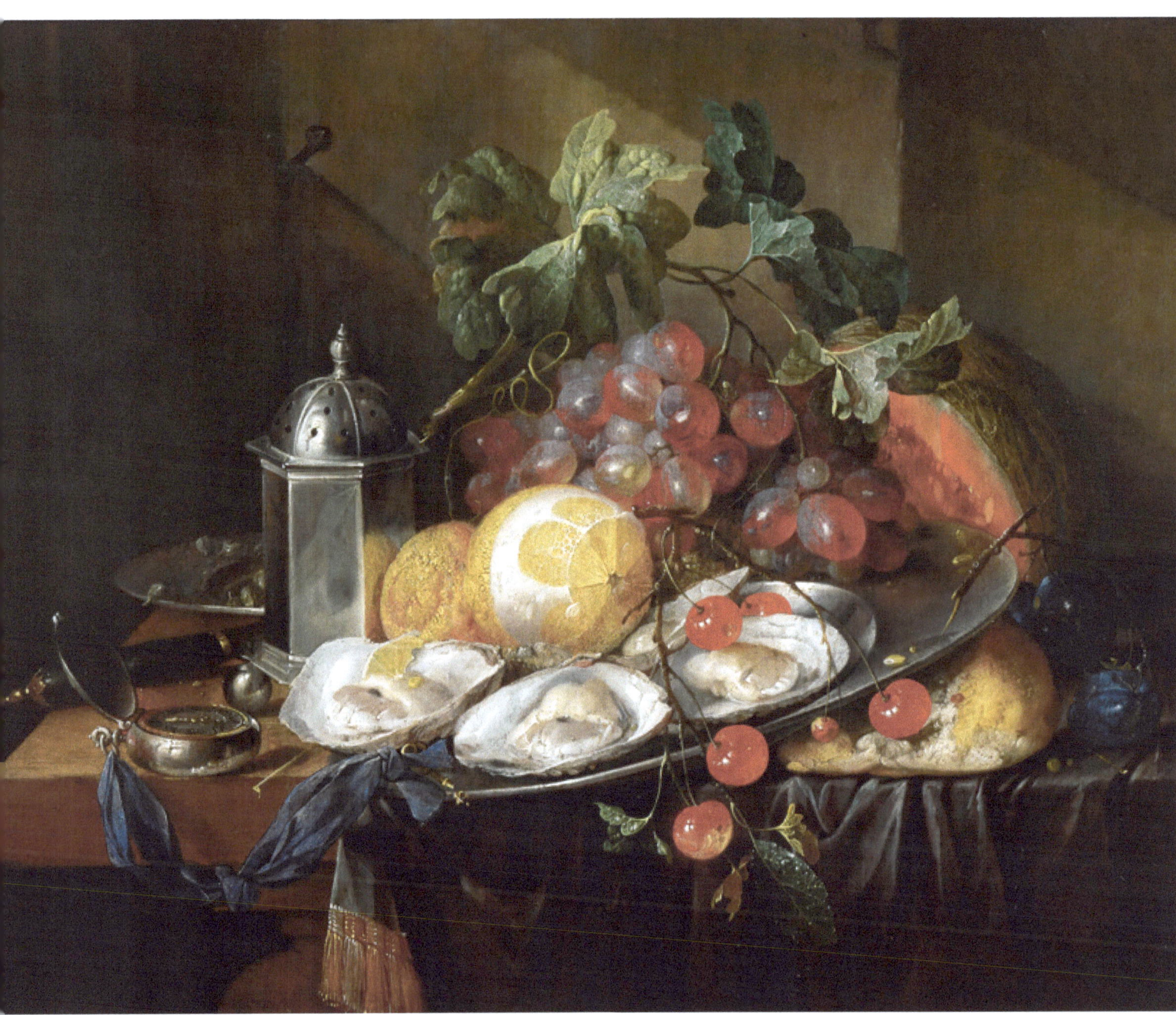

Still life with fruit, oysters and pocket watches 34 x 41 cm

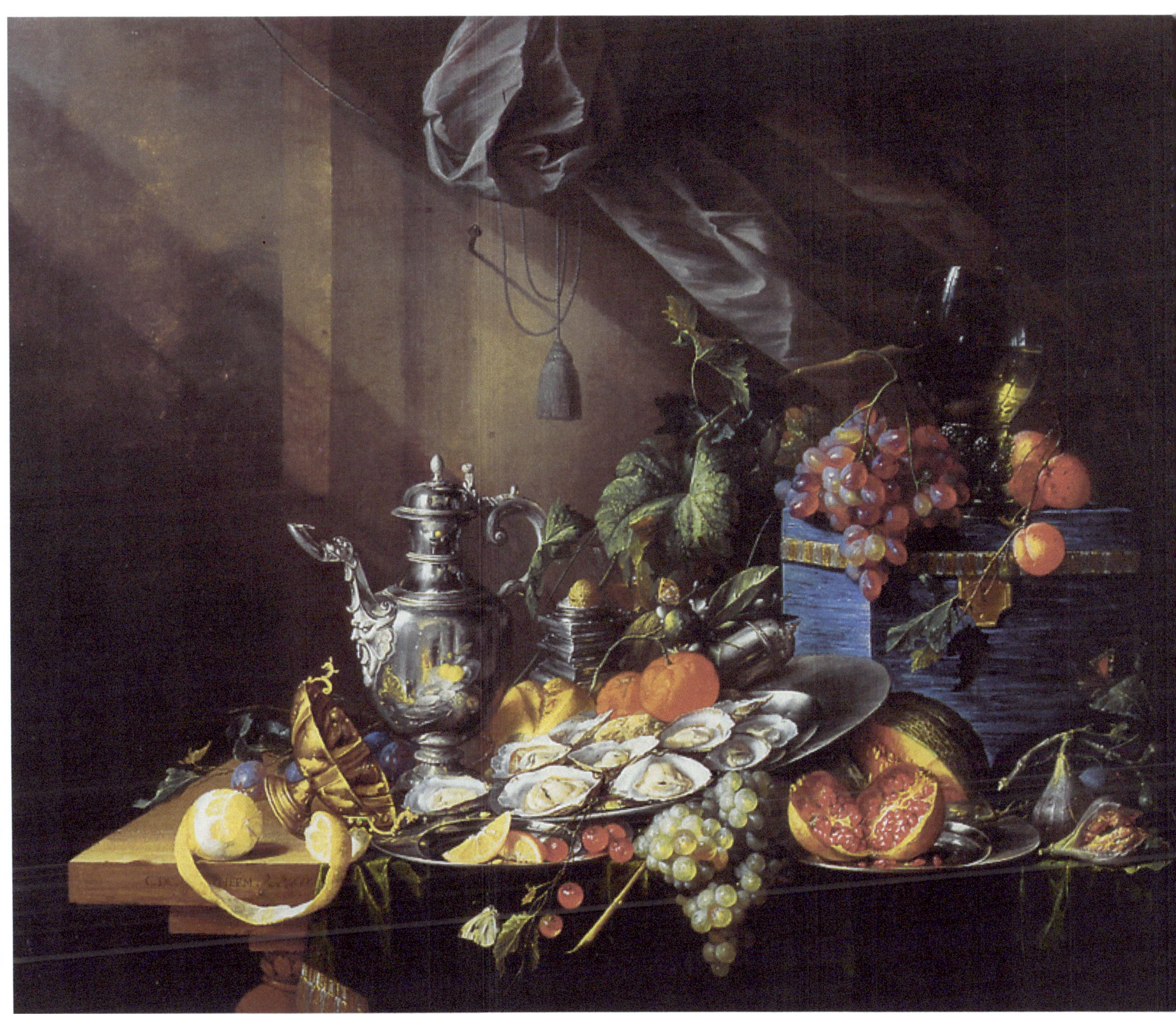

Still Life

27

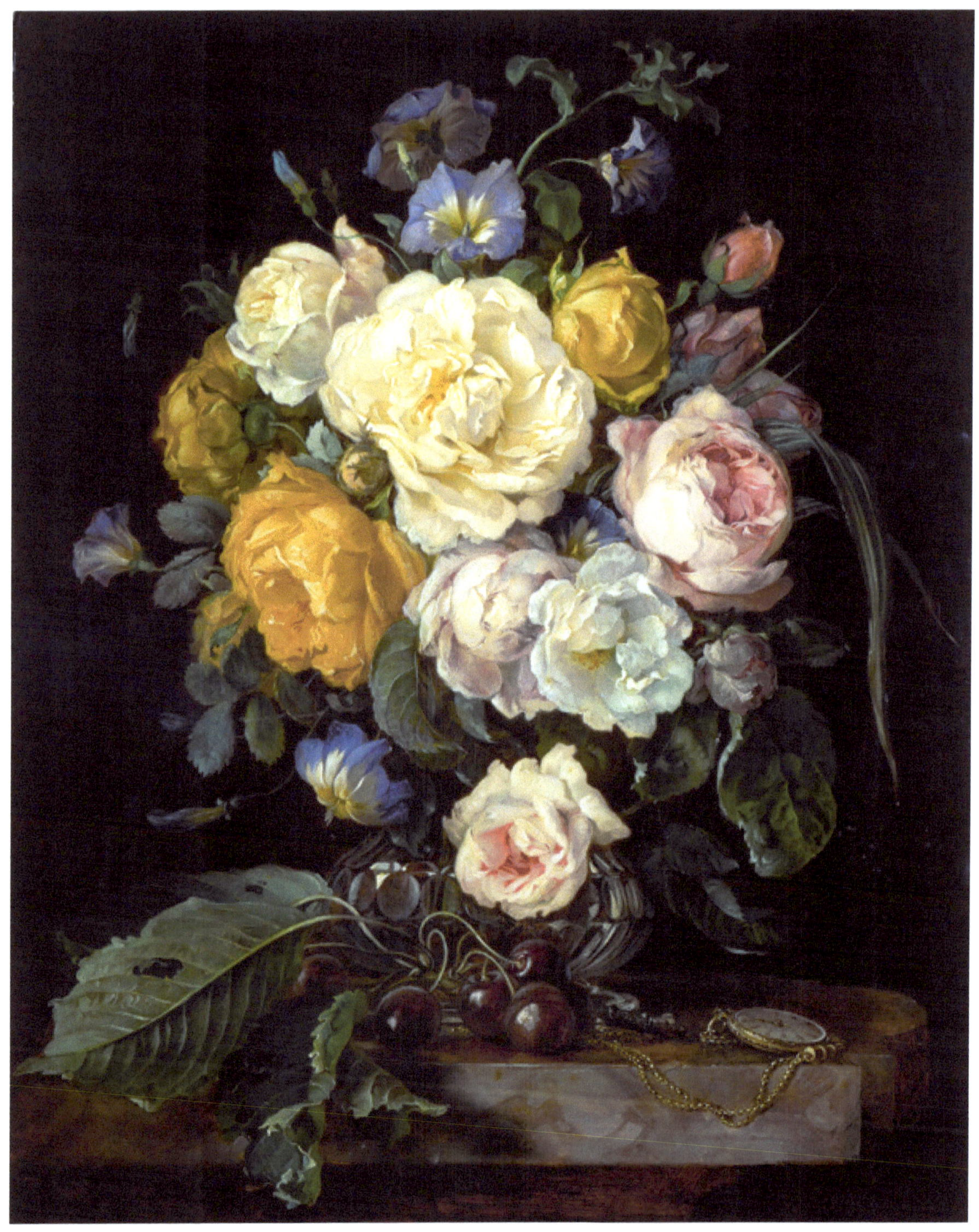

Still-life with a bouquet of flowers, cherries and a clock

Cornelis Kick

1634 - 1681

   Cornelis Kick is a Dutch painter famous for flower still life born in Amsterdam, the Netherlands in 1634. He took art education from his father, Simon Kick, a famous painter with Schuttersstukken(voluntary city guard or citizen militia).

   He painted flower still life which was a popular genre in the Dutch golden age following the details and styles with the lively composition of his teacher Jan Davidsz. De Heem. The kick, specializing in still life, has gained a reputation for describing various materials such as flower arrangements, fruits, andeveryday objects. The still life of the kick showed a meticulous approach and the ability to capture the texture, color, and complex details of the described objects. His work is often characterized by careful elements, balanced lighting, and harmonious sensations. His painting was collected by collectors and supporters who highly appreciated the beauty and symbolism found in still life genres.

   The Cornelis Kick has been a lifelong still life painter, leaving works that show the richness and diversity of the 17th-century Dutch still life. He passed away in 1681, and his work contributed to the rich tradition of the 17th-century Dutch still life.

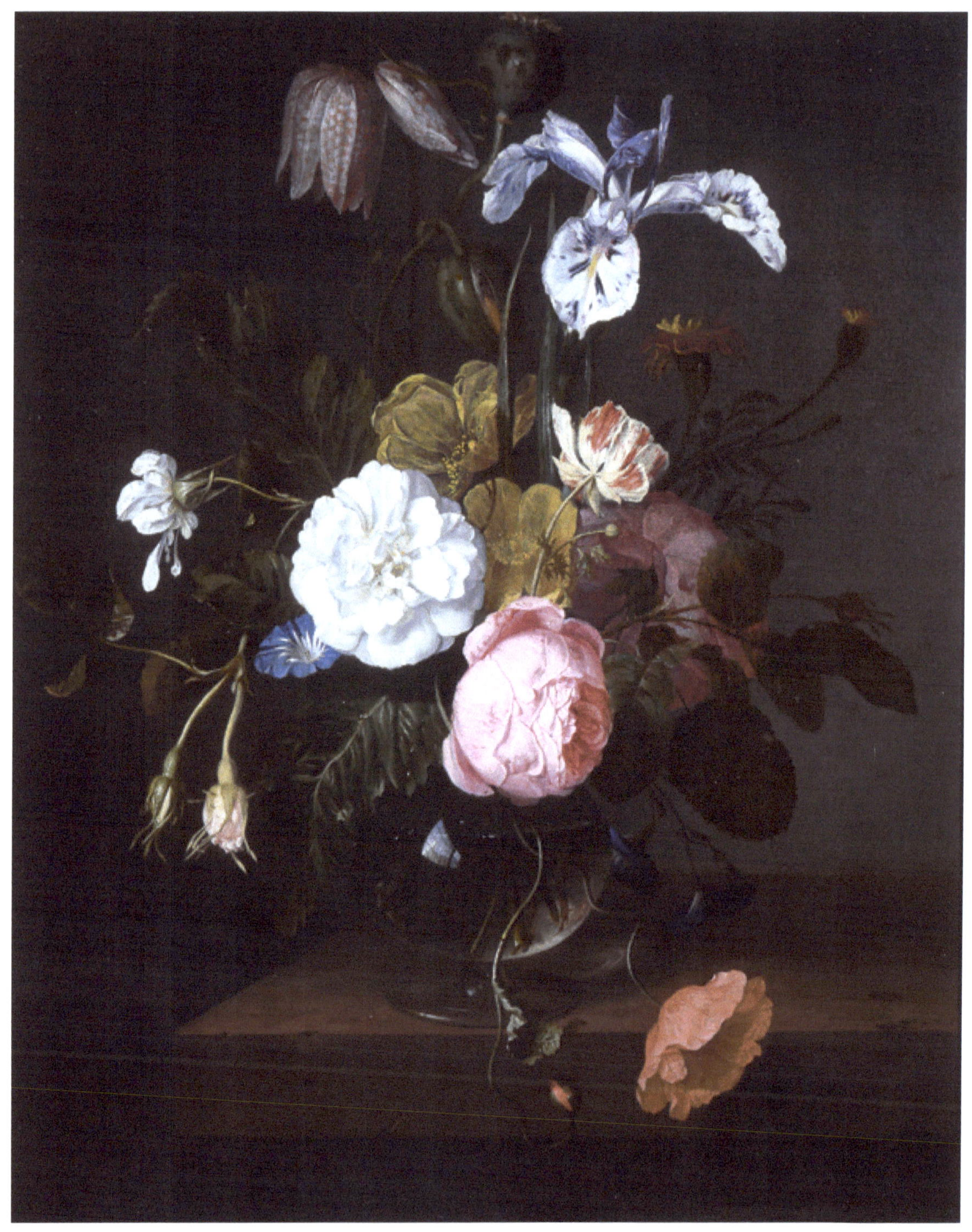

Bouquet of flowers in a glass vase

Frans Ykens

1601 - 1693

Frans Ykens is from an artist family, and his father was a famous painter Pieter Ykens the Elder. Frans Ykens was educated at Antwerp and became a member of the Guild of St. Luke in 1618. Afterward, he moved to Italy and studied the works of Italian masters to further develop his artistic skills.

Ykens focused mainly on still life, especially flower still life. His work is often lively arranged with flowers, fruits, and other objects, and it is expressed carefully with delicate details, sharp colors, and composition. His flower paintings showed his technical masterpiece with a variety of elements harmoniously balanced.

In addition to still life, he drew a genre scene that depicts everyday life and the inside of the family. His genre paintings often featured scenes of family, musicians, and people in various tasks. Ykens was talented in capturing the subtleties of human expressions and bringing intimacy to the work.

Ykens's paintings were highly regarded in his lifetime and were sponsored by prominent individuals and institutions. He was very interested and loved by collectors and was commissioned for the altar and decorative panels. Frans Ykens's artistic style evolved throughout his career. At first, he was influenced by the tradition of Franders still life, and later integrated the elements of Italian Baroque art, such as dramatic lighting and dynamic composition.

Today's work can be found in various museums and collections around the world, including the Royal Art Museum of Antwerp and the St. Petersburg Hermitage Museum. His contributions in the fields of Flander Baroque arts, especially in still life and genre painting, is recognized for his techniques, attention to detail, and ability to capture the beauty of everyday life.

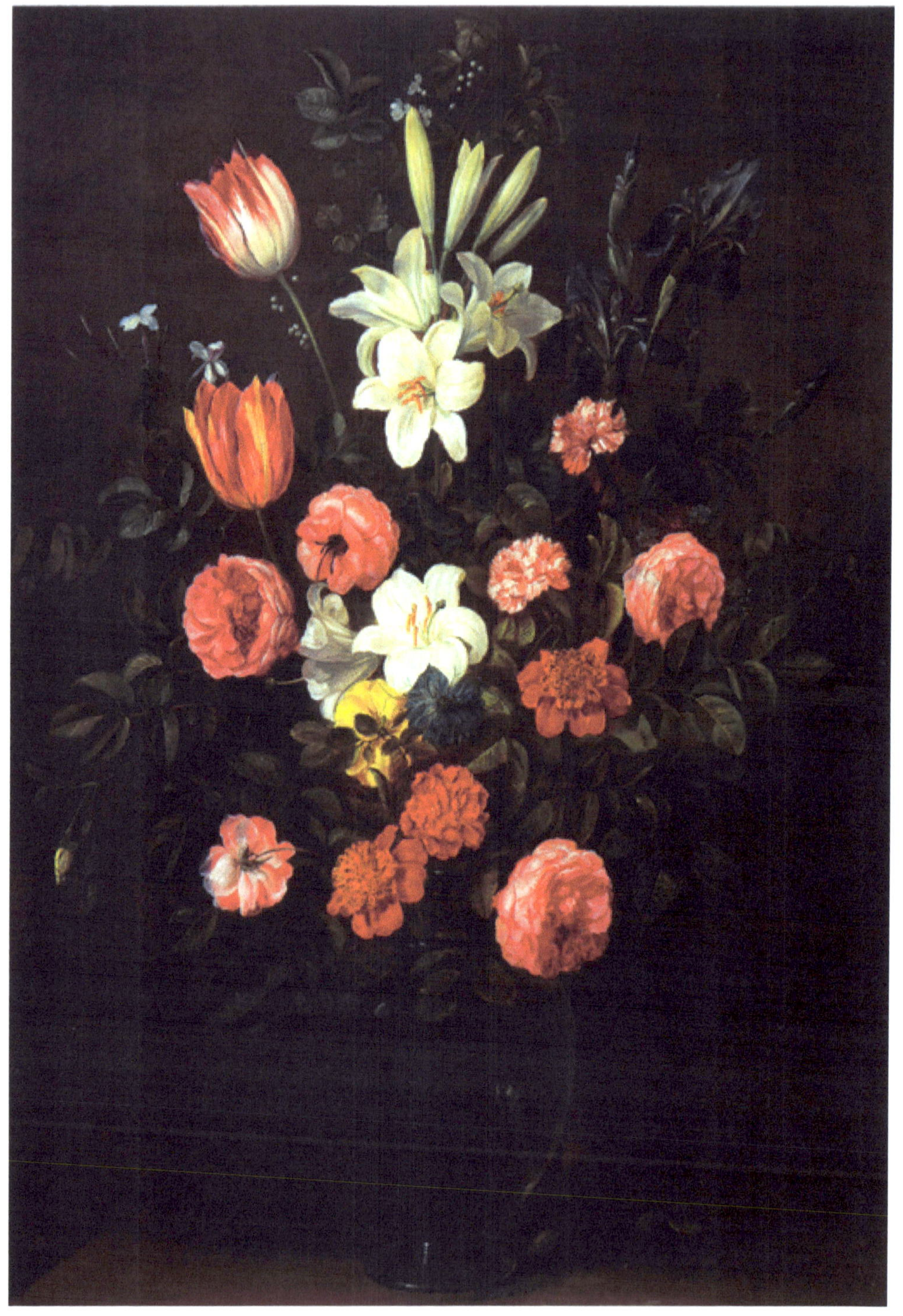

<table><tr><td>**Bouquet of flowers in a glass vase**</td><td style="text-align:right">**90 x 64.5 cm**</td></tr></table>

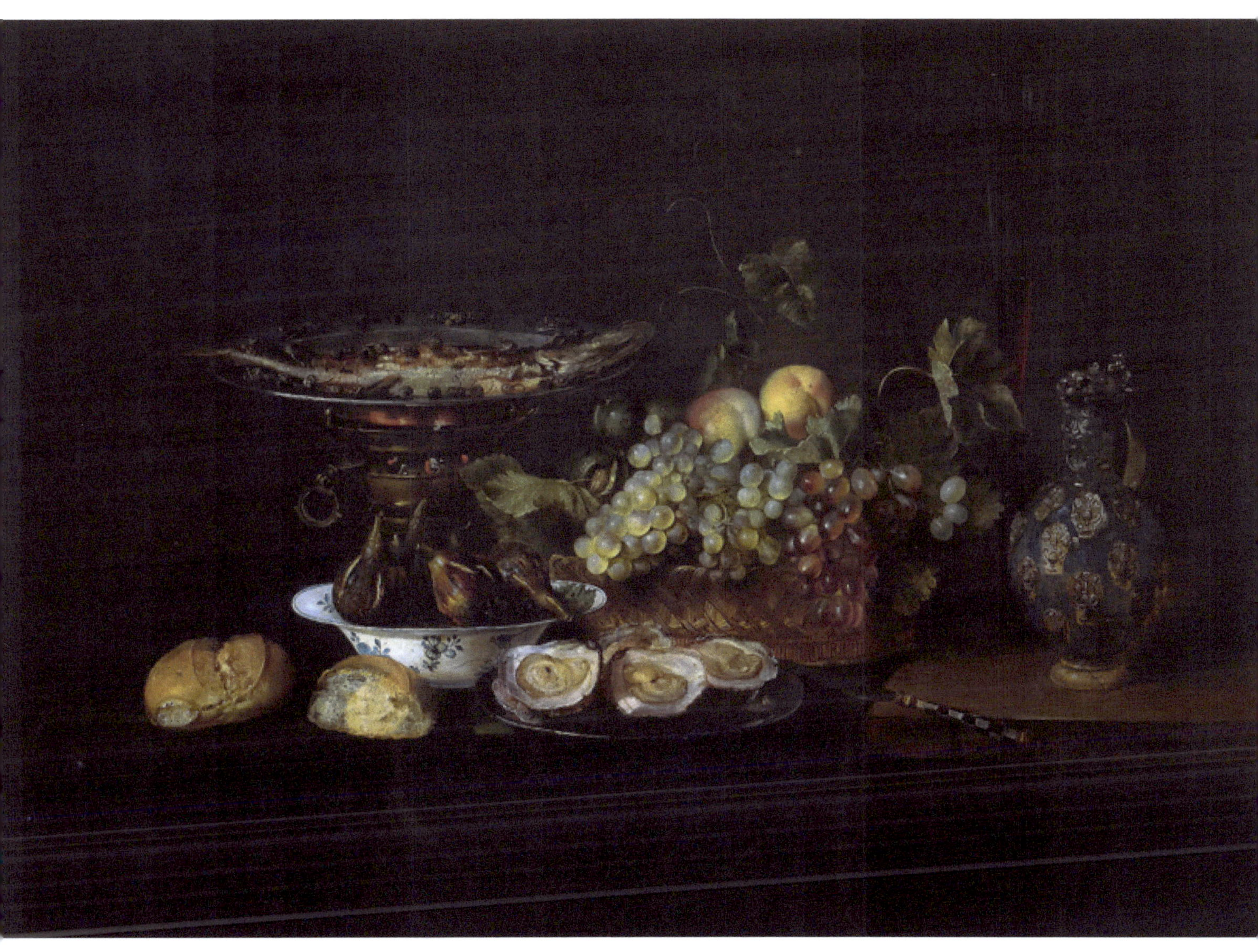

Still Life, 1646   74 x 105 cm

Jan Brueghel The Elder
1568 - 1625

Jan Brueghel is a painter of Franders, who is famous for his contribution to life still and landscape progress in the late 16th century and the early 17th century. He is the son of the prominent painter of Franders, Pieter Brugel the Elder, and became one of the most important characters of the artist in the Brueghel dynasty. Brueghel, a young painter since childhood, was initially trained by her grandmother, Mayken Verhulst. In 1589, Jan Brueghel studied abroad in Italy and studied the works of Italy Renaissance masters for many years. He visited Rome, Naples, and other prominent cities was famous for art, and traveled around Italy extensively. The natural teaching of Italian art had a great influence on his style and subject. Returning to Antwerp, Jan Brueghel has become a highly skilled and popular painter. He collaborated with several prominent artists from the time, building close cooperation and friendship, and exchanged portraits and landscapes in each other's works with Peter Paul Rubens. Jan Brueghel has made artistic achievements that encompass various themes such as landscape, still life, mythical scenes, and the Bible story. His still life is especially famous for his careful details and rich visual textures. He often integrated flowers, fruits, and small animals into the works to create a harmonious and visually attractive array. Brueghel's landscape painting is characterized by capturing natural beauty in the surrounding world with its atmosphere of perspective and lively color. He showed the ability to describe various natural elements such as wood, water, and rocks with amazing accuracy and techniques.

He did not draw a lot of explicit Vanitas still life but often dealt with elements that imply the fleeting life and the flow of time. For example, he often painted flowers in various flowering stages, ranging from fresh flowers to petals that symbolize the circulation of birth, old age, sickness, and death, the four phases of life. Brueghel often included small creatures such as insects and butterflies. These creatures can symbolize the fleeting life or the necessity of death. Brueghel's contribution to the Vanitas still life genre is not as wide as other artists, but the integration of symbolic elements and focus on the time essence of life is consistent with the subjects explored in Vanitas paintings. His work has been highly regarded as a harmonious composition and the ability to reflect on the fleeting essence of human beings. Jan Brueghel passed away in Antwerp in 1625. His work can be found in major museums and collections around the world and is evidence of his talents and continuous influence on the art of the Dutch golden age.

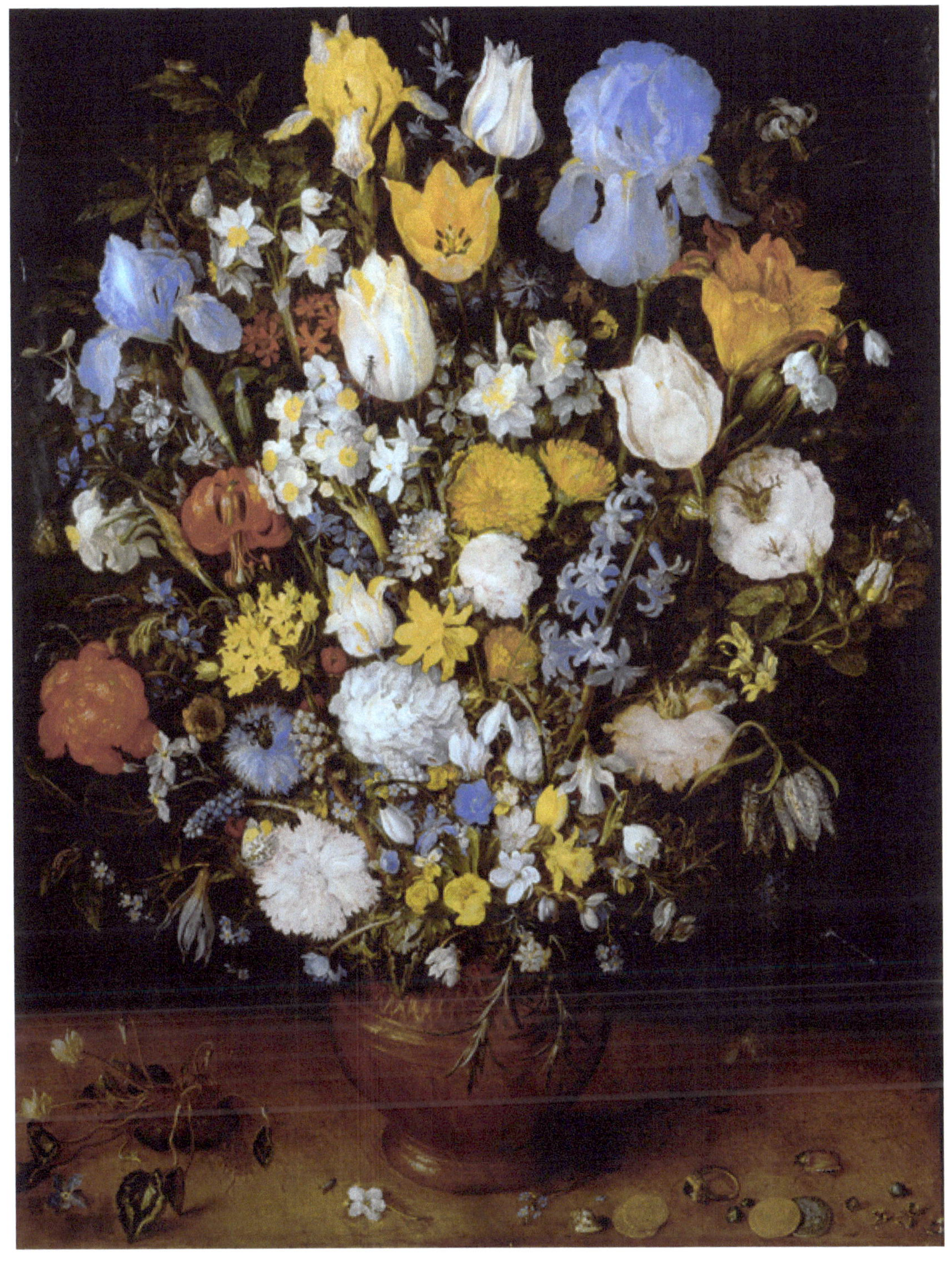

Bouquet, c.1607

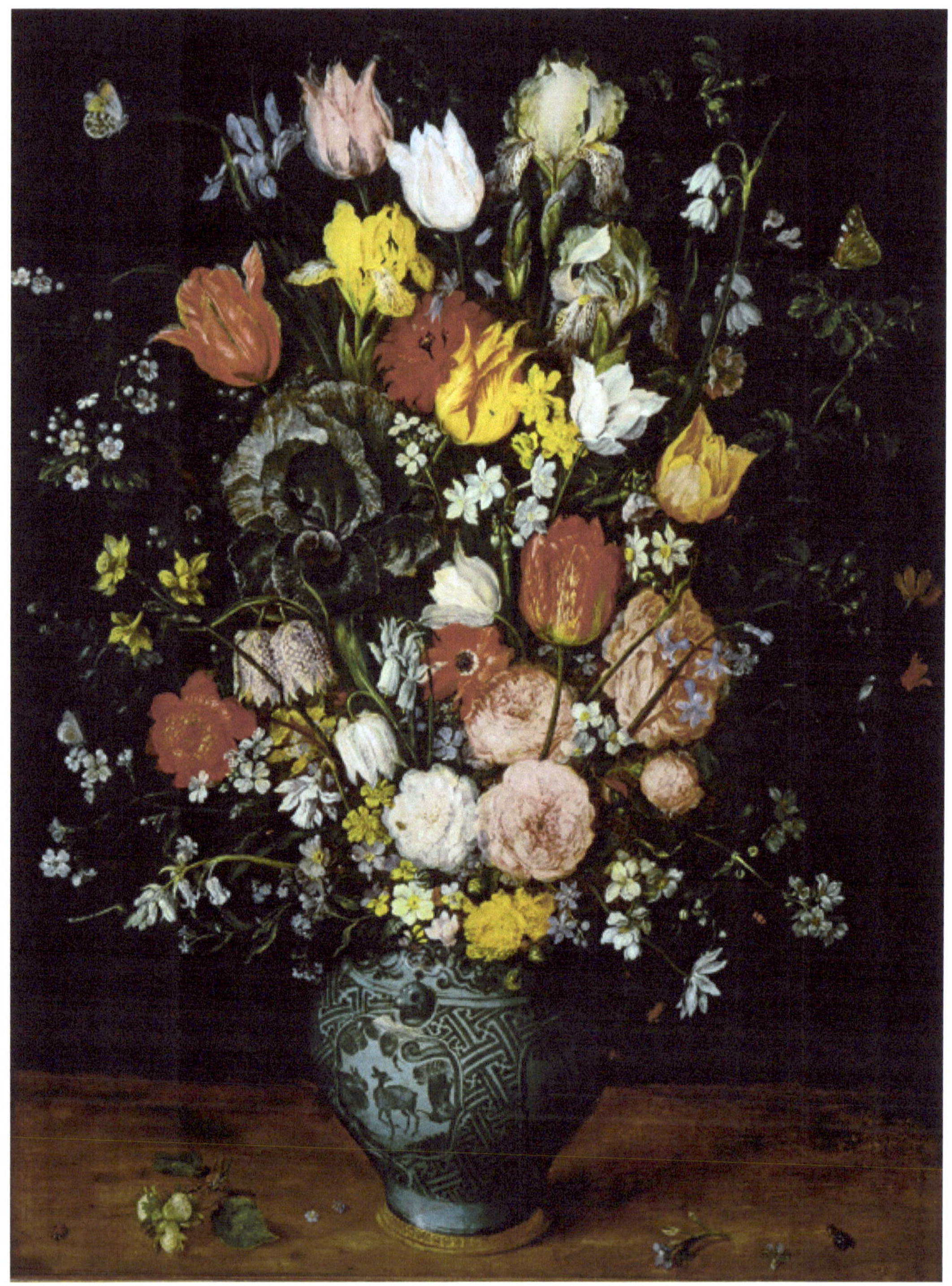

Bouquet of Flowers in a Blue Vase, 1608

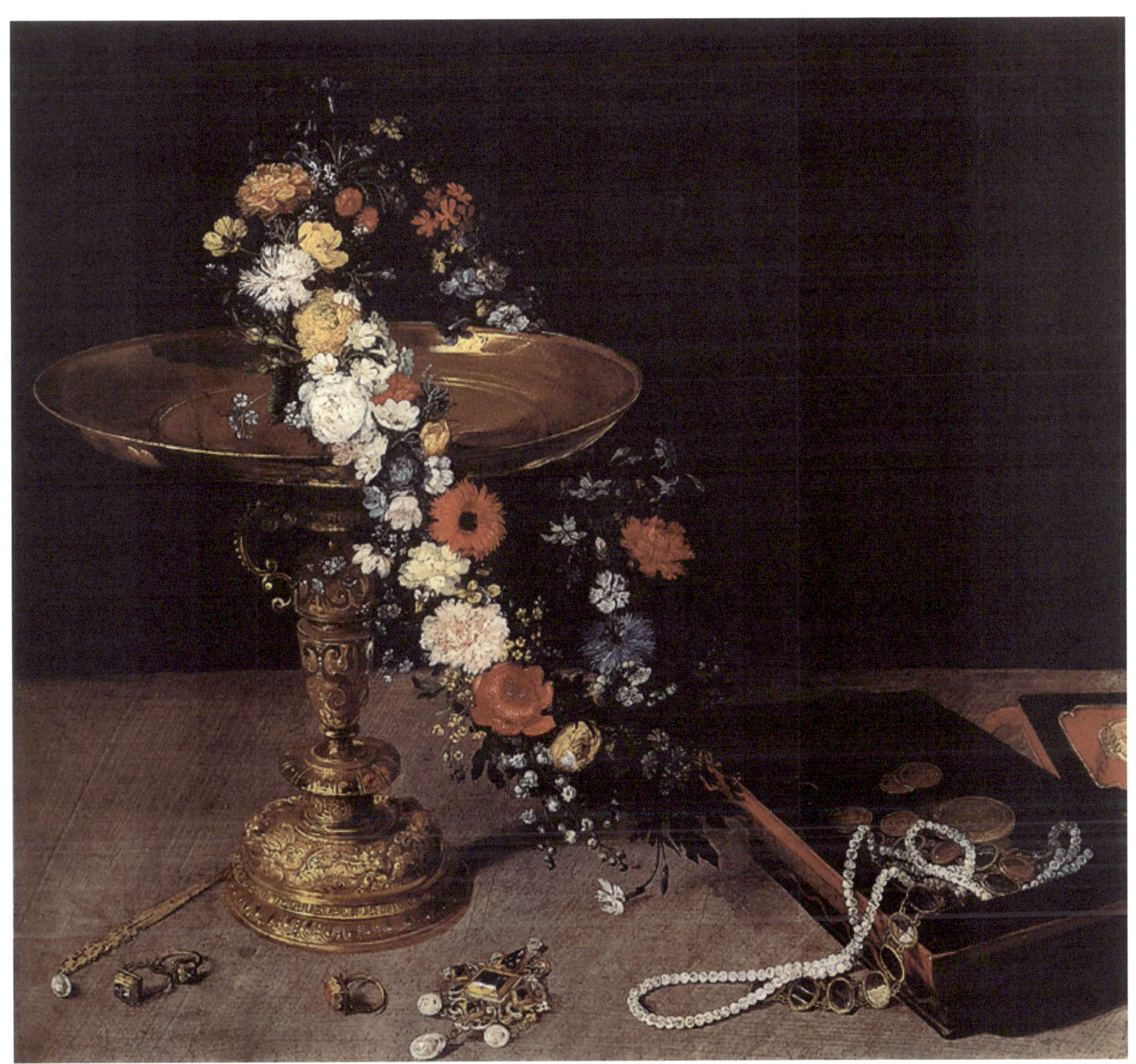

Still Life with a wreath and gold vase

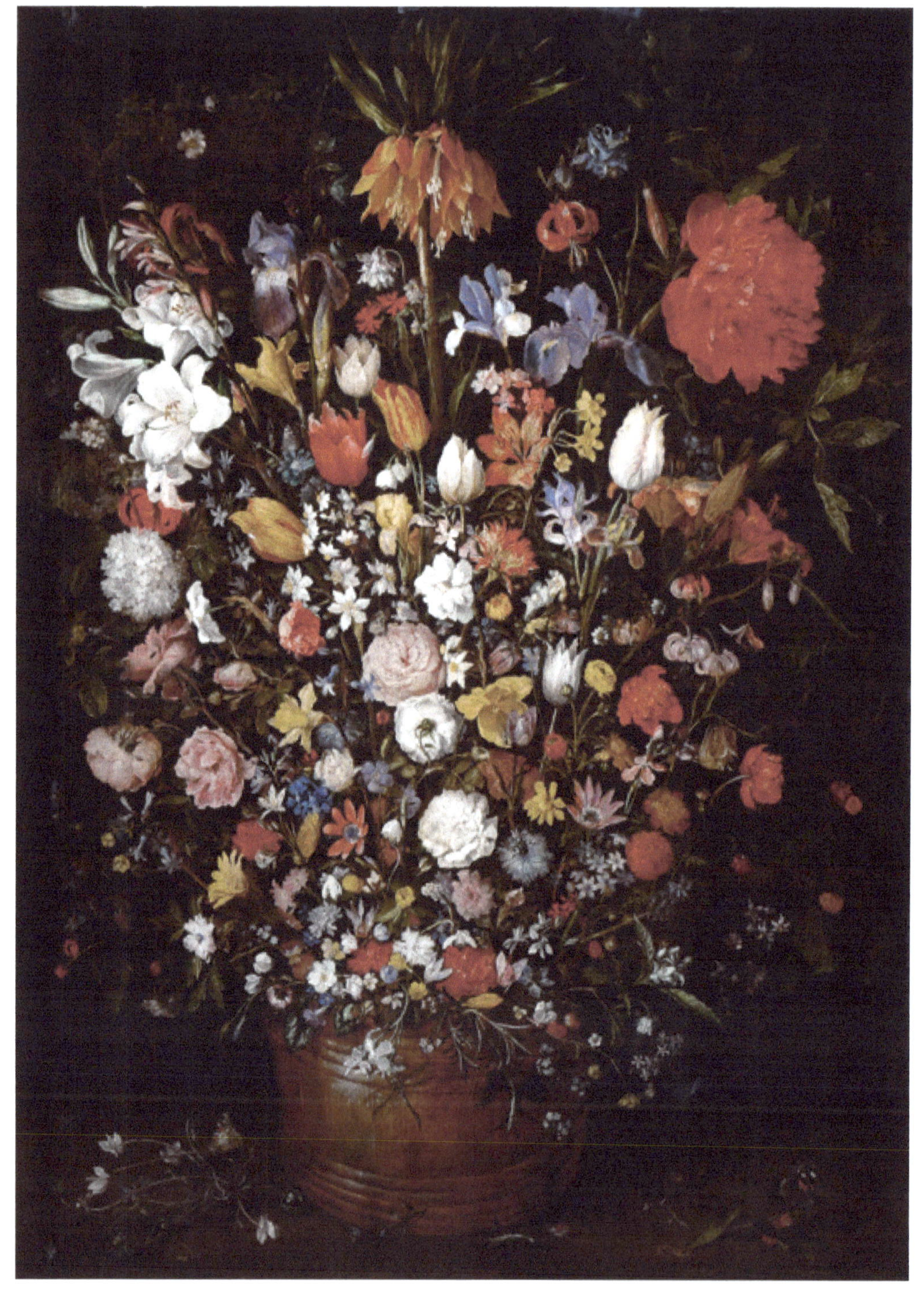

Still Life with Flowers, 1607

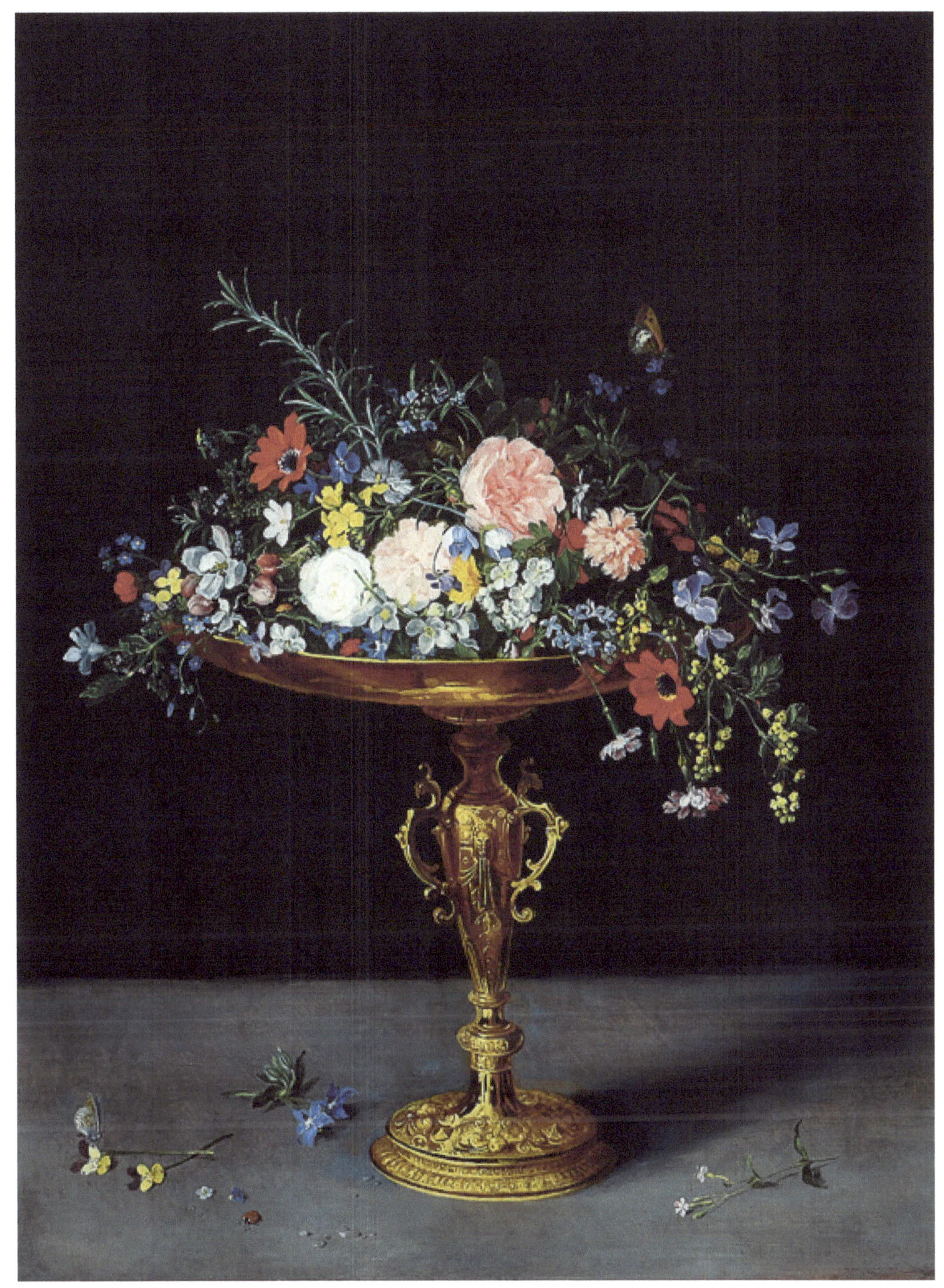

Vase of Flowers, c.1620

Jan Brueghel II (the Younger)

1601 - 1678

Jan Brueghel the Younger was the painter of Franders, who followed his father, Jan Brueghel the Elder. Although he inherited his father's artistic talent and became a successful painter, there is a distinct difference in the style and focus of the two.
Jan Brueghel the Younger received art education from his father and initially worked in his father's studio. He mainly focused on continuing his father's traditions by producing landscape paintings, still life, and fable scenes. His father, Yan Brueghel the Elder, who was good at describing a variety of textures and was also called 'Velvet Brueghel', was famous for his complex and delicate landscape paintings and still life. He was a painter with a keen view of capturing nature such as landscapes, sea landscapes, and flower still life. His work was filled with small and delicate elements, giving a wealthy and rich feeling. In addition, panoramic landscapes appeared in landscape paintings, and still life was carefully placed on the accuracy of plants. Jan Brueghel the Young, on the other hand, walked a similar artistic path but developed his unique unique style.

He closely imitated his father's composition and technique and sometimes worked with other artists to replicate his father's work. However, the young Brueghel's painting is generally less stylish and is considered to have a lack of exquisite details and techniques of his father's work. Jan Brueghel the Elder was a master of many genres such as landscape painting, still life, and fables, but Jan Brueghel the Young focused on continuing his father's legacy in the field of still life. He has painted numerous flower still life and also contains the Bible and mythological themes in his works. His work features a larger scale element and a simple array compared to the complex details found in his father's painting. Jan Brueghel the Young's work did not achieve the same technical masterpiece as his father, but he had great success in his life. He received a lot of commissions from the Habsburg royal family and other prominent supporters, which firmly established his reputation as an experienced painter. Jan Brueghel the Young sometimes introduced the Vanitas element to the still life work along the father's footsteps and the artistic tradition of the time. Examples are the works that describe the delicate flowers in the stages of various flowering and withering sounds, expressing the circulation of life and reminding the fleeting of beauty.

Jan Brueghel the Young's work was widely distributed and widely distributed to the collectors, aristocrats, and art lovers of the time, which influenced the development of still life and landscape painting throughout the 17th century.

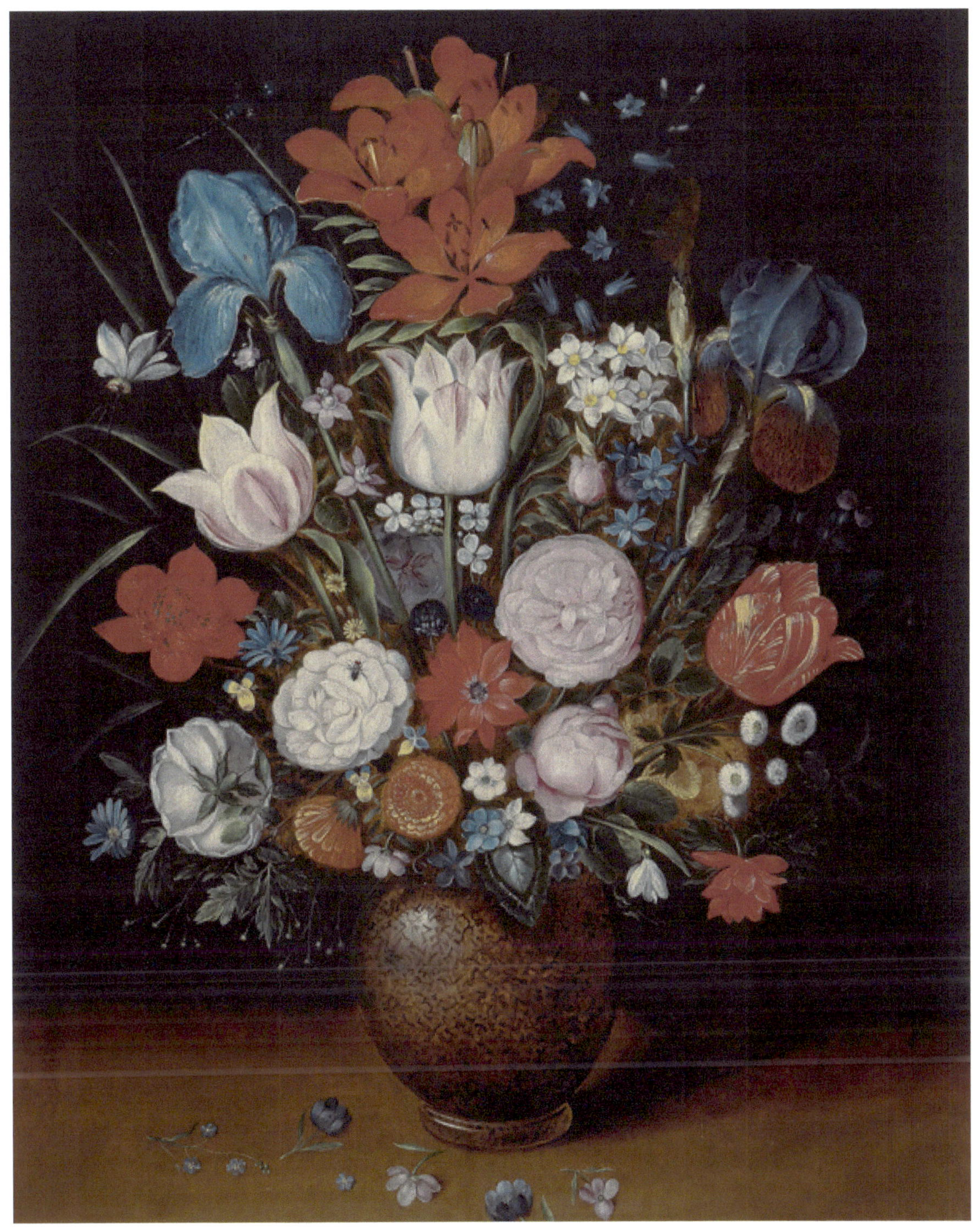

Bouquet of flowers in a vase

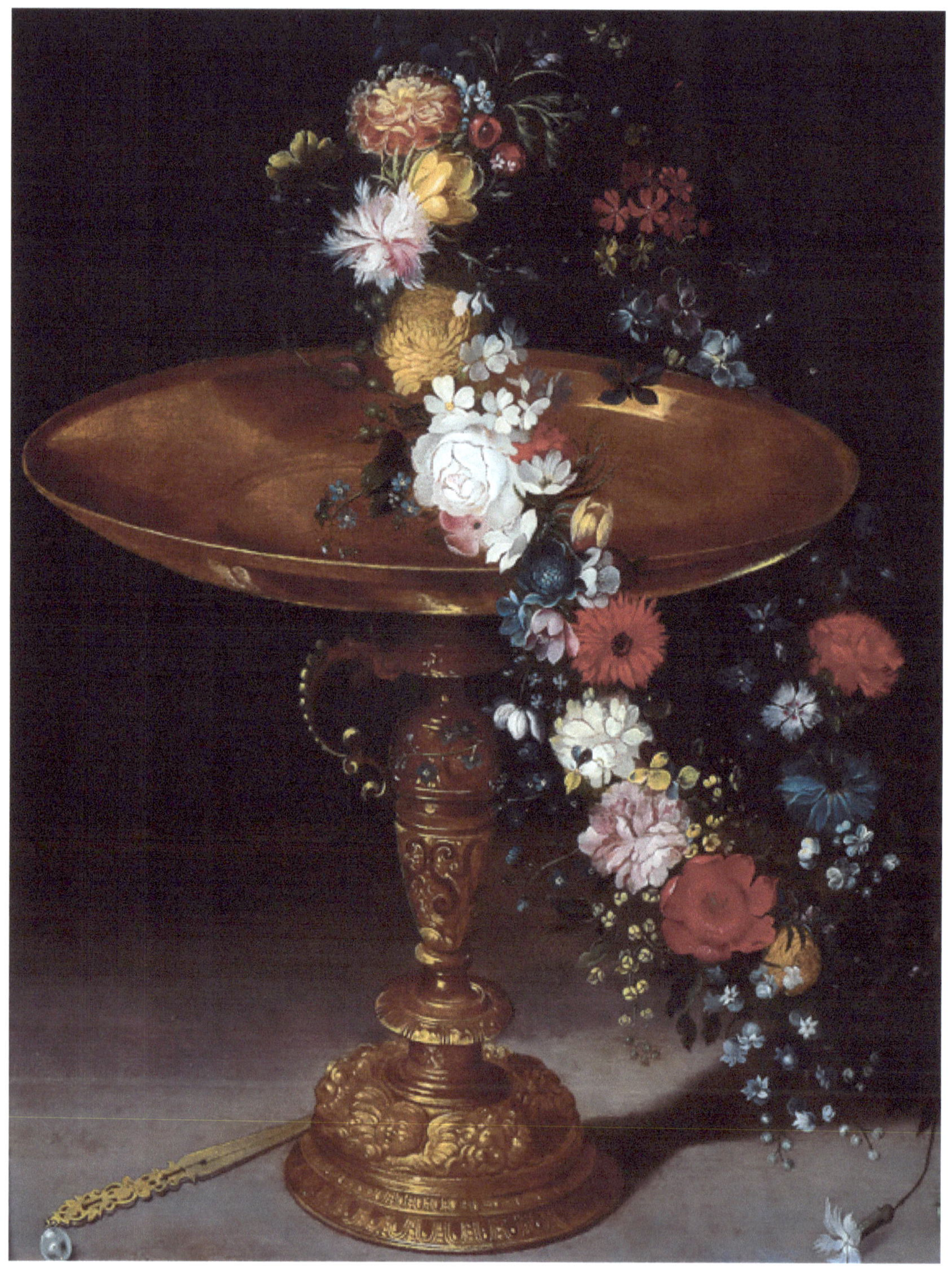

Bowl with wreath

Into the details

With Exotic flowers_Flower Still Life

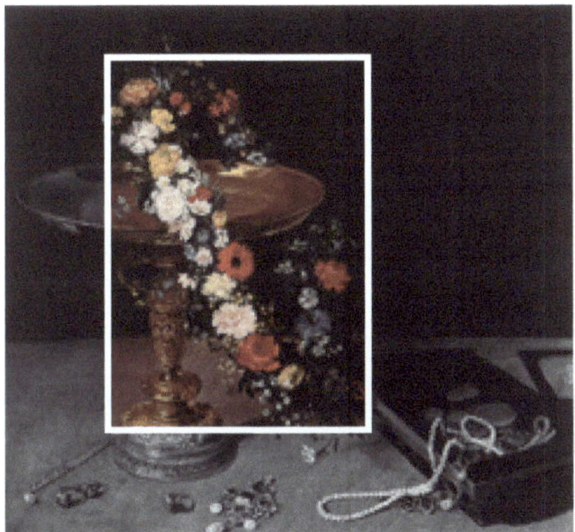

Still Life with a wreath and gold vase p.37
Jan Brueghel The Elder

Exotic flowers have become a popular material for still life for various reasons In the Dutch golden age.

Exploration and World Trade

Through exploration and trade, the Dutch people encountered new and exotic plants in distant lands such as Asia, America, and Africa. Exotic flowers such as tulips, hyacinths, and various tropical flowers captivated the imagination of both artists and supporters.

Symbol of Wealth

Rare exotic flowers with vivid colors, and unusual forms have additional symbolic meaning. Exotic flowers were considered to reflect the wonders of the natural world and the wealth and prosperity of the Dutch Republic. By including exotic flowers in still life, it delivered a message of admiration for the wealth, exploration, and beauty of nature.

Progress of Horticulture

Horticultural knowledge and its progress were famous in the Dutch golden age. Innovative cultivation technologies have been developed, such as using greenhouses to grow and preserve rare and delicate flowers.

Support and market demand

The rich merchants and collectors in the Netherlands were willing to buy still lifes from artists as their perception of art increased. Exotic flowers were popular because they added visual interests and diversity to composition.

Aesthetics

Exotic flowers provided visual attractions in still life. Artists such as Ambrosius Bosschaert the Elder, Jan Davidsz de Heem, Jan Brueghel The Elder excelled at capturing the delicate details and brilliance of the flowers, showed off their techniques, and made the overall attractions of paintings stand out even more.

Maria Theresia van Thielen

1640 - 1706

Maria Theresia van Thielen is a famous still life painter of Franders, especially with the flower still life. Although she is not known about her childhood and education, she is likely to have been taught by the famous painters of the time.

Van Thielen specializes in flowers and flower arrangements. Her works are characterized by a delicate and very detailed description of flowers. She showed excellent techniques in capturing the vivid colors and textures of flowers. van Thielen's still life often appears with colorful vases or flowers with bouquets in a basket. She made a harmonious composition that delivered an elegant and beautiful feeling by paying attention to the arrangement of flowers. Her works showcase meticulous details that emphasize the nuances of each flower.

Maria Theresia van Thielen's career has been active for decades and has been active as a painter until he died in 1706. van Thielen is still highly regarded as a contribution to exquisite descriptions and still life genres.

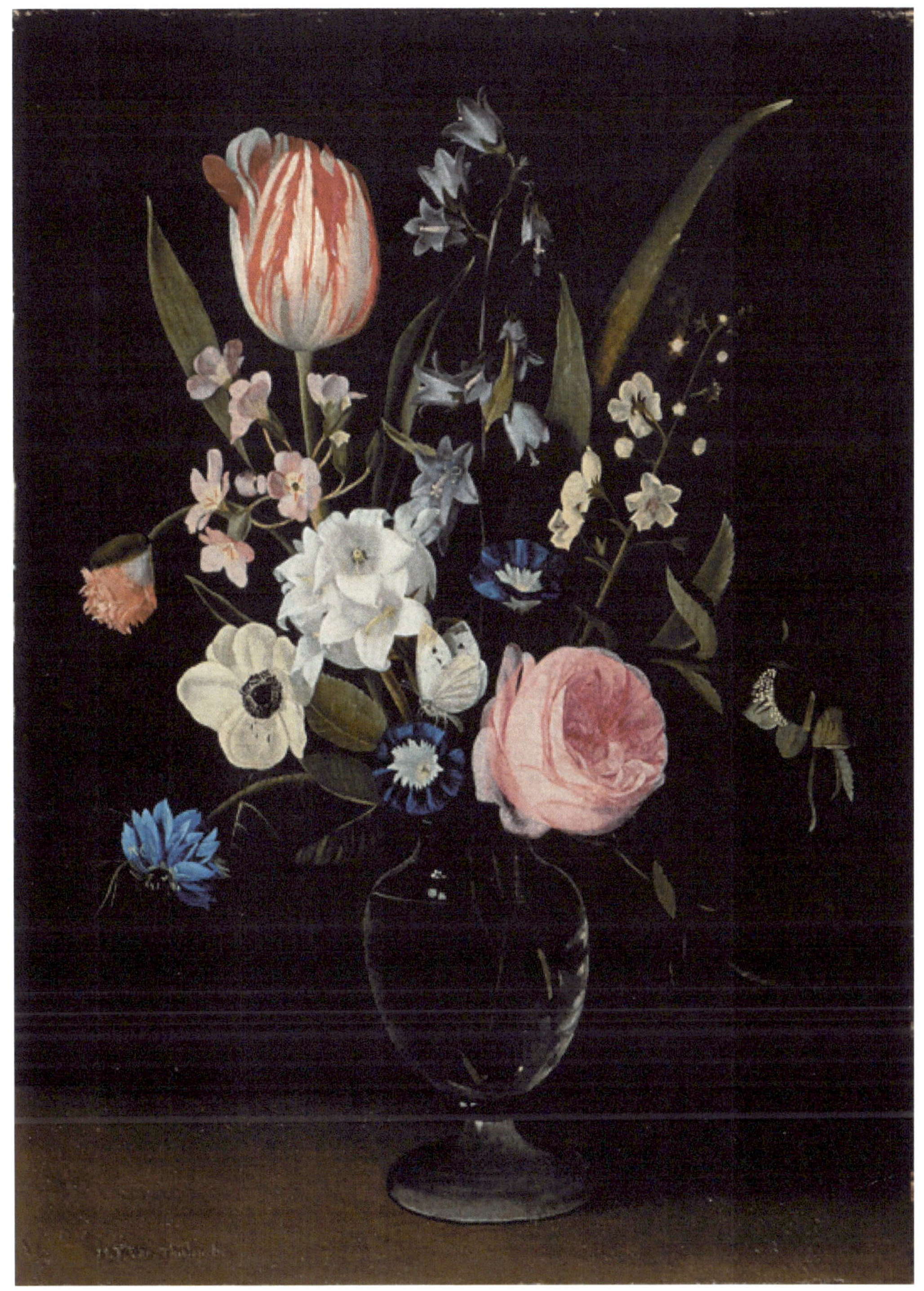

Bouquet of flowers in a glass vase, c.1660   47x 35.3 cm

Maria van Oosterwijck

1630 - 1693

Maria van Oosterwijck is a famous female painter who is skillful and detailed in still life and portrait during the Dutch golden age.

She was born in Nootdorp near Hague, the Netherlands in 1630. She took art education from her father who was a goldsmith. Since then, She was taught by the famous still life painter Jan Davidsz. de Heem and his influence are clearly revealed in her work. She was absorbed in drawing flowers focusing on capturing the delicate texture and vivid colors of flowers.

In the still life of the van Oosterwijck, carefully arranged bouquets in vases and baskets often appear. She had a keen eye to capture the light and shadows of the plant and completed the deep composition and realistic work based on him. High levels of techniques and attention to detail stand out in her work.

The bouquet in the vase is the classic motif of still life. Certain flowers selected for the configuration may have a symbolic meaning. In addition, various flowers are associated with various concepts and emotions. For example, roses often symbolize love and passion, lilies are purity, and tulips are wealth and prosperity. Van Oosterwijck chose insects for another motif. The depicted insects may have different meanings depending on the specific types, culture, and time. She also painted portraits in addition to still life. She was especially good at expressing the complex details of lace and cloth and capturing the appearance and features of the subject.

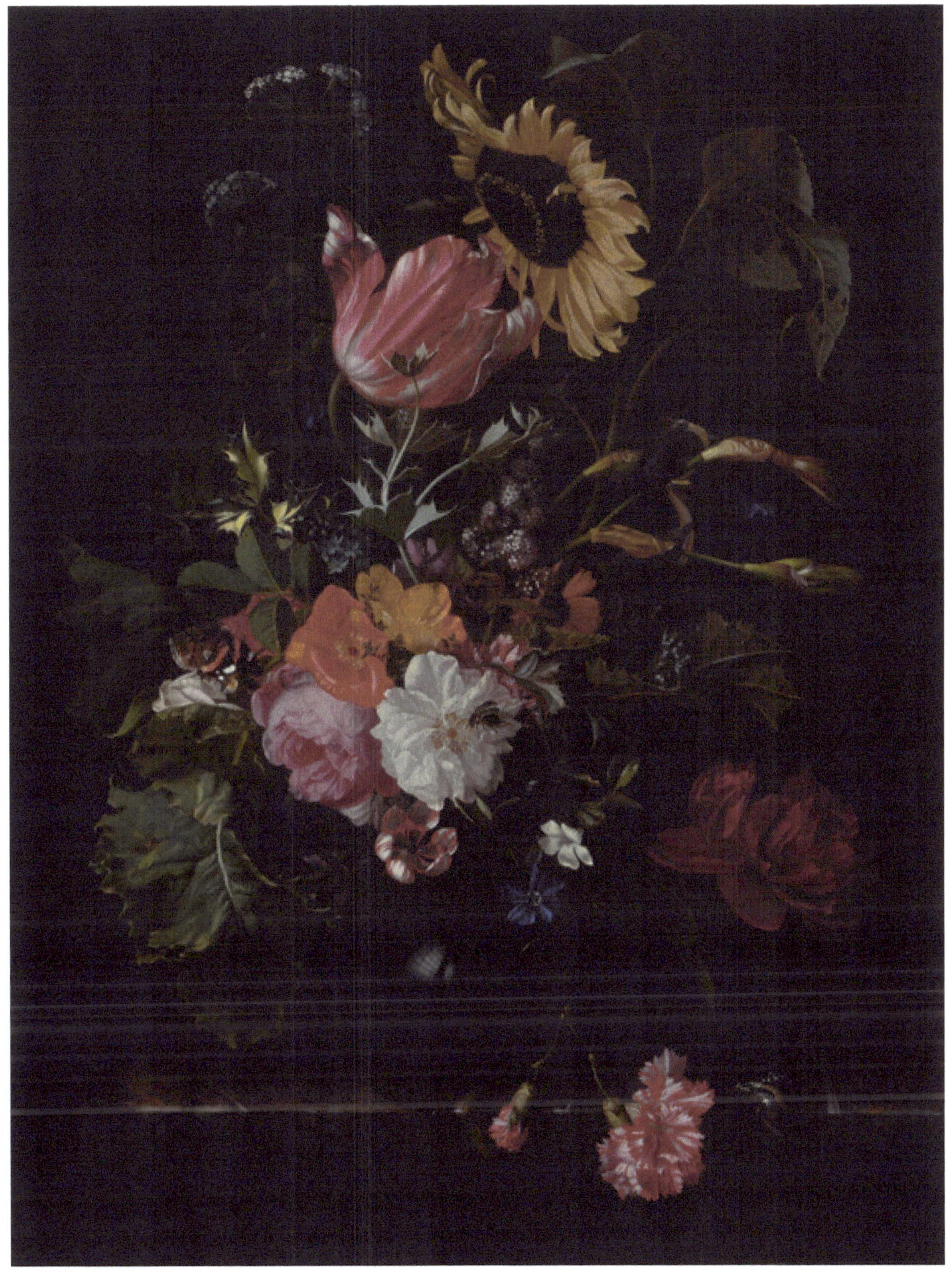

Bouquet of flowers in a vase, 1670   73.6 x 55.8 cm

Pieter Casteels III

1684 - 1749

Pieter Casteels III is a painter of Franders, and is especially famous for its elaborate still life depicting flowers and fruits. He was born in an artist family in Antwerp, Belgium in 1684. His father, Pieter Casteels II, was also a famous painter. Peters Casteels III has been trained by his father and is likely to have learned still life. He developed a unique style that features careful attention to detail, vivid colors, and depth and realism of composition.

Casteels III's works often feature precise and delicately arranged bouquets. He had a keen eye for capturing the delicate details of each flower, and lively expressed petals, leaves, and textures on the canvas. He used light and shadows skillfully to add depth and dimension to the paintings. In addition to flower still life, Pieter Casteels III also painted fruit works based on various fruits such as grapes, peaches, and melons. These works showed his ability to express a variety of textures and surfaces, from the smooth skin of the pear to the rough shells of the orange.

He continued to paint notable works until he died in 1749. His legacy is considered technical accuracy, sophisticated details, and transcendental masterpieces.

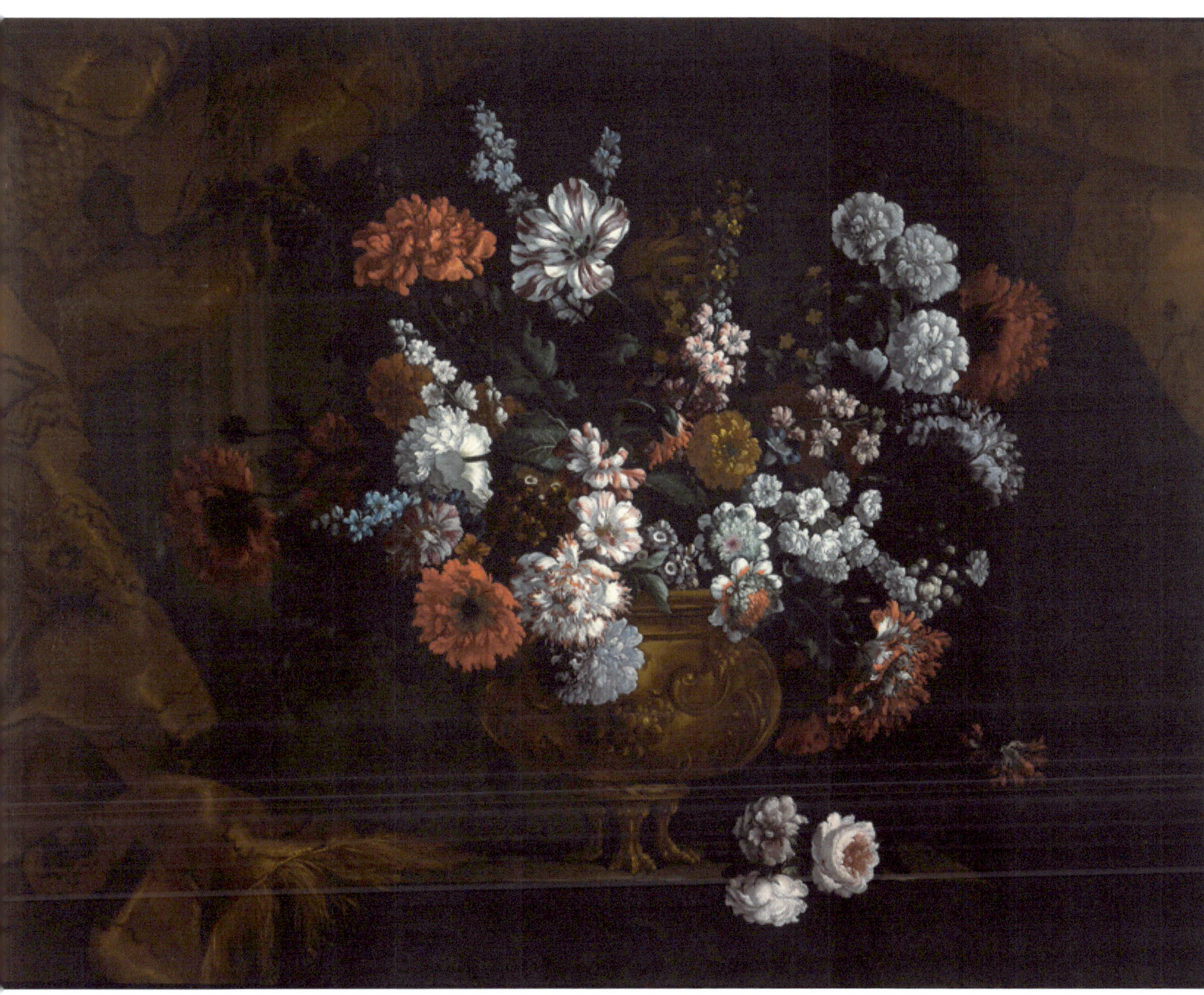

Bouquet of flowers in a bronze urn

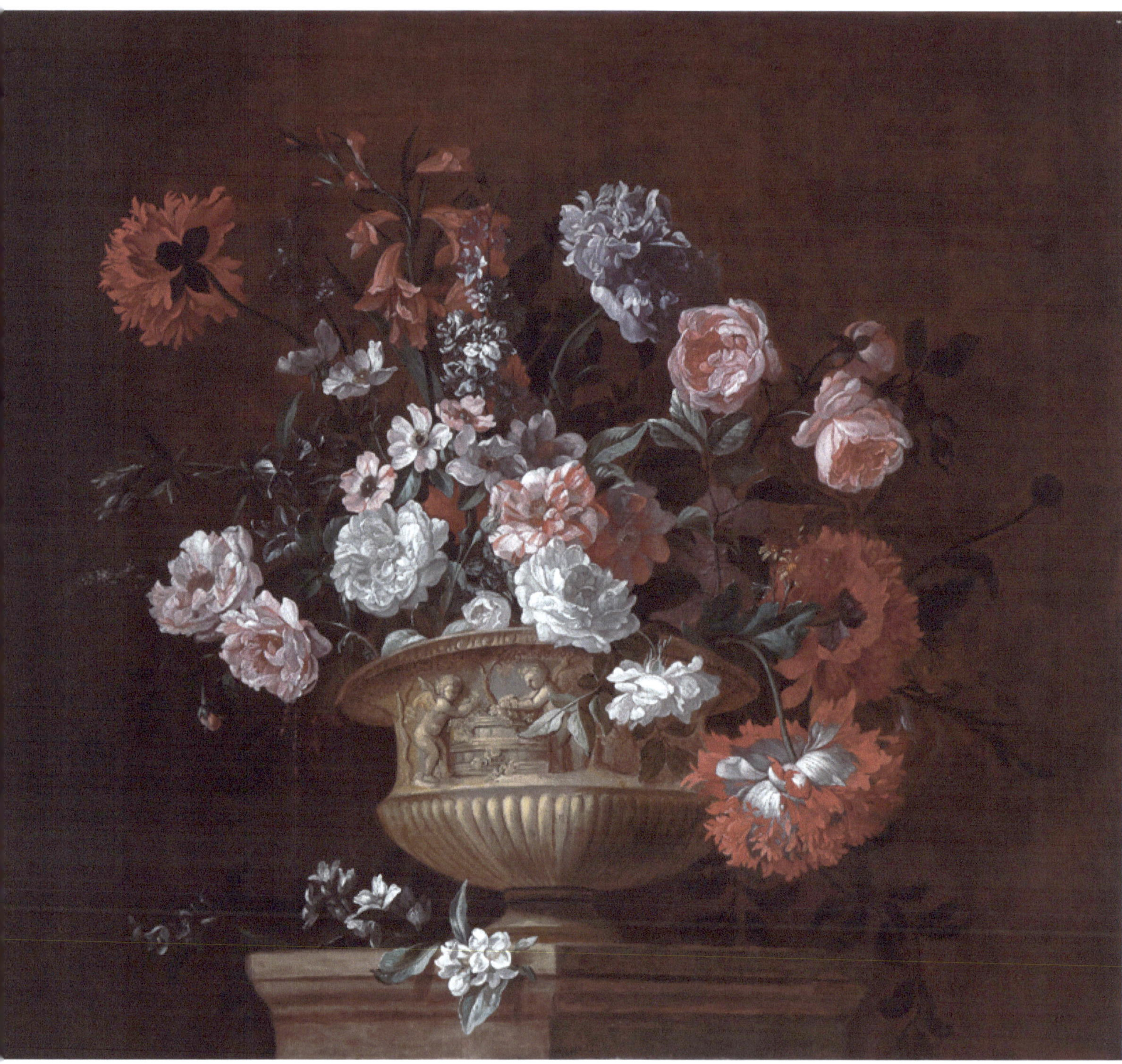

Bouquet of flowers in an urn on postamente

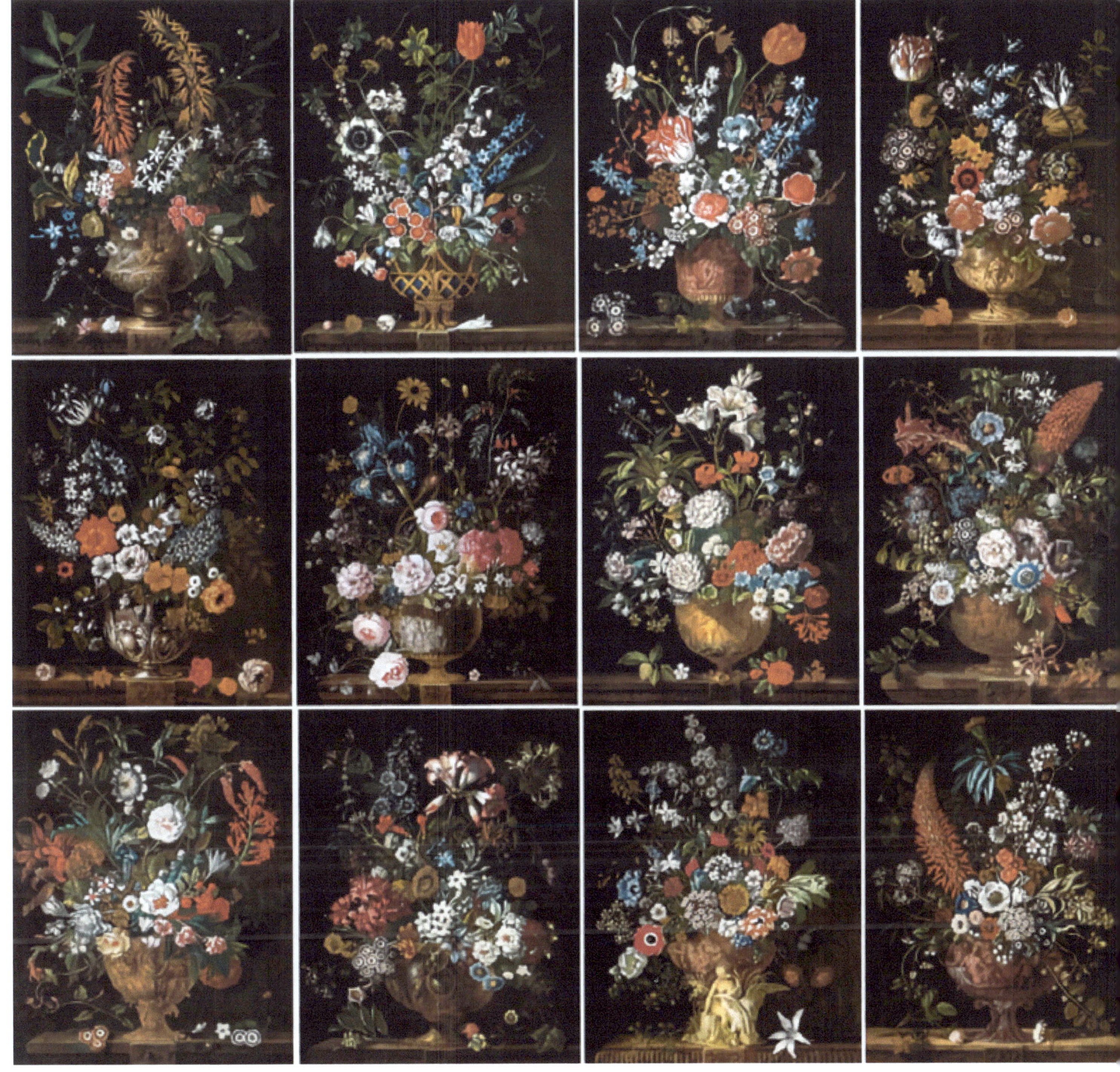

Johannes Goedaert

1617 - 1668

Johannes Goedaert is a Dutch naturalist, entomologist, and painter who is famous for his achievements and insect illustrations that contribute to insect science. At the age of 18, Goedaert became a member of the Saint Lucas Guild and participated in the art community. He worked at the same time as other artists of Middelburg, including Adriaen van de Venne and Christoffel van den Berghe. In particular, Goedaert has made a groundbreaking achievement in the field of insect science. He directly observed and experimented with the growth and perverts of insects and recorded them from 1635 to 1667. His findings and illustrations were published in three books, 'Metamorphosis Naturalis', which was famous for its detailed description of the life cycle of insects and insects. This study has led to one of the early writers in the field of insect science and contributed greatly to insect research in the Netherlands and Europe. It is not clear who taught Goedaert painting and drawing, but there is a possibility that Christoffel van den Berghe was his teacher who combines insect paintings into his work.

His particular picture depicts a small bouquet in Chinese vases, which was quite popular in the 17th-century Netherlands. Still life often shows the artist's skills that capture the beauty and complexity of various objects such as flowers, fruits, and other daily goods. Goedaert, an entomologist, was not only excellent in expressing insects precisely but also excellent in describing the structure and function of flowers. The inclusion of Chinese vases suggests that the prosperous trade between the Netherlands and Asia recognized the high value of exotic imports in the Dutch golden age. The flowers and insects in his work are likely to show off their skills as a painter and capture the aesthetic charm of flower arrangements. It may also reflect the influence of international trade and exotic objects in the 17th century.

Johannes Goedaertert has contributed to insect studies and natural history, especially due to the initial exploration of careful illustrations and insect life cycles.

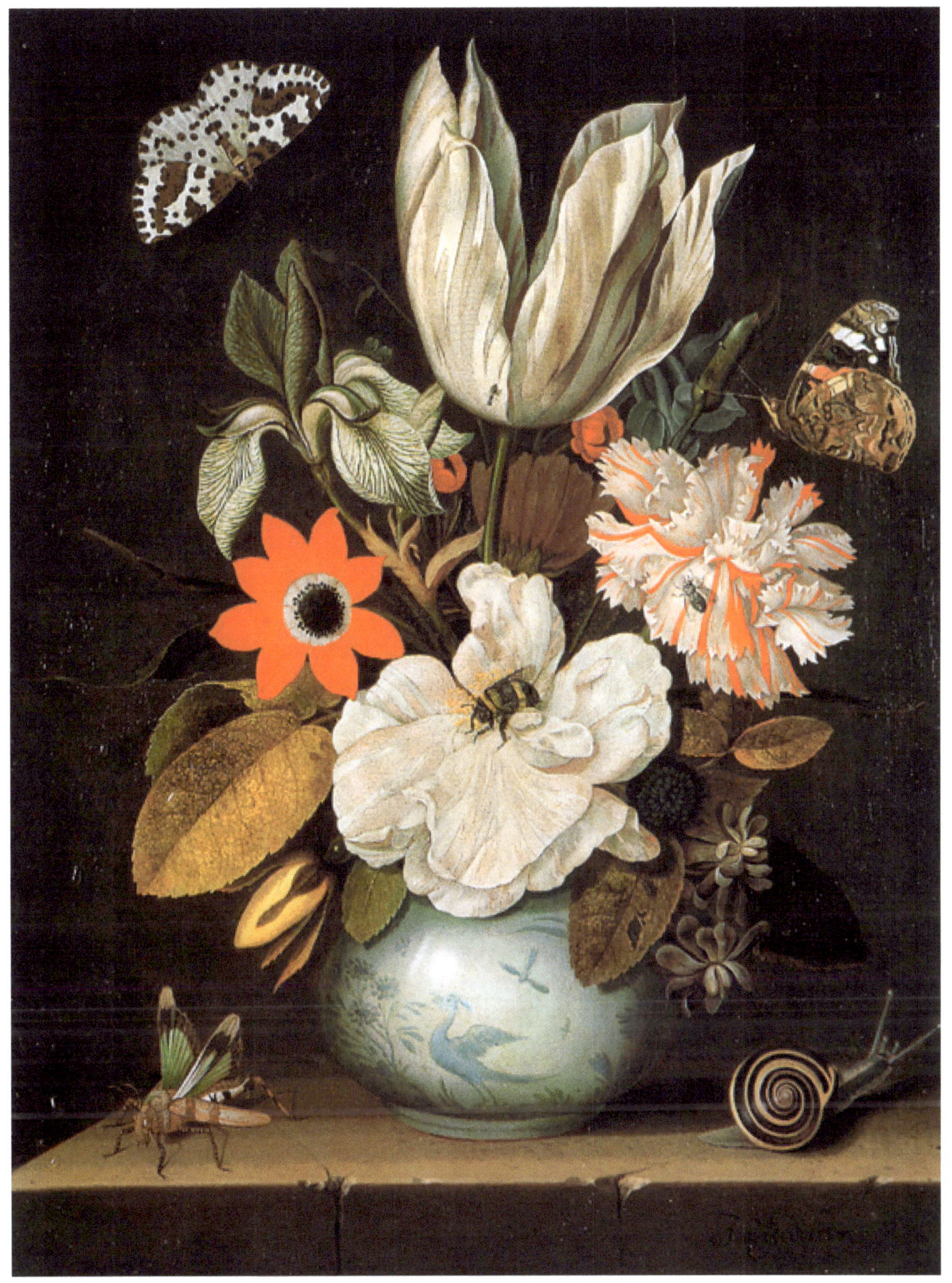

Small bouquet of flowers in a Chinese vase 28 x 22 cm

Nicolaes van Gelder

1636 - 1676

Nicholas van Gelder is a Dutch golden age painter famous for still life genre.

He was born in Amsterdam, the Netherlands in 1636. It is known that Nicholas van Gelder was influenced by prominent 17th-century Dutch still life painters Jan Davidsz. de Heem and Willem Kalf. Jan Davidsz. de Heem was famous for its colorful and very delicate still life, based on luxurious objects, sophisticated flower arrangements, various fruits, insects, and other natural elements. His work is characterized by rich colors, sophisticated brush touches, and careful attention to light and shadows. In van Gelder's work, you can see the influence of de Heem such as detail, lively color, and including various natural elements in the work. Willem KALF, on the other hand, was famous for its still life of things such as glass bowls, silver bowls, and Chinese pottery. In particular, it was also famous for the careful expression of texture, accurate reflection, and balanced composition. Van Geler's still life shows the style of Willem Kalf, especially in interest in the choice and detail of things. Van Gelder also developed his unique unique style and approach. His work shows the unique ability to capture the texture of things, color, and light, and shows a visually attractive and technically complete composition.

Van Gelder died in 1676 at the age of 40 in Amsterdam. Despite his relatively short life, his work is still praised for his contribution to techniques and lively composition and the 17th-century Dutch still life tradition.

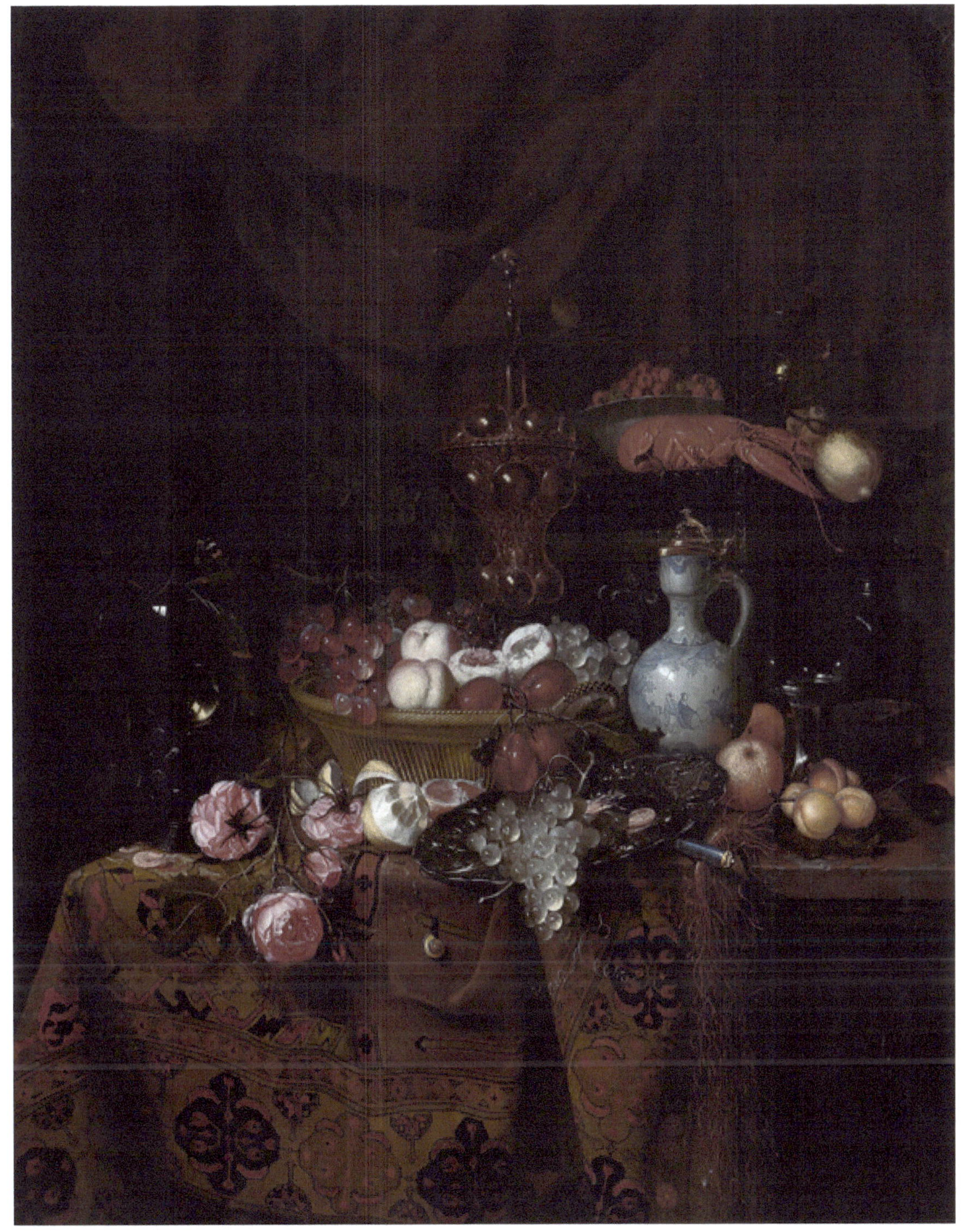

Still Life, 1664

Into the details

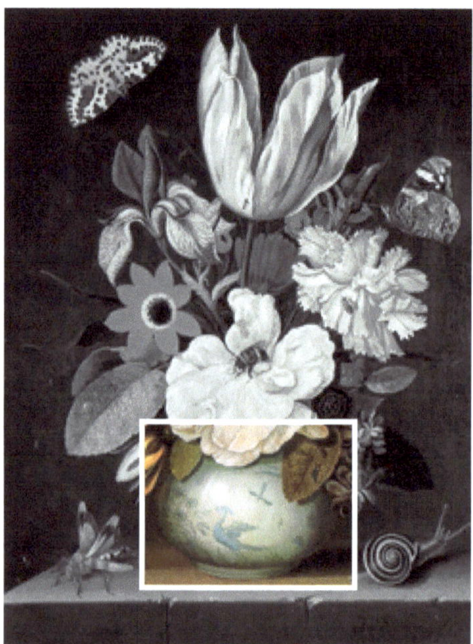

Small bouquet of flowers in a Chinese vase ^{p.53}
Johannes Goedaert

Trade played a decisive role in the economic success of the Dutch Republic. One of the important things about this trade was the import of Chinese pottery, which gained high popularity and fame among Dutch elites. Chinese pottery with sophisticated craftsmanship and delicate beauty had tremendous values and symbols of wealth and sophistication. The Dutch East India company

Vereenigde Oostindische Compagnie pioneered a trade route to Asia, especially China, to get coveted products such as spices, tea, silk, and pottery, and the Dutch were fascinated by Chinese pottery. Chinese pottery still life has emerged as a genre of Dutch golden age arts, and Artists such as Johannes Goedaert, Willem Kalf, Jan Janz Trek described the arrangement of pottery on the table.

Still life which mainly describes Chinese pottery was used for various meanings and purposes. First, it was used to symbolize the wealth and status of the Dutch elite class that can buy valuable and exotic objects. Second, these paintings showed the delicate details of Chinese pottery and the artistic skills of Dutch painters who express the glossy glaze. Artists have demonstrated their skills by capturing the complexity of pottery patterns and creating a picture of realism and charm. Lastly, it was emphasized that the Dutch Republic was interconnected with a wider world and is a hub of international commerce by including Chinese pottery in the work.

Floris van Dyck

1575 - 1651

Floris van Dyck is a Dutch golden age painter famous for his portrait, historical paintings and still life. Van Dyke was educated in Haarlem and became a member of the St. Luke in 1613. He was influenced by the works of Franders and Dutch painters, especially Caravaggio and Hendrick Goltzius, and then integrated Dutch naturalism into the work to adopt a more sophisticated and restrained approach.

As a portrait painter, van Dyke was very good at capturing the appearance and personality of the subject. The upper class and the individual of the Dutch aristocracy appeared in his portraits, He paid attention to detail and texture and created a realistic and expressive description. Van Dyke also inspired classical mythology and religious stories to draw scenes in history and the Bible. His historical paintings often showed his techniques by combining dramatic composition, vivid colors, and sophisticated details. Van Dyke was famous for his portraits and historical paintings, especially "breakfast works". This still life depicts a visual arrangement of food, dishes, and other objects.

Today, Van Dyke's paintings can be found in various museums and collections around the world, including the National Museum of Art in Amsterdam, the Louvre in Paris, and the London National Gallery. His contribution to Dutch golden age art is highly regarded for his techniques, expression, and unchanging artistic values.

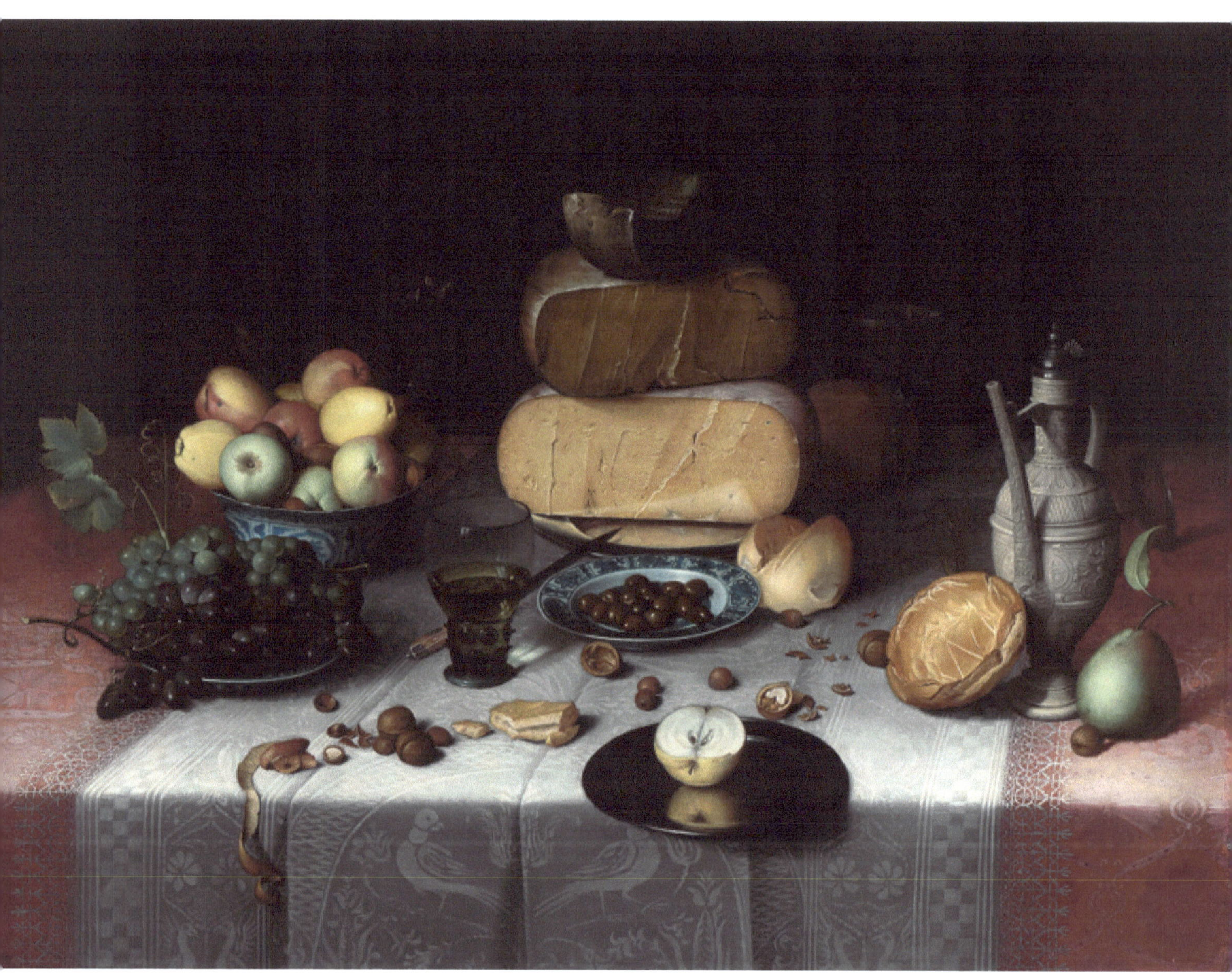

Still Life with cheese, c.1615   82.2 x 111.2 cm

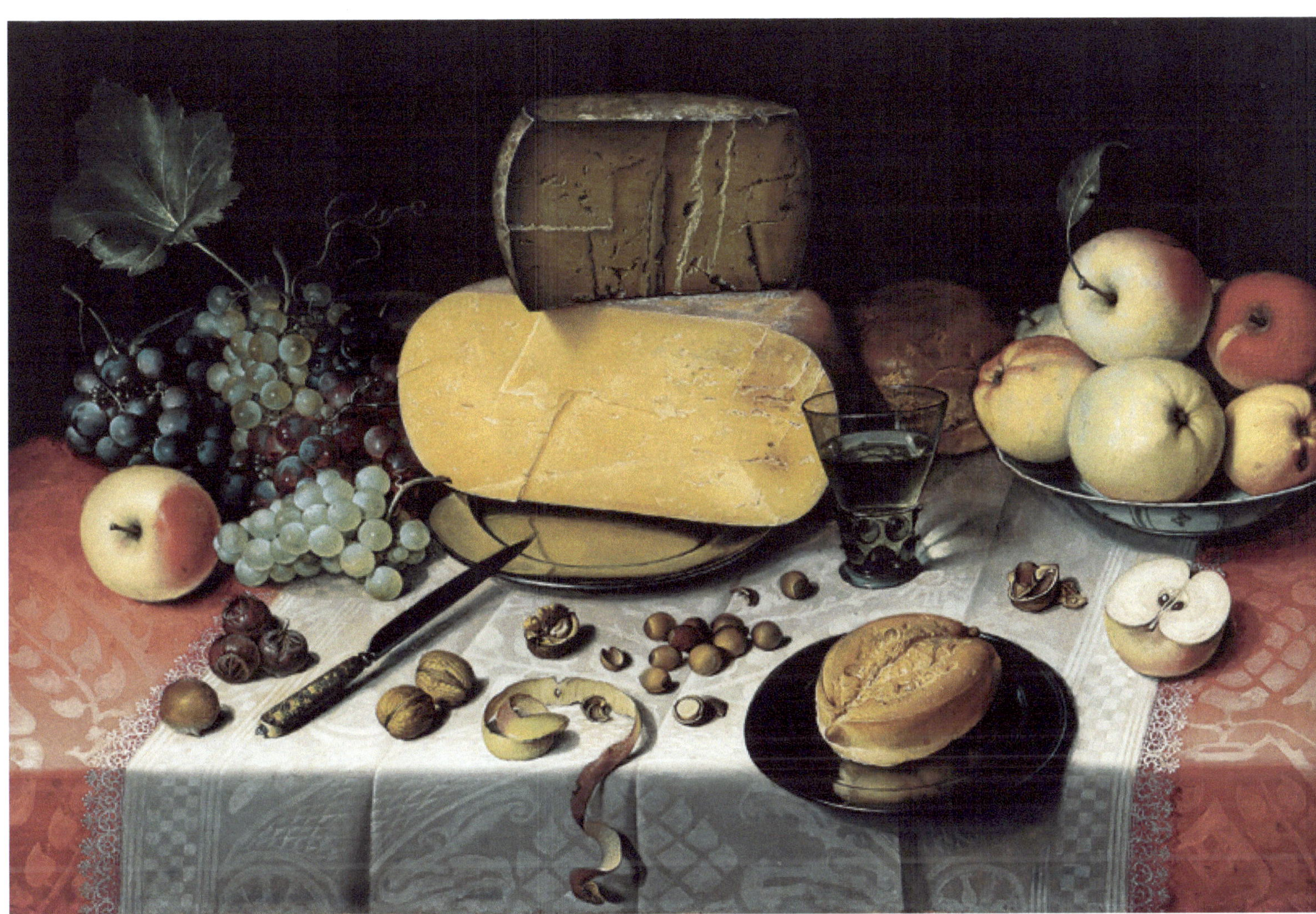

Still Life with cheese, c.1613   49.5 x 77 cm

Nicolas Gillis

1595 - 1632

Nicholas Gillis is a Dutch still life painter, famous for fruit and flower still lifes, and is one of the early Dutch still life painters of the genre of 'Banketje' or 'Breakfast still life'. He was influenced by the famous Dutch painter Floris van Dyck. Gillis was born in 1595 and married in Haarlem, the Netherlands in 1615, and lived there until he died. He specialized in still life, especially in fruit and flower arrangements. His work is characterized by describing a variety of fruits, flowers, and other objects in detail and often in an informal and naturalistic way.

Unfortunately, Nicholas Gillis's life ended in 1632 at the age of 37. Despite his relatively short career, his contributions are noteworthy in still life genre, especially in breakfast still life. Today, his work is highly regarded for his contribution to his experienced techniques and attention to detail, and for contributing to the rich tradition of Dutch golden age still life.

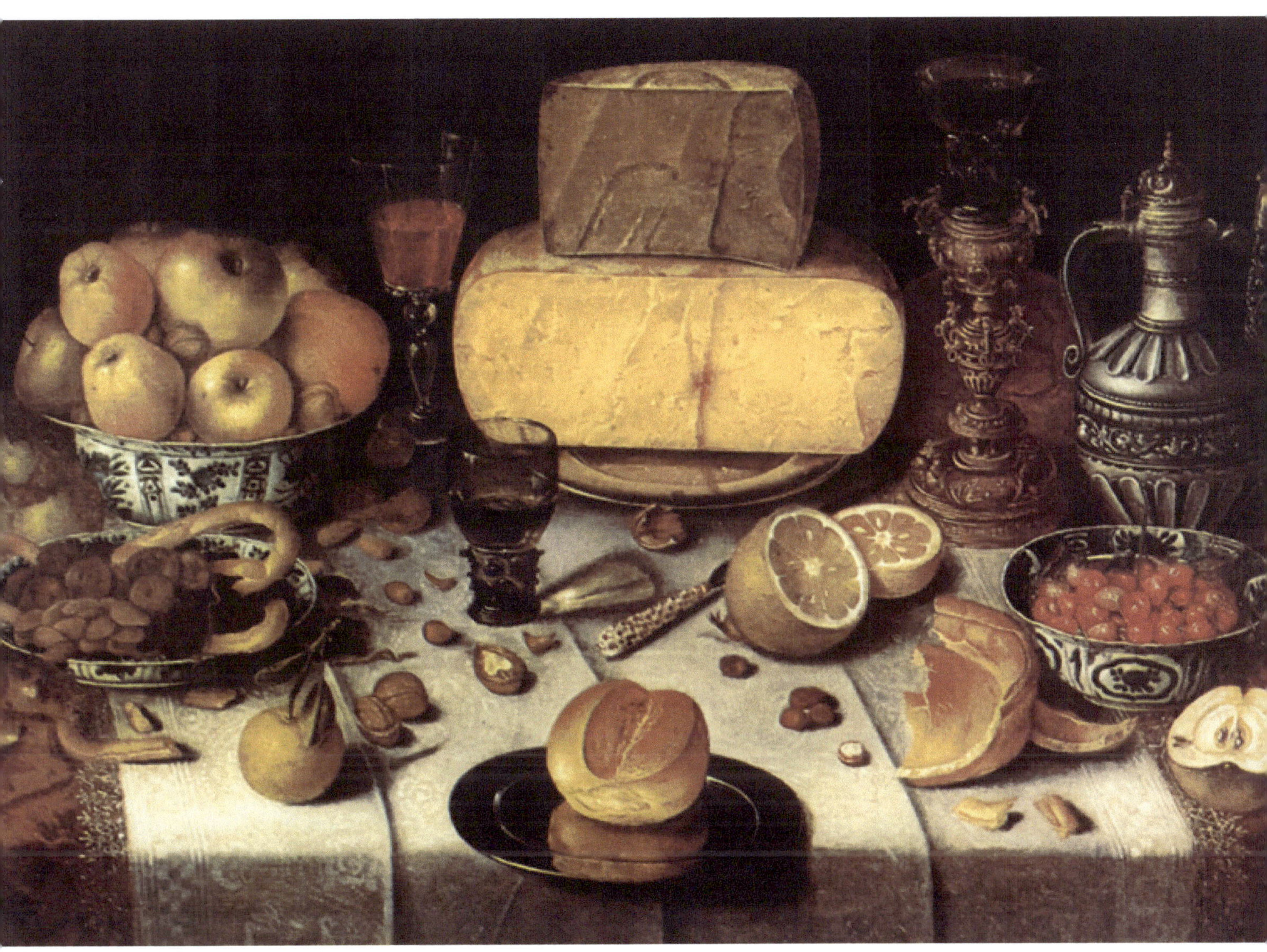

Covered table, 1611   59 x 79 cm

Clara Peeters
c.1588/94 - 1621

   Clara Peeters is believed to have been born in Antwerp, Belgium, around 1588 or 1594. She is a female artist who worked in Antwerp, the center of 17th-century art production.

   Peeters specializes in the scenes on the top of the table where various objects are arranged in the still life genre, especially balanced and harmonious composition. In her paintings, objects such as fruits, seafood, bread, glass, and elegant dishes often appeared.

   Peeters' work shows excellent aspects of female artists who worked in male-oriented fields. Her work shows a high level of techniques and artistic sense and shows a keen view of capturing the texture, reflection, and play of light on various surfaces. Peeters' paintings have been highly praised in her lifetime and are still praised for their quality and artistic value. Her works currently belong to prominent museums and collections, including the Prado Museum in Madrid Prado, The Royal Museum of Fine Arts Antwerp, and the Mauritshuis Museum of Hague. As an experienced still life painter, her contributions had a continuous influence on the art world. Her work was evidence of her talent, and later opened the way to other female artists.

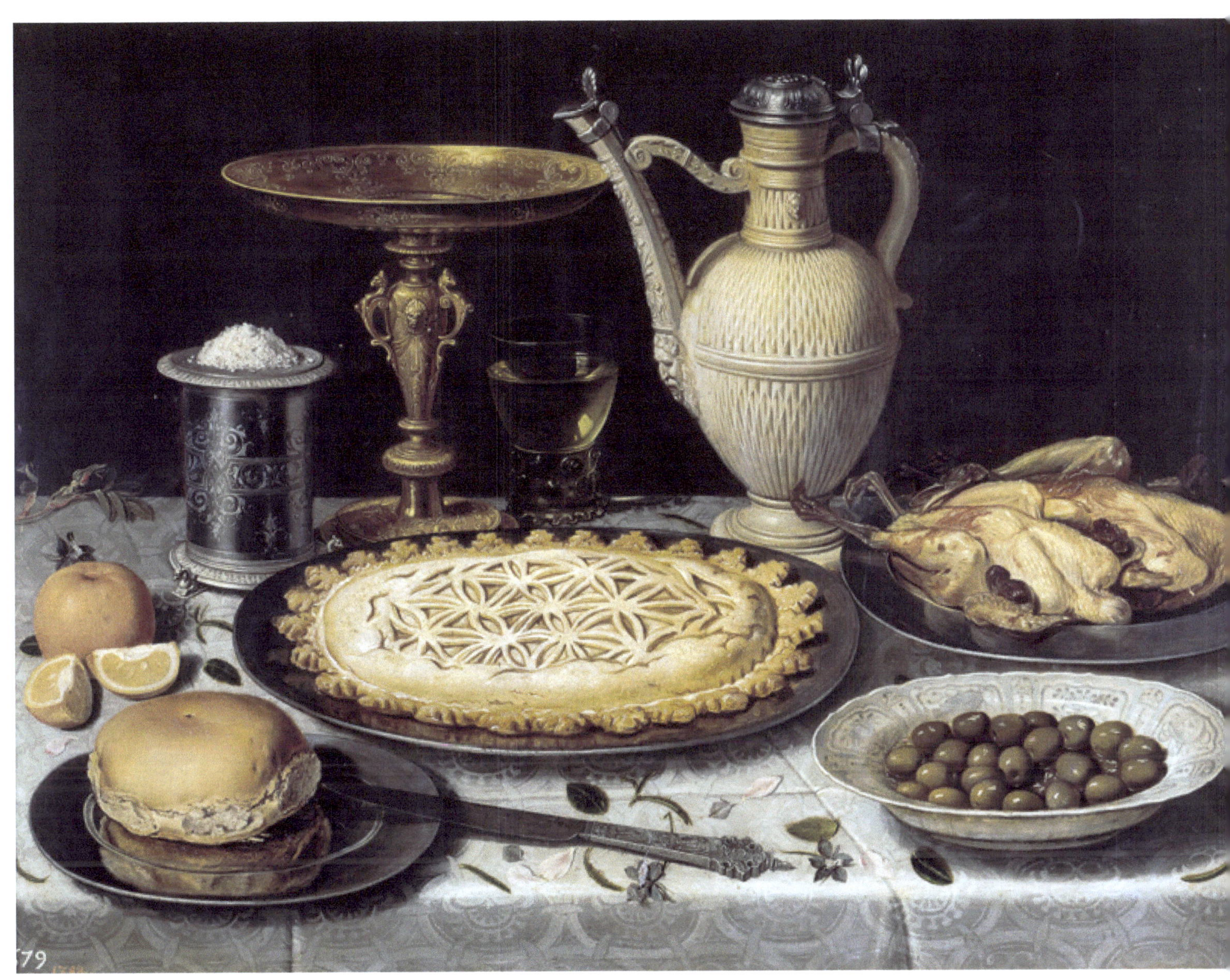

Still Life, 1610-15   55 x 73 cm

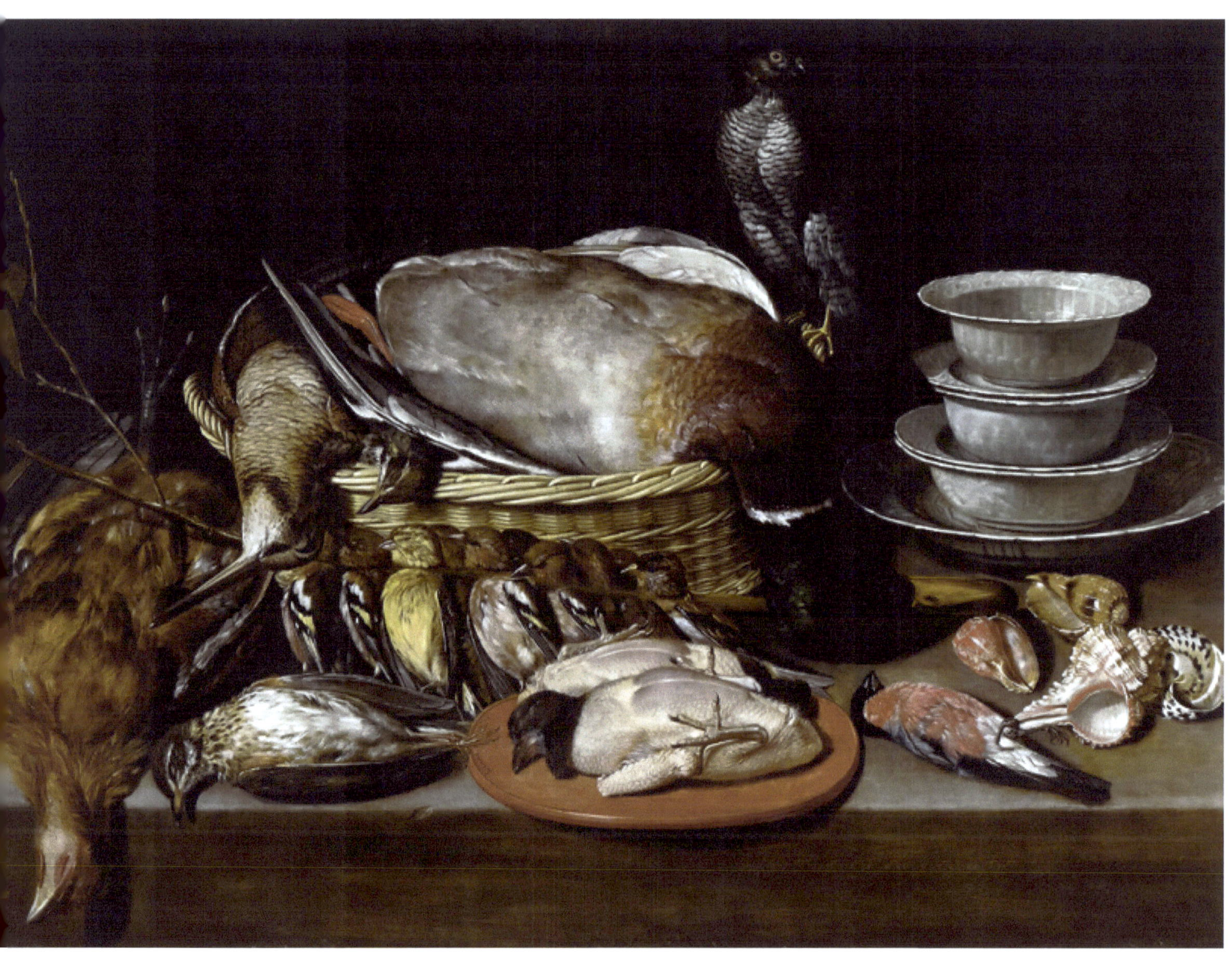

Still Life, 1611   52 x 71 cm

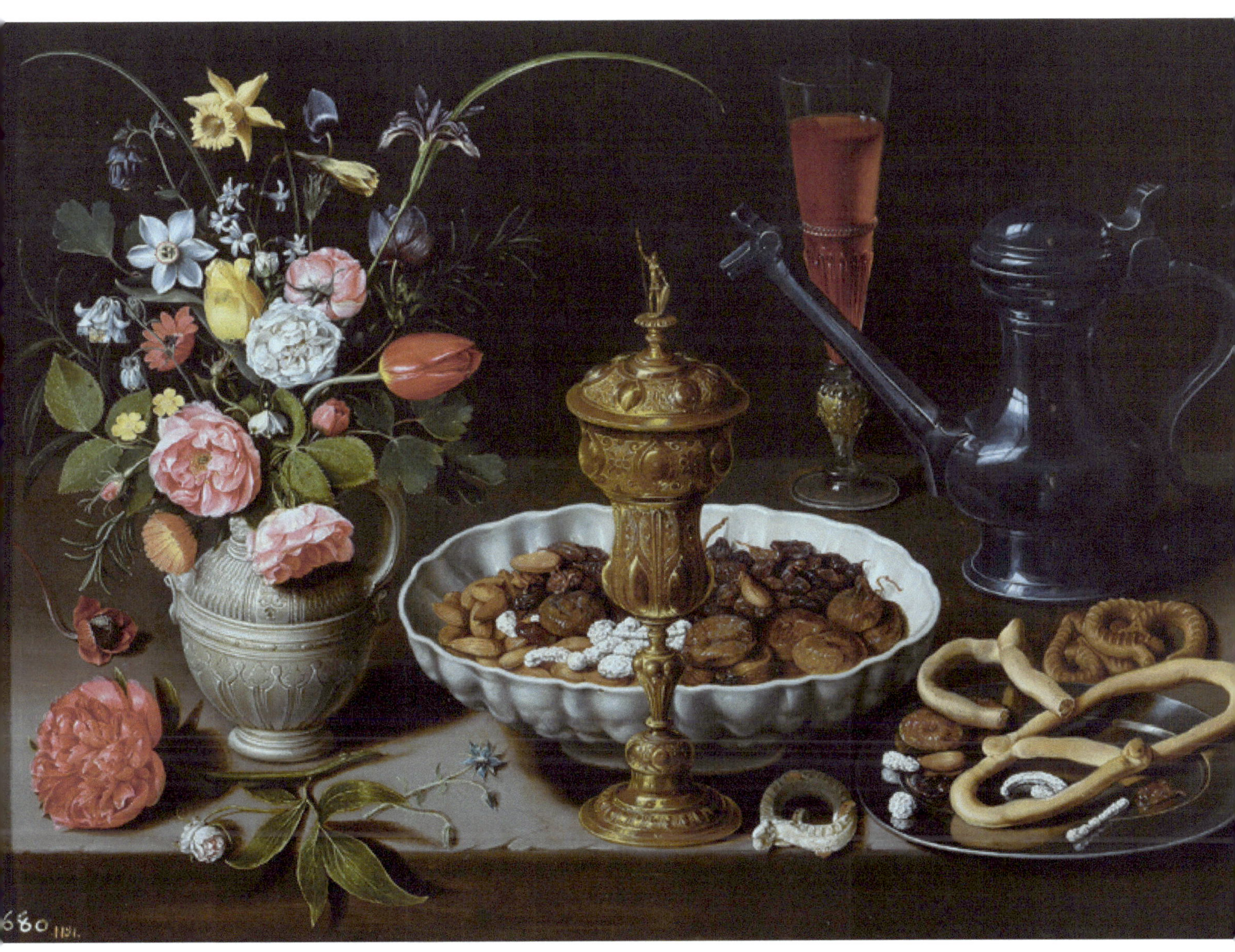

Still Life, 1611   52 x 73 cm

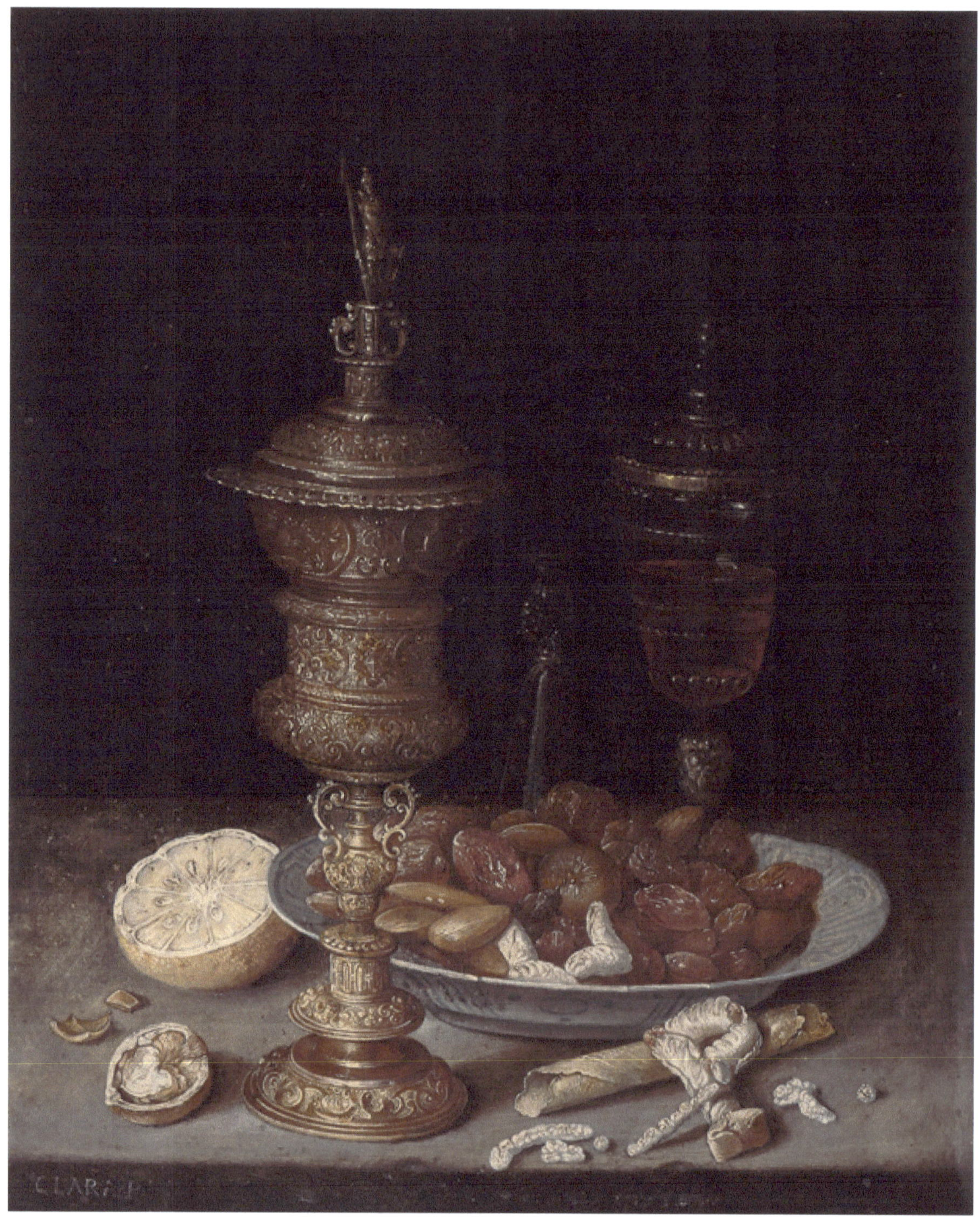

Still life with gilt vessel

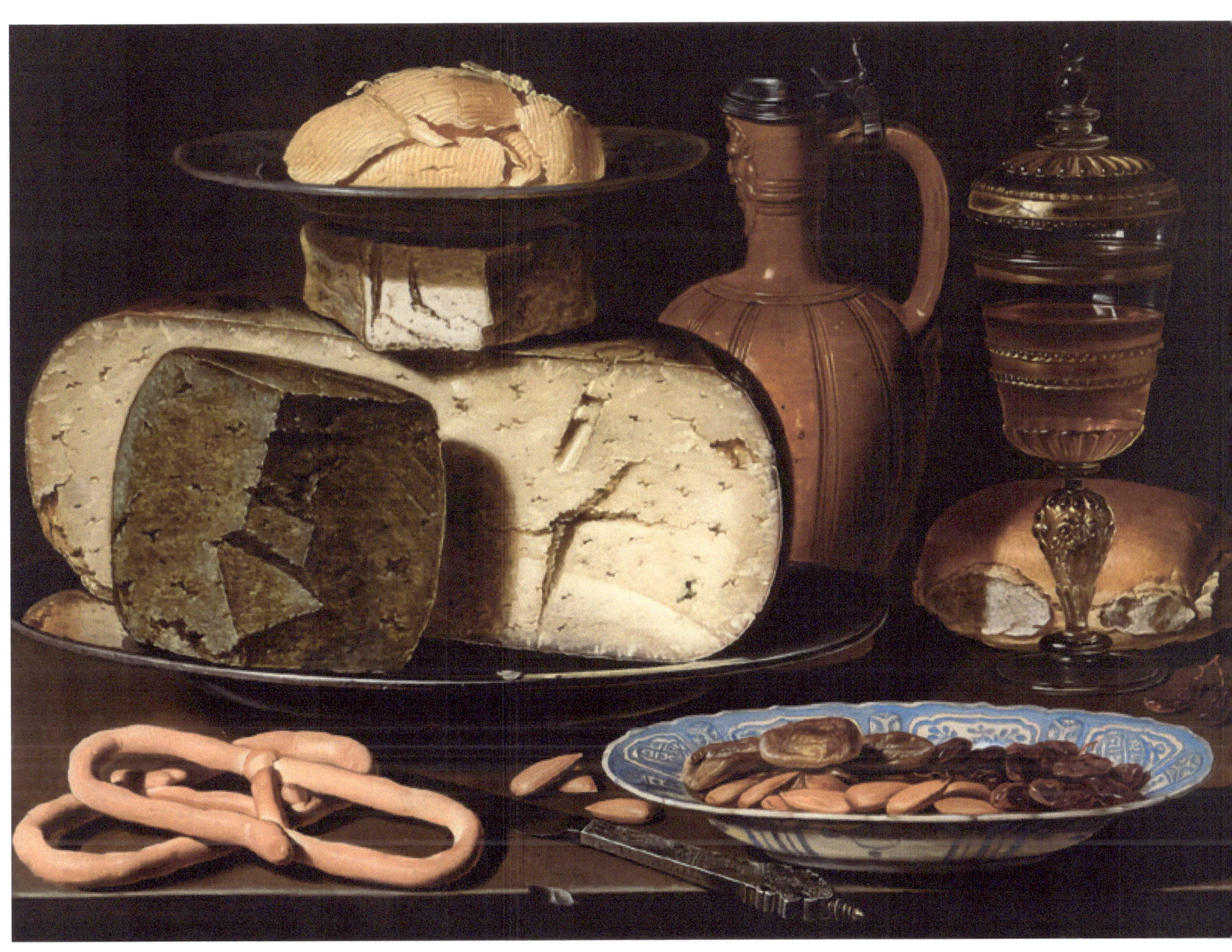

Still-life with cheese, almonds and pretzels, c.1613

35 x 50 cm

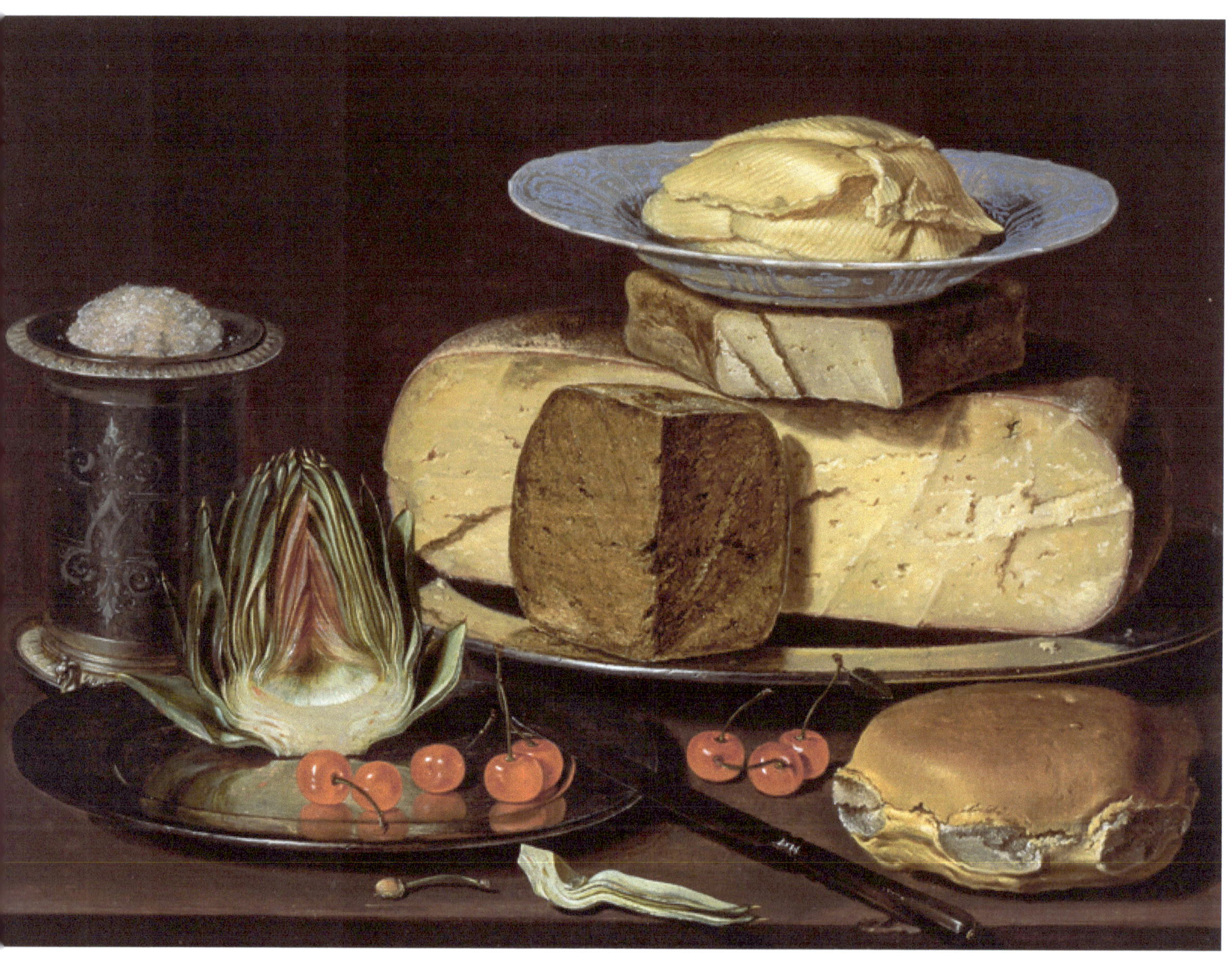

Still-life with cheese, artichokes and cherry   34.5 x 49.5 cm

Into the details

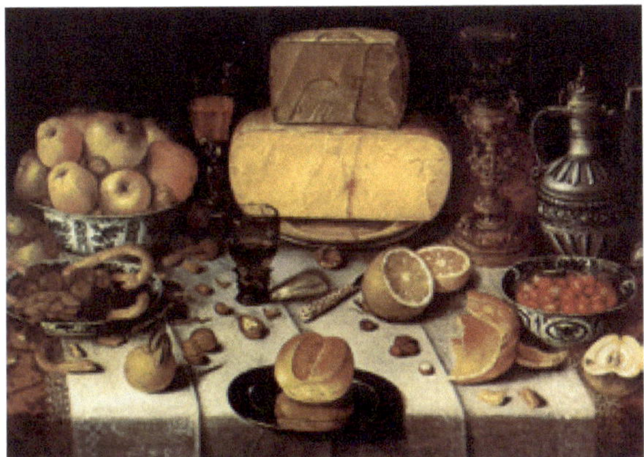

Covered table p.61
Nicolas Gillis

Ontbijtjes' is a professional term that refers to a picture depicting breakfast in the Dutch golden age. This was derived from the Dutch 'Ontbijt', which means breakfast, and 'Stillevens', which means still life. Breakfast in the Dutch golden age is generally composed of items such as bread, rolls, butter, cheese, fruit, milk, ale, wine, sometimes seafood or meat. The artists focused on displaying various foods and creating a visually attractive composition. In general, it depicts table settings with a variety of foods and drinks. The work was often depicted by paying attention to the details and strongly emphasizing light and shadows. In the typical Dutch golden breakfast still life, there are various objects on the table, and generally covered with a clean white tablecloth.

In Nicholas Gillis' work <Covered Table>, you can see a table covered with a clean white tablecloth. There are a variety of objects on the table: pottery bowls or plates with bread and rolls, kettles, silver or pewter cups, and small vessels or plates with apples and red ripe fruits. Gillis focused on the composition and added realism to the painting so that tableware tools can be harmonized with food naturally. It was common to give a subtle shadow and emphasize the texture of objects using soft light from the window. Gillis who was influenced by Floris Van Dyck paid careful attention to the rendering of each element, using detailed and precise techniques that capture the vivid colors and textures of fruits, flowers, and other objects.

Abraham Hendrickz. van Beyeren

1620 - 1690

Abraham Hendrickz. Van Bayeren is a painter in the Netherlands in the mid-17th century and is famous for his still life. His work is characterized by gorgeous decoration of everyday objects such as food, dishes, and luxury goods, especially colorful displays. Van Beyeren was educated in Hague under the guidance of his uncle, painter Pieter de Putter. Afterward, he moved to Delft and joined the Guild of Saint Luke to improve his skills as a still life painter. Van Beyeren's still life is characterized by abundant and colorful expressions, and complex details with rich food, and luxurious dishes. He created a work that conveys a colorful and rich feeling with well ripe fruits, shiny oysters, and complex table settings. Vanitas elements, such as withered flowers and rotting fruits, can be found in his work. Van Beyeren's paintings mainly praise the pleasure of senses and the material abundance of the natural world. His work, which focuses on rich color, delicate texture, and luxurious objects, reflects the desire to show the beauty and richness of life.

One of the remarkable achievements of van Beyeren was the ability to capture the play of light on a variety of surfaces, from sparkling silver products to glossy fruits and glass products. He skillfully expresses the texture of various materials and adds a sense of depth and realism to the painting by using strong contrast. He became very popular with sophisticated details, skilled techniques, and rich feelings, and attracted wealthy sponsors and collectors who wanted to own his work. Van Bayeren was famous for his still life, but he also explored other genres such as landscape and sea landscape. But what he left a deep impression on art history is his still life work, especially the Vanitas still life.

He married Sara van der Linde and they had a daughter named Maartje. Abraham Hendrickz. van Bayeren died in 1690 at the age of 70 in Alkmaar, the Netherlands. His legacy continues with the excellent still lifes that capture the hearts of art lovers and collectors around the world.

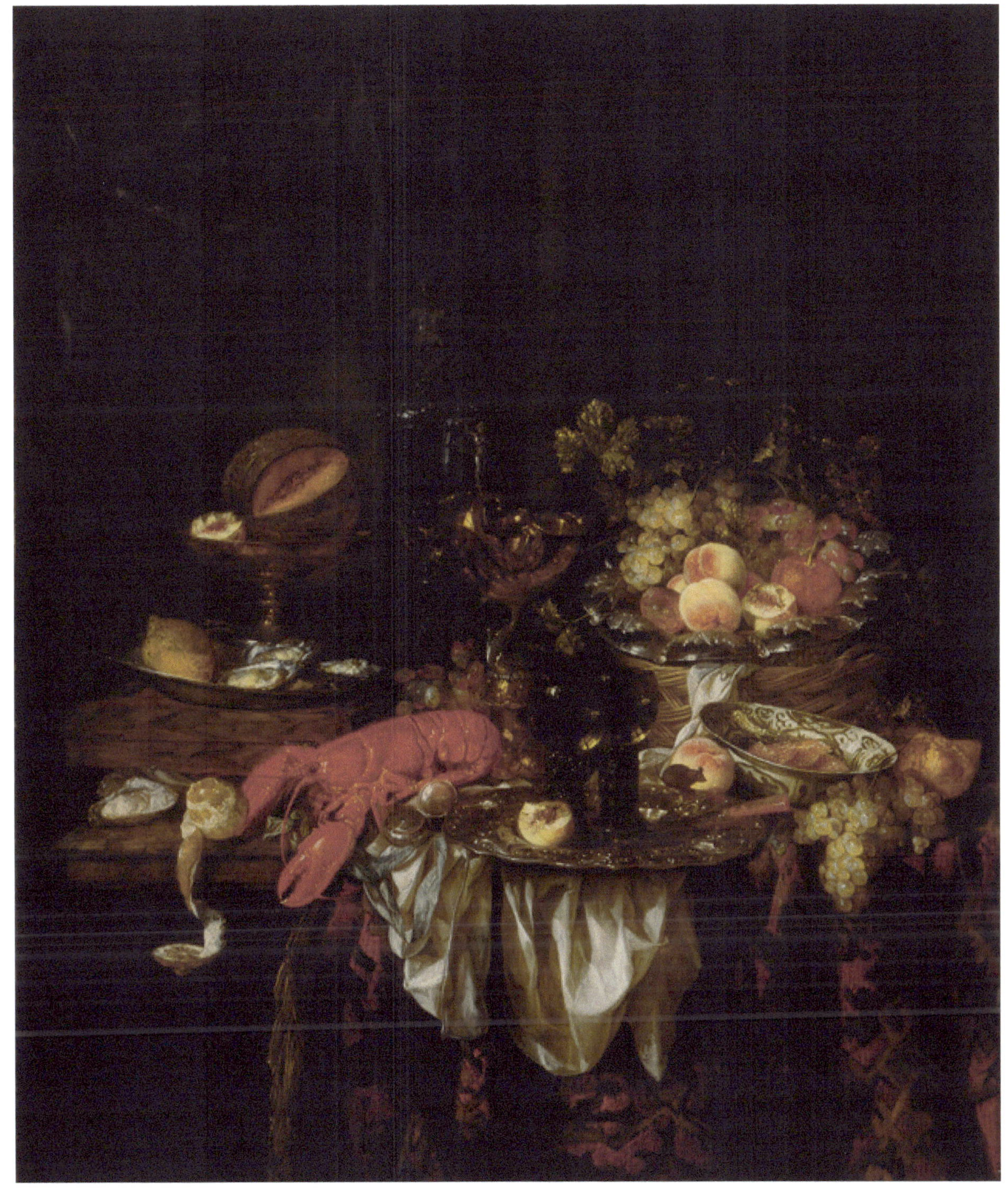

Banquet, 1667   *141 x 22 cm*

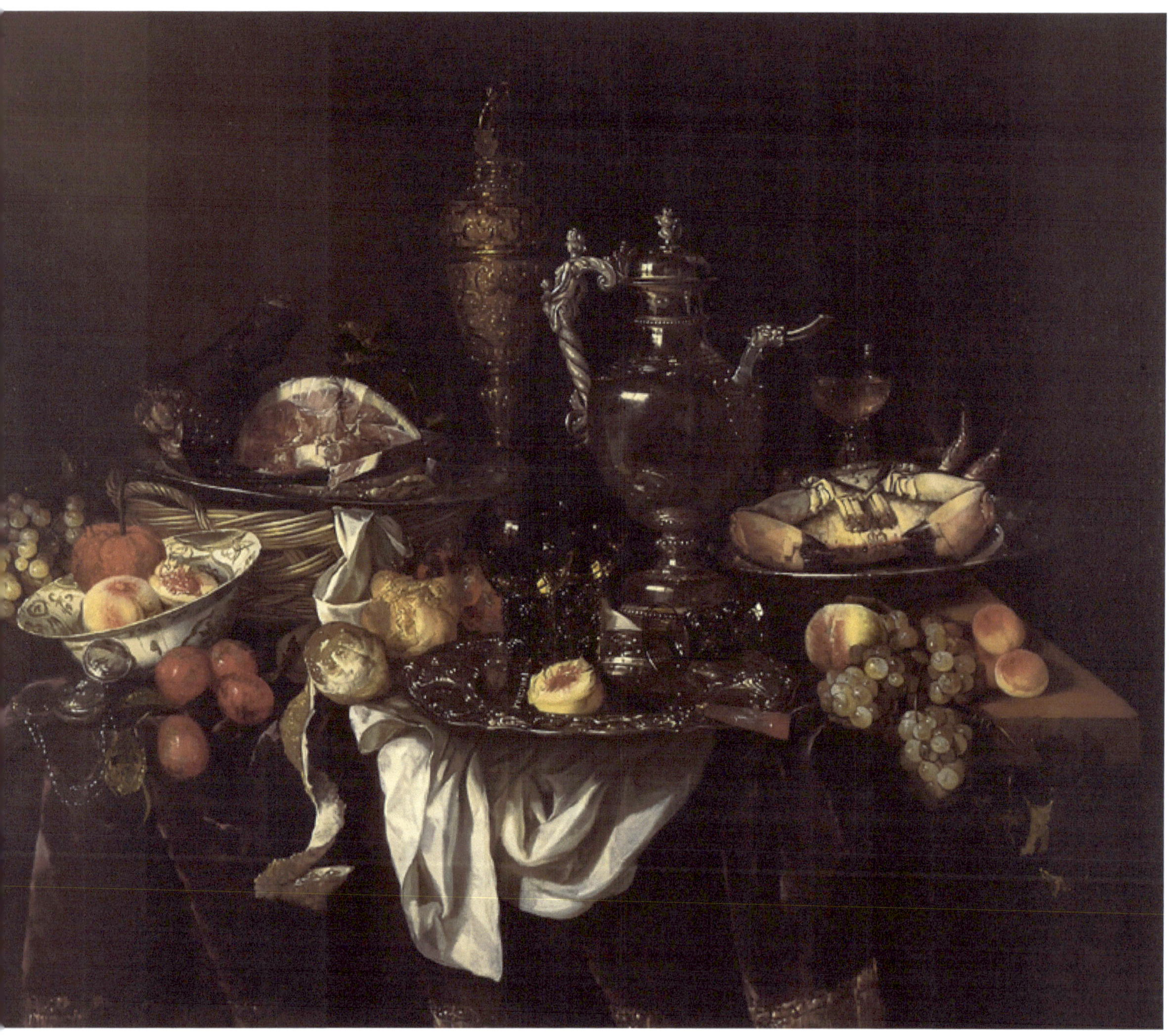

Banquet, 1655   99.5 x 120.5 cm

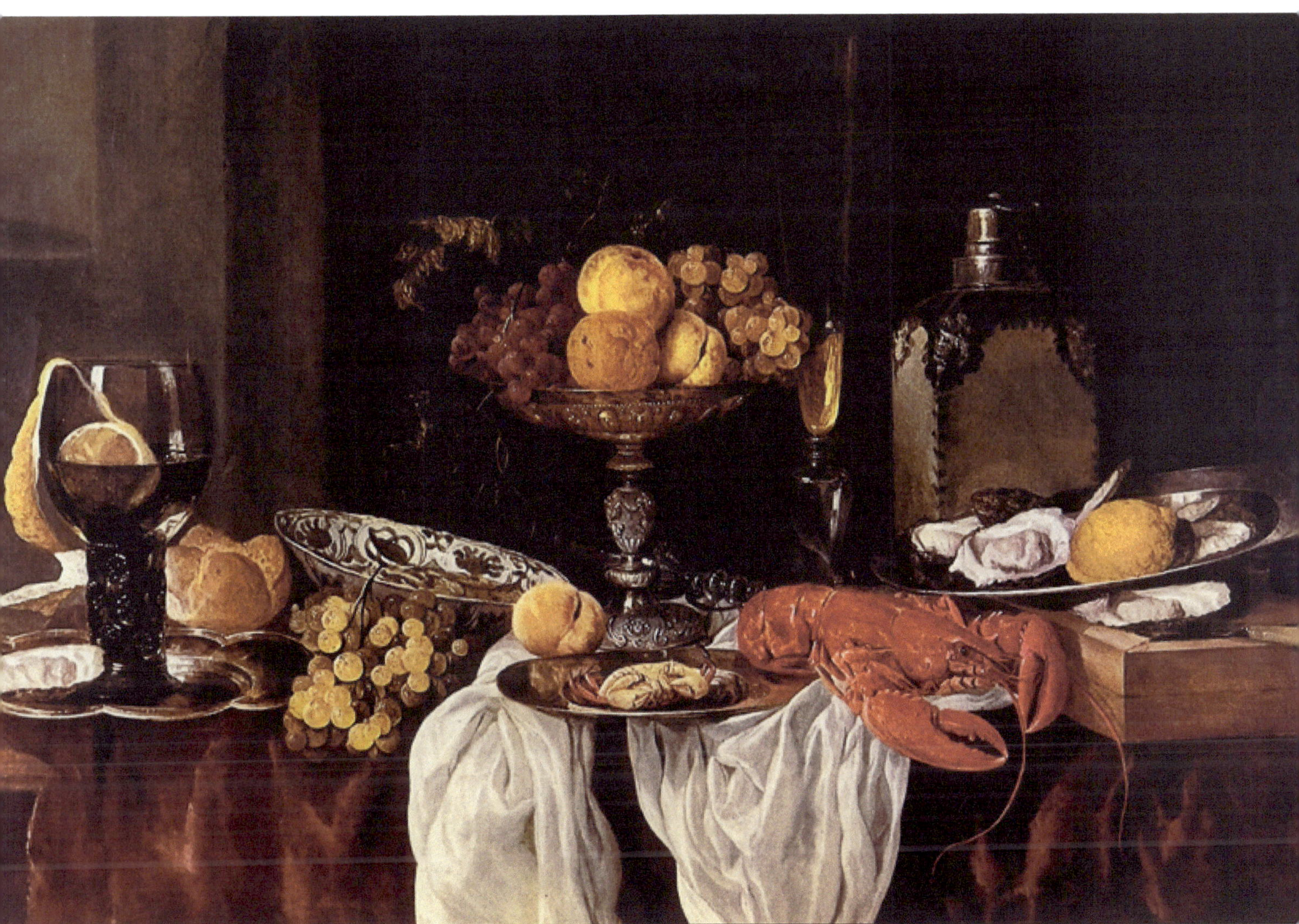

Banquet

73

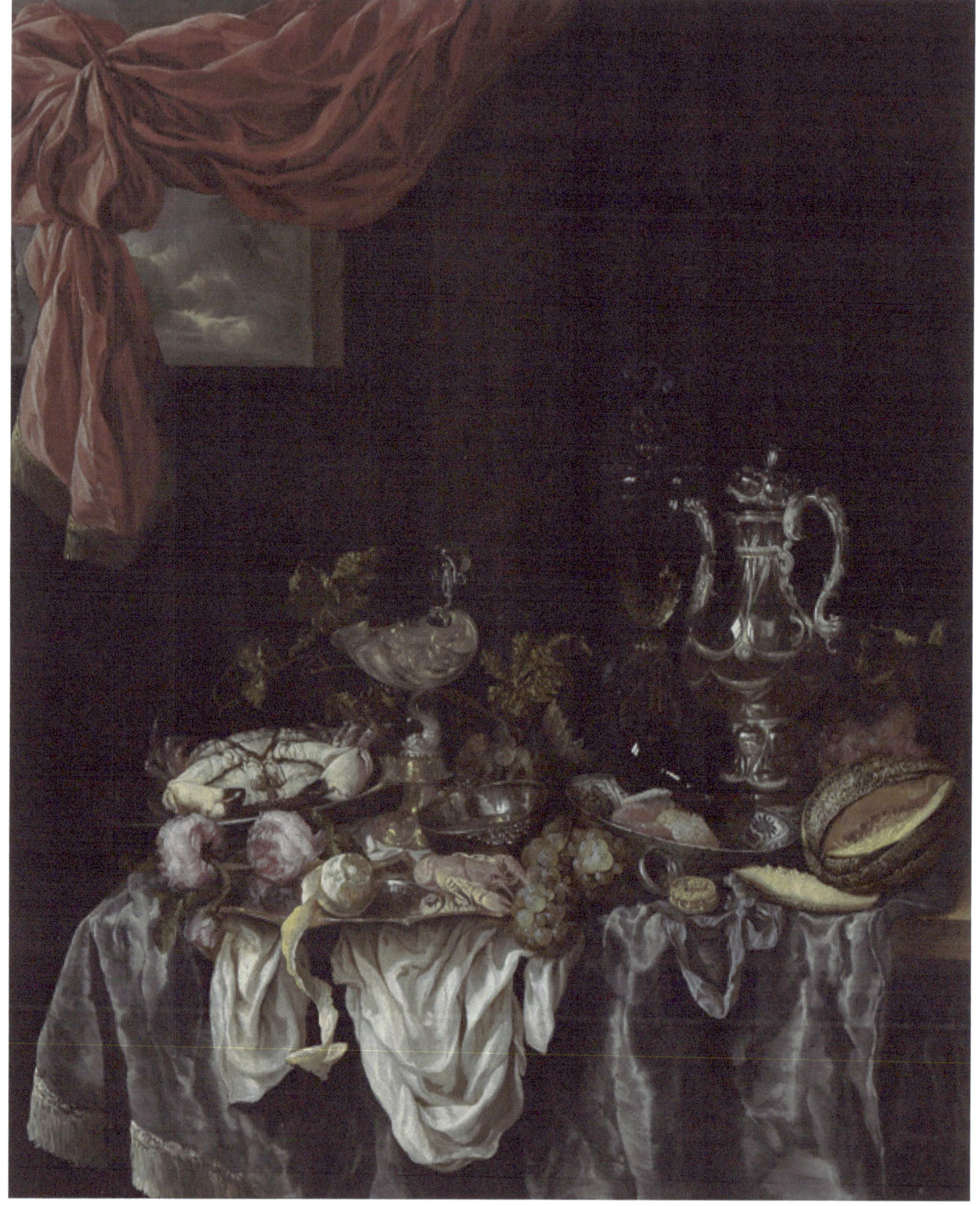

Luxury Still Life, 1654

126 x 106 cm

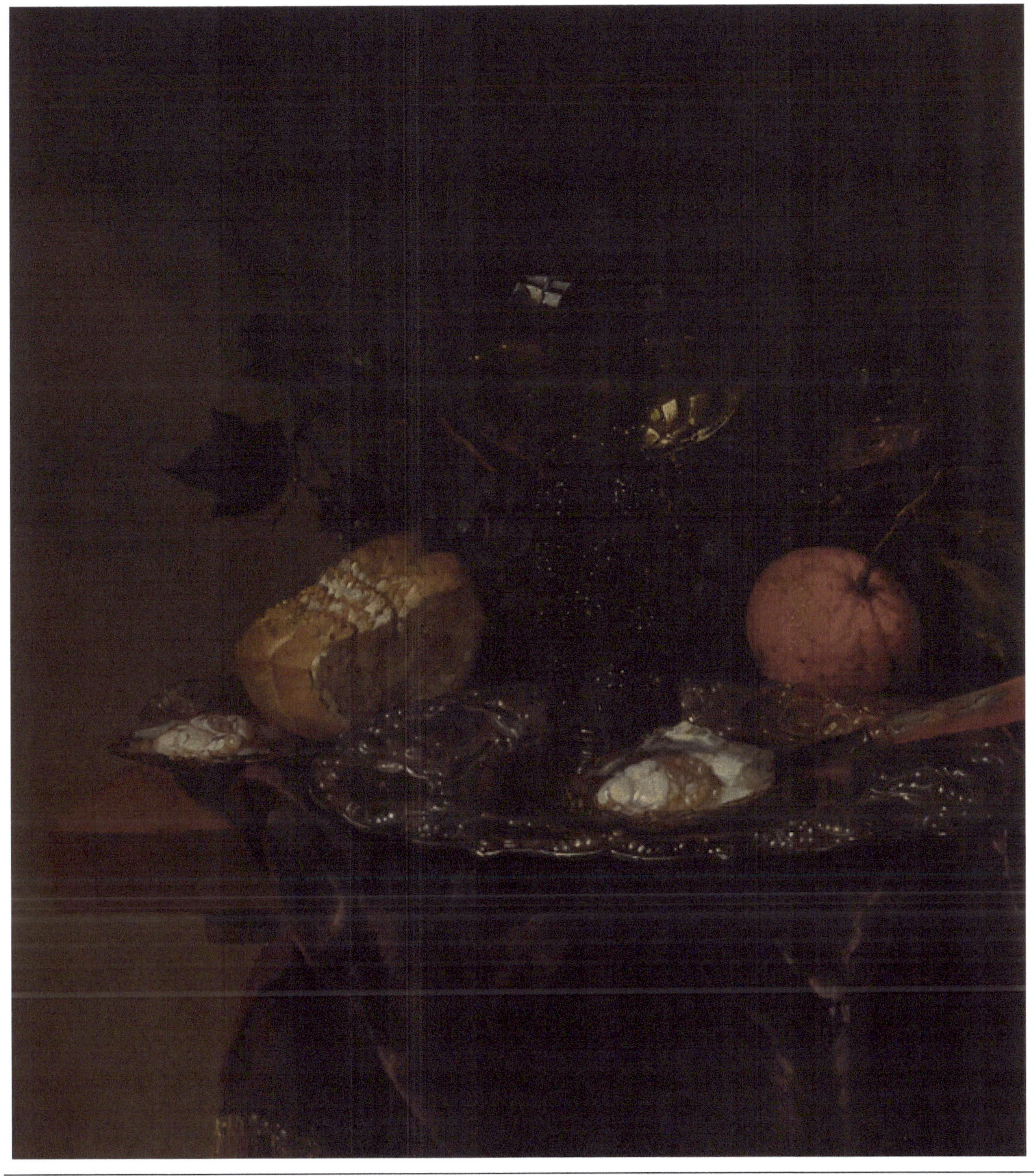

Still life, 1640   **57 x 52.5 cm**

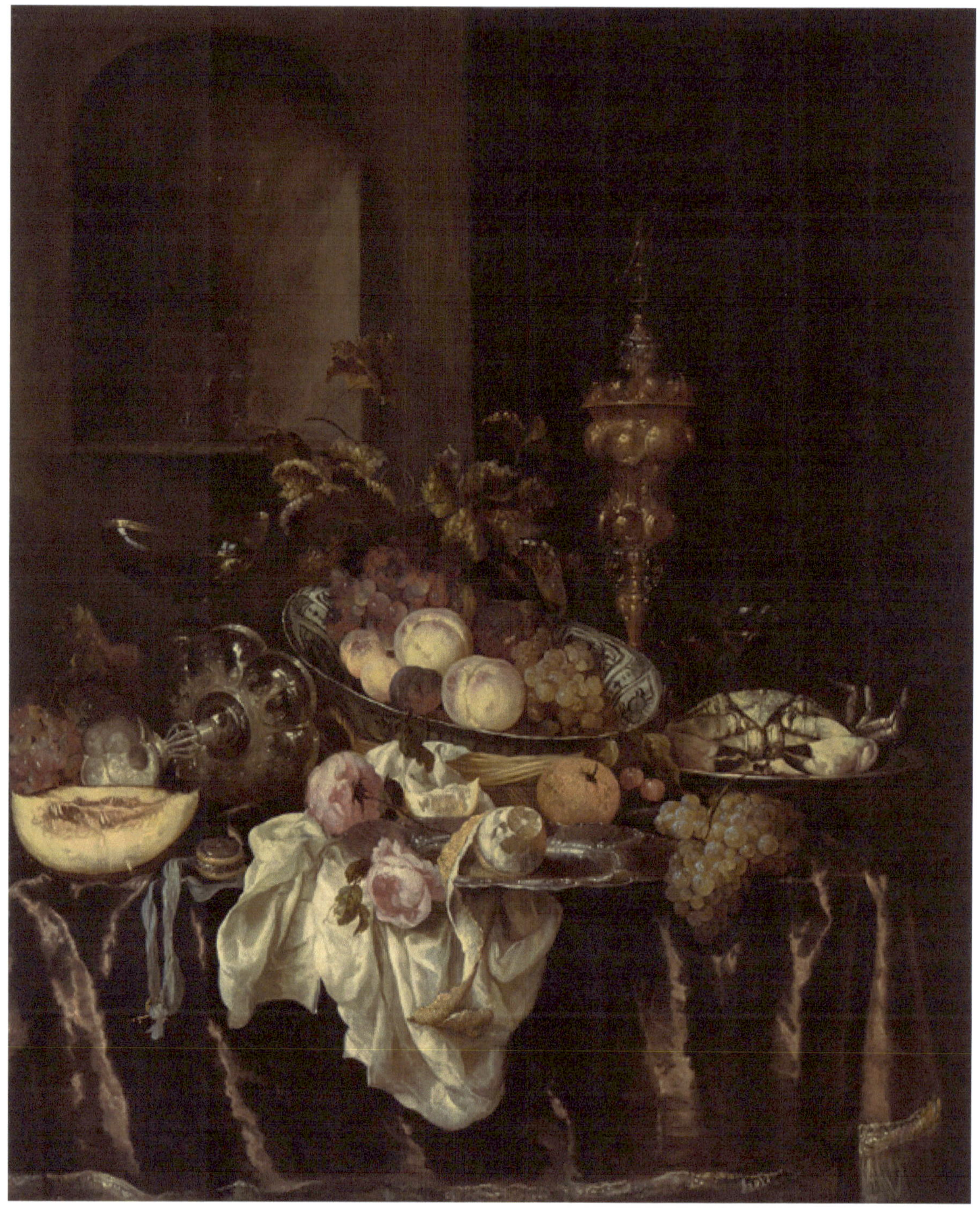

Still life, 1640

126 x 106 cm

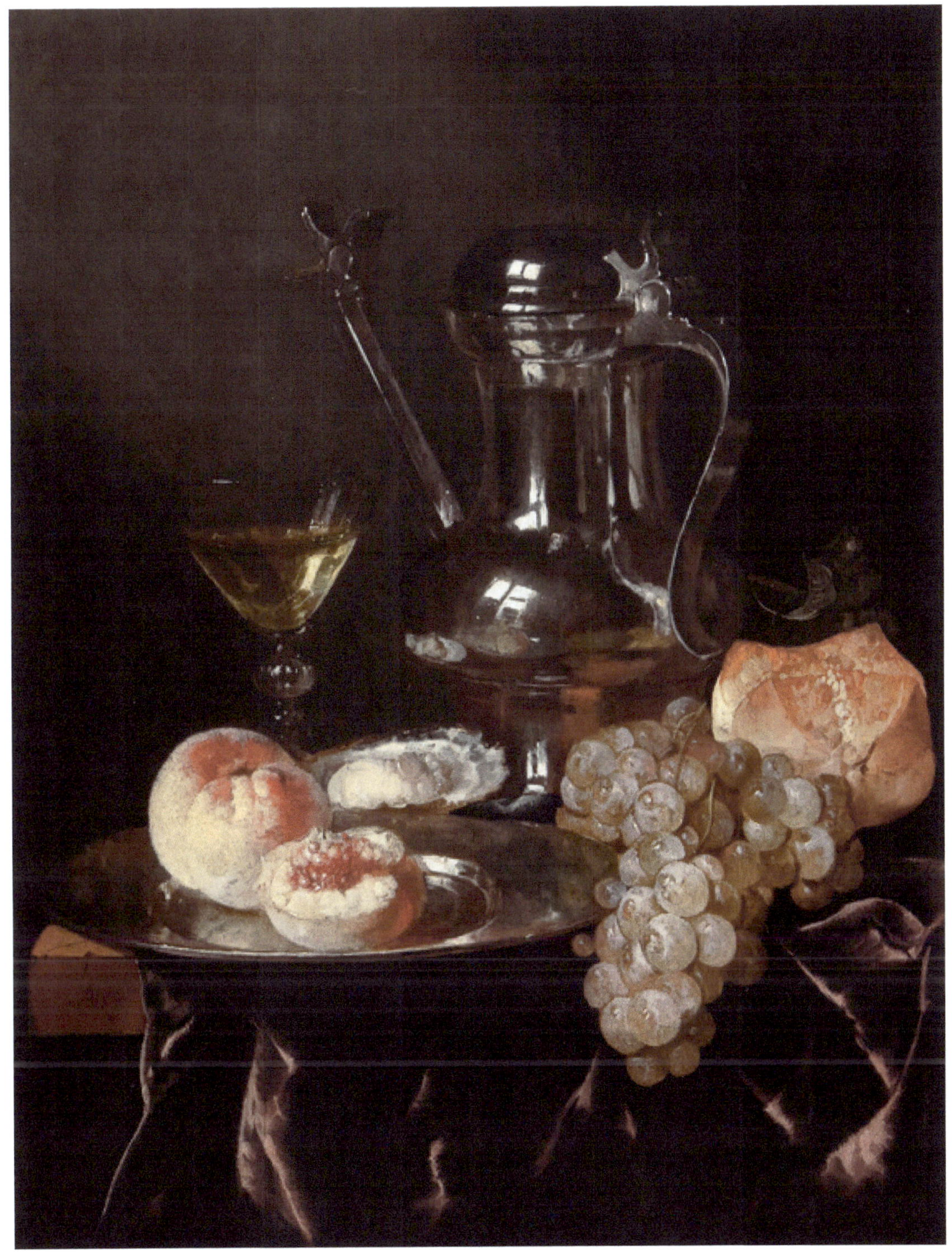

Still life with a pewter jug　　　　　　　　　　　　　　　49.2 x 37.2 cm

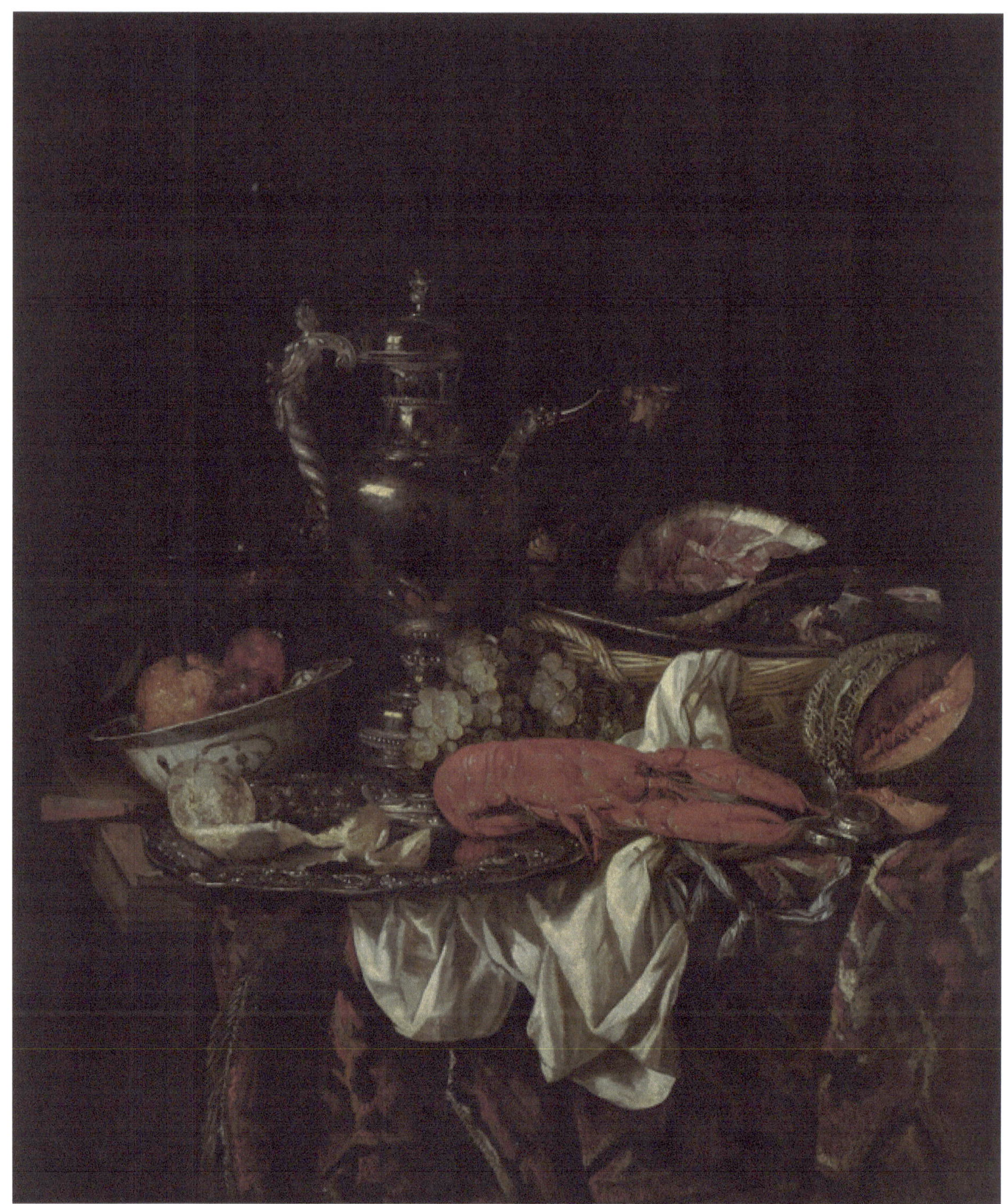

Still life with a silver pitcher, 1660-65   102.5 x 88 cm

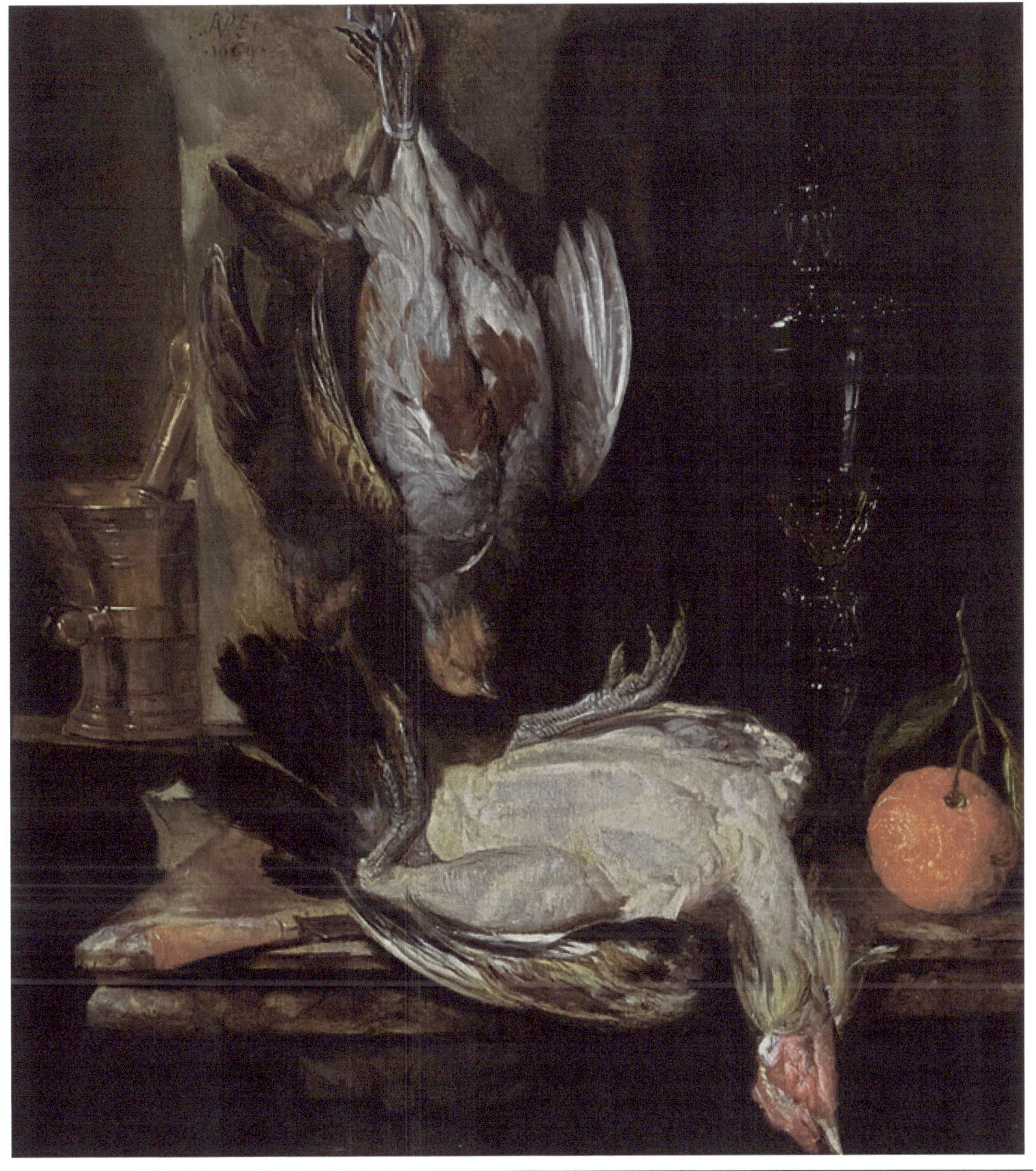

Still life with birds, 1664   64 x 59 cm

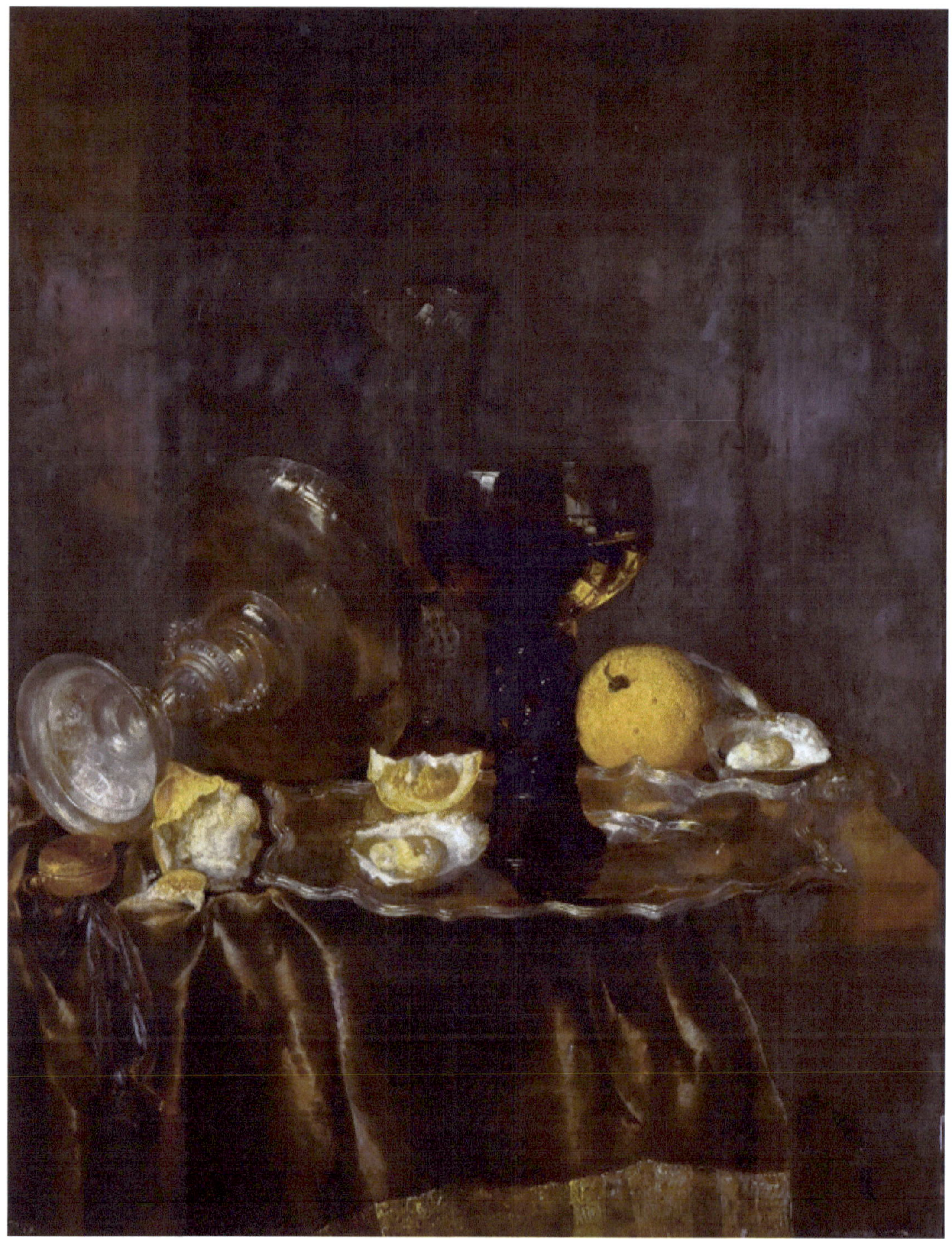

Still life with breakfast, 1666 74 x 57.4 cm

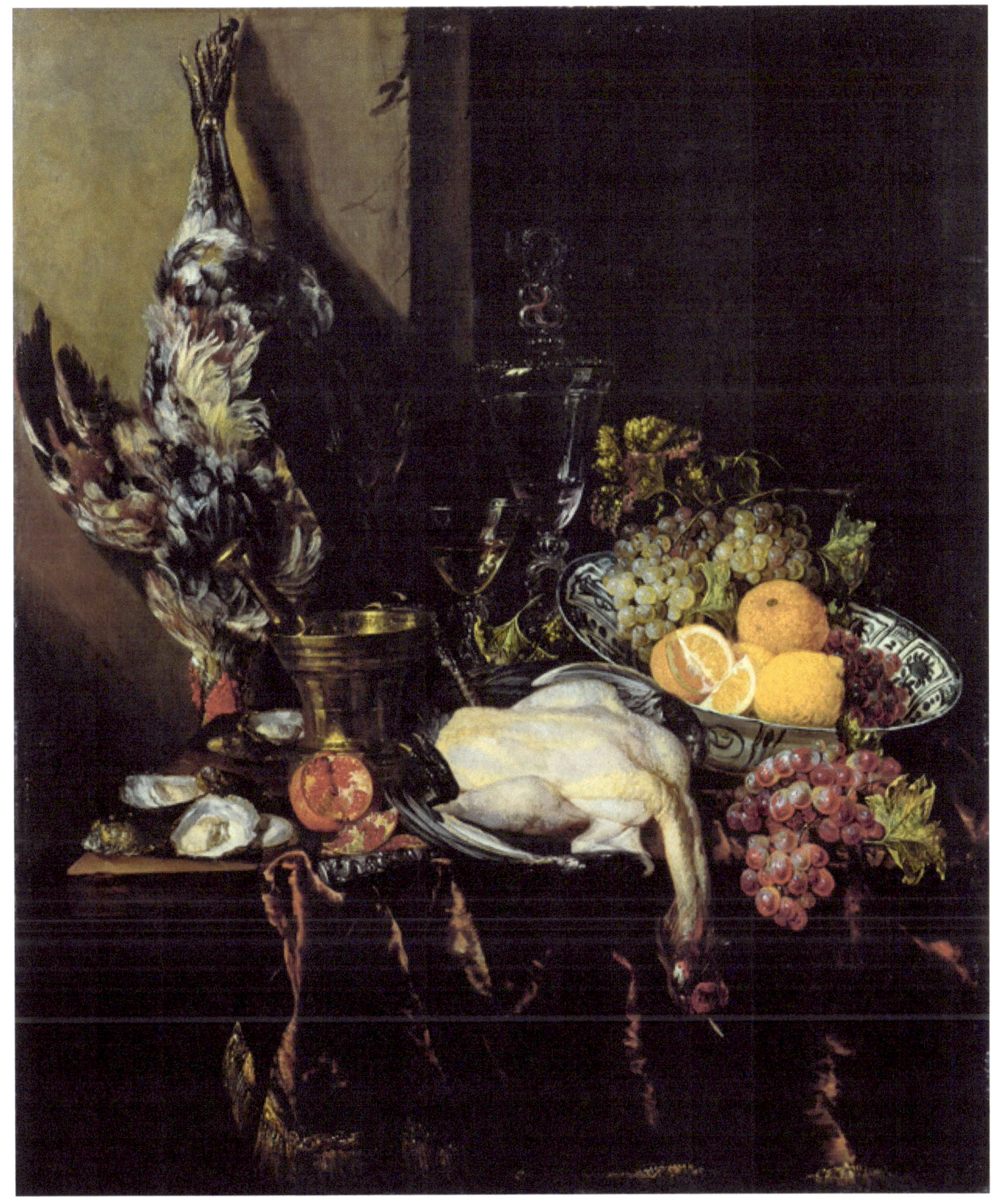

Still life with Fruit and bat bird, 1651   104 x 88.8 cm

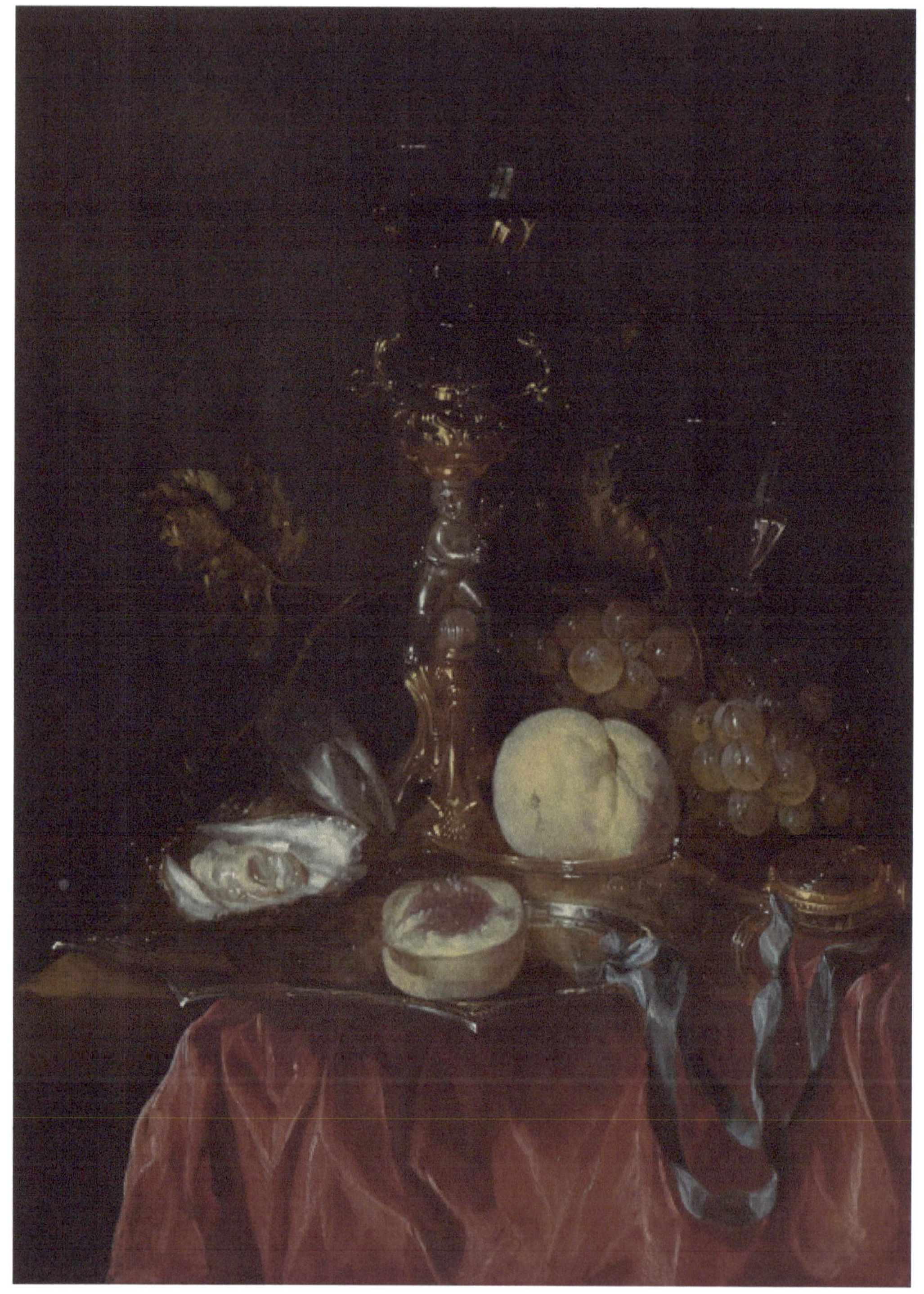

Still life with gilt stand and Jug, 1640

50.2 x 36.3 cm

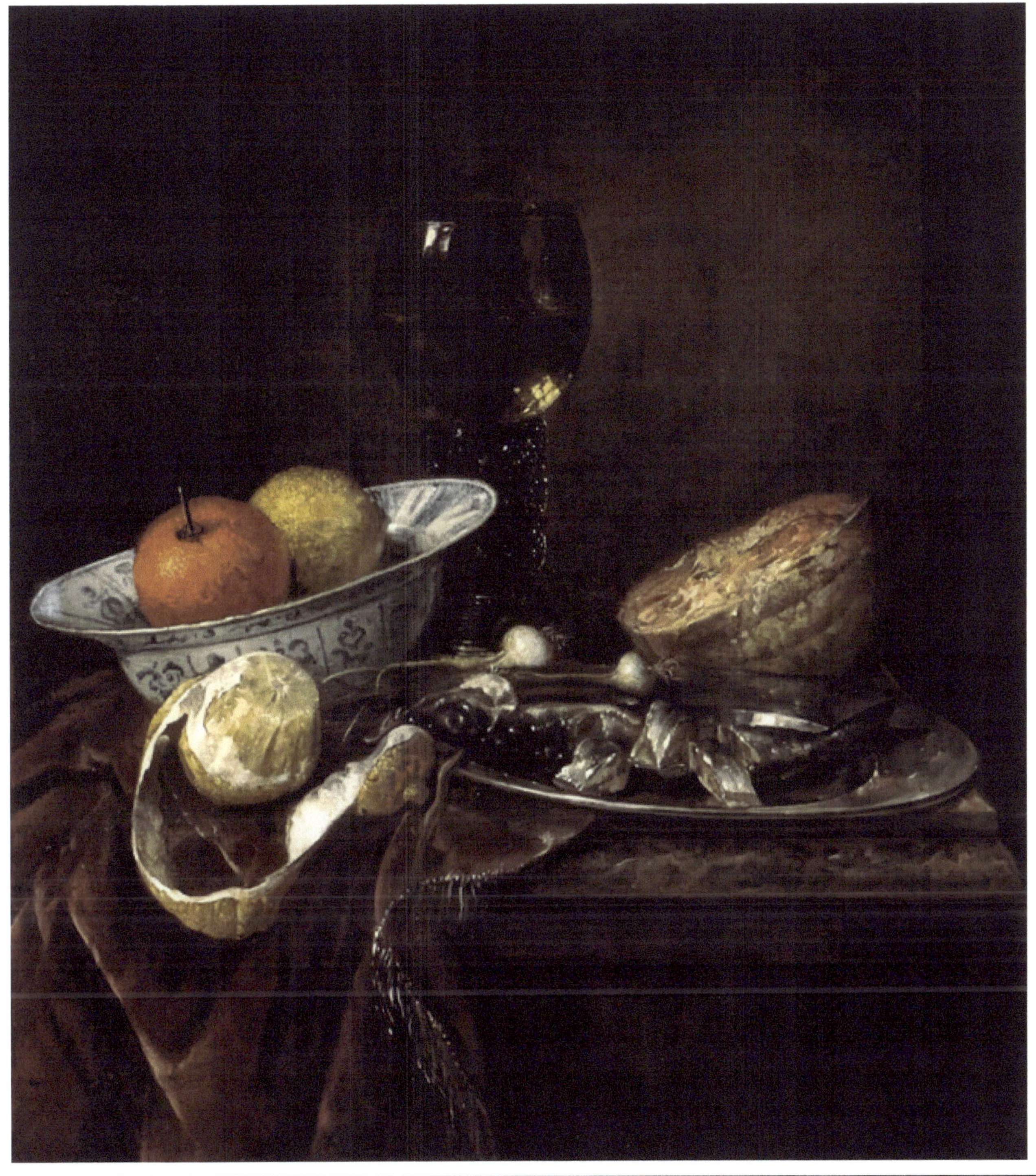

Still life with Jug

57 x 51 cm

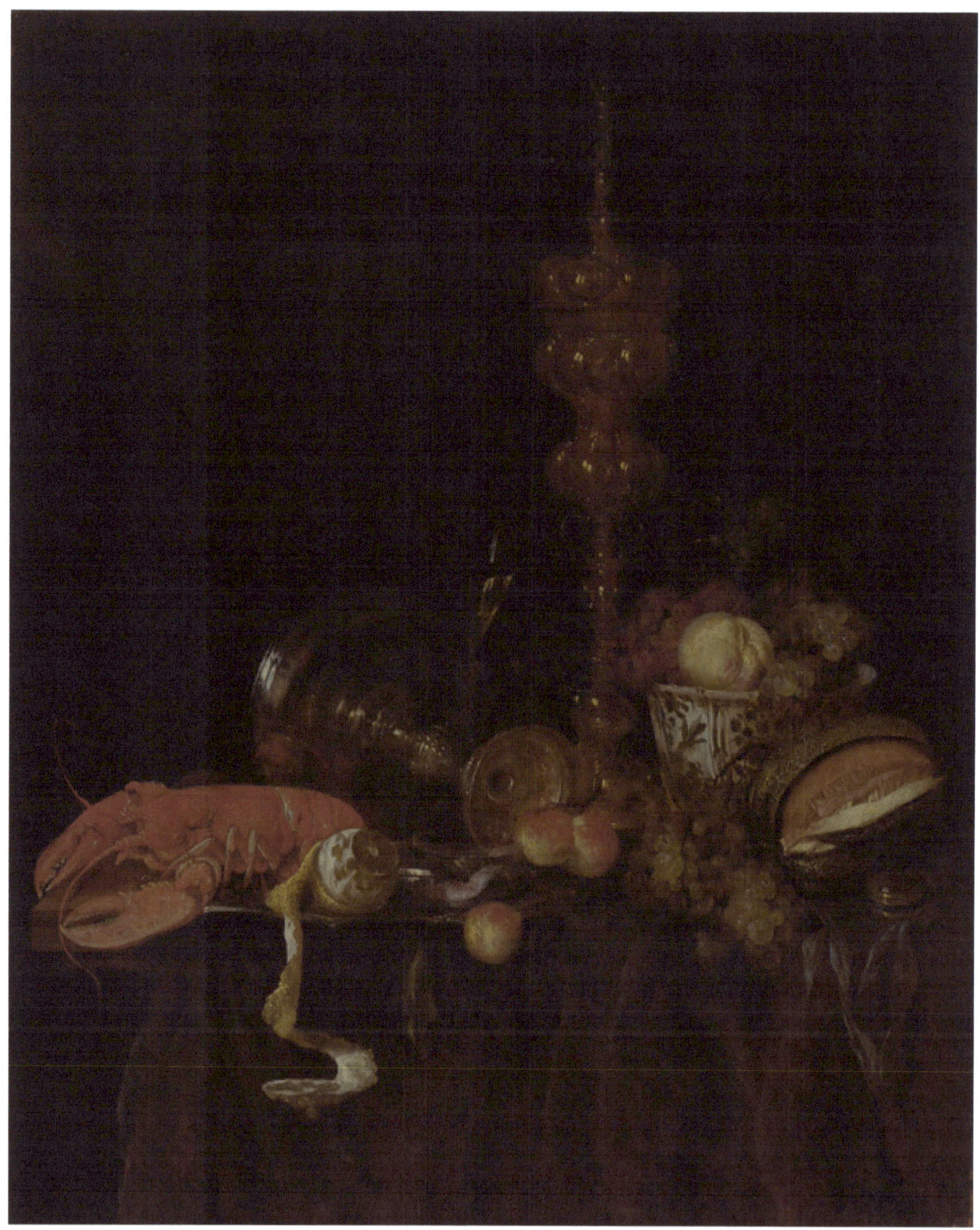

Still life with Lobster and Fruit, 1650s

96.5 x 78.7 cm

Willem Van Aelst

1627 - 1683

Willem Van Aelst is a still life painter born in Delft, the Netherlands on May 16, 1627. He is a painter who shows the complex and inspiring composition which is the features of the Dutch golden age, including praise of wealth and the meditation of Vanitas. Van Aelst began artistic training under his uncle Evert van Aelst, a prominent still life painter. Later, He became an apprentice of his relative Jan Davidsz. de Heem who was an influential still life painter of the time. Under the guidance of the two, Van Aelst improved techniques and developed his unique unique style. In 1643, at the age of 16, he was recognized as a professional painter as a member of the Guild of St. Luke in Delft. Afterward, he moved to France and worked at the palace of Louis XIV and worked as a painter for the French king for a while. After living in France, Van Aelst returned to the Netherlands and settled in Amsterdam. He has a significant reputation and success as a still life painter, especially with the ability to describe very realistic textures and complex details.

His work often features luxurious objects, exotic flowers, fruits, hunted animals, and other symbolic elements. It shows wealth through the description of various objects related to hunting, such as animals for hunting, hunting tools, and lush vegetation. Vivid colors, sophisticated details, and meticulously arranged elements contribute to the overall wealth and visual splendor. Meanwhile, you can also feel that the Vanitas has been included.

The body of the animal shows off its beauty even in death and reminds us of human death and fleeting life. The juxtaposition of life and death, wealth and decline make the audience think that existence is fleeting and worldly success is ultimately meaningless.

Willem Van Aelst died at the age of 56 in Amsterdam on December 8, 1683. As a prominent still life painter of the Dutch golden age, his legacy belongs to museums around the world and private collections.

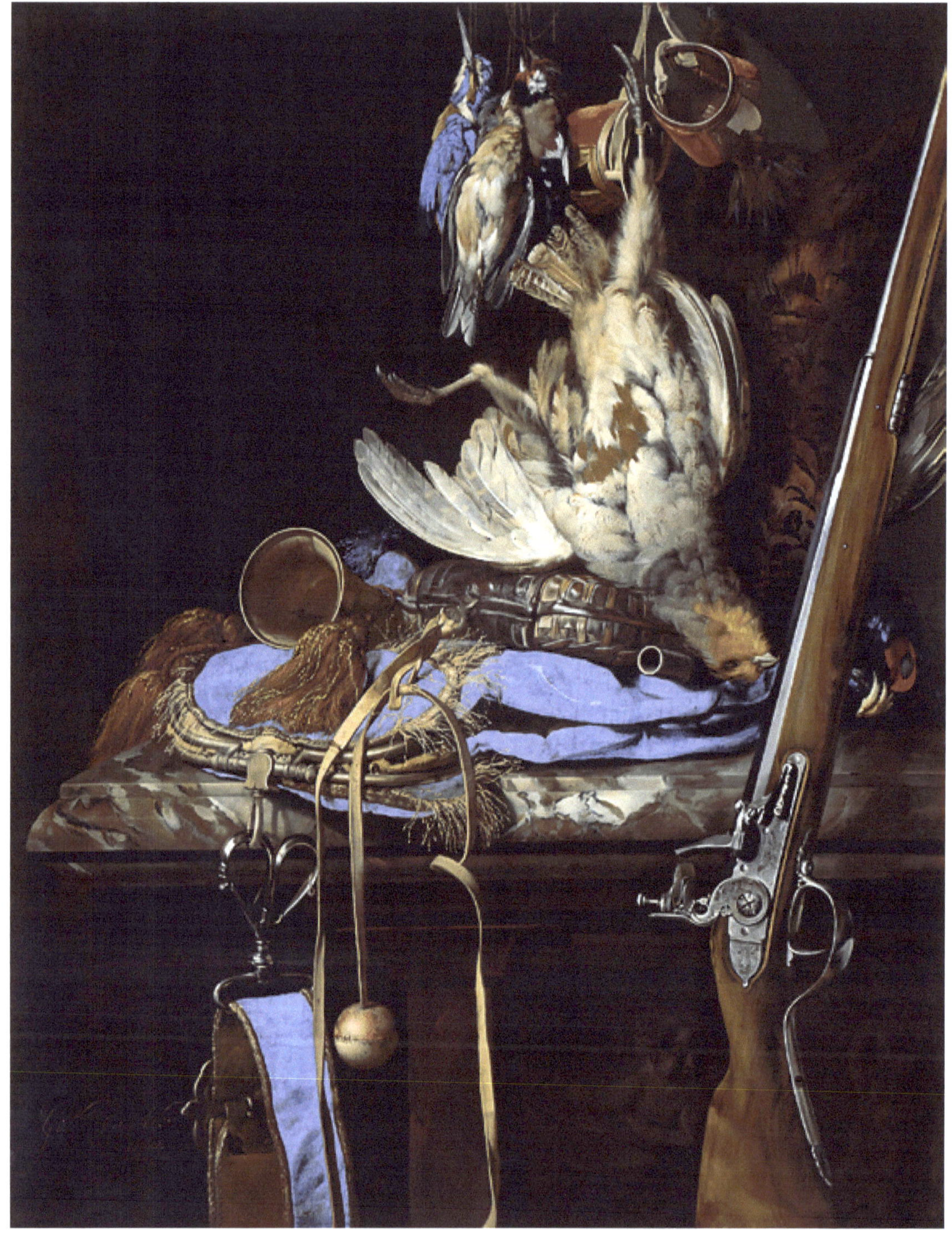

Hunting Still Life, 1664   68 x 54 cm

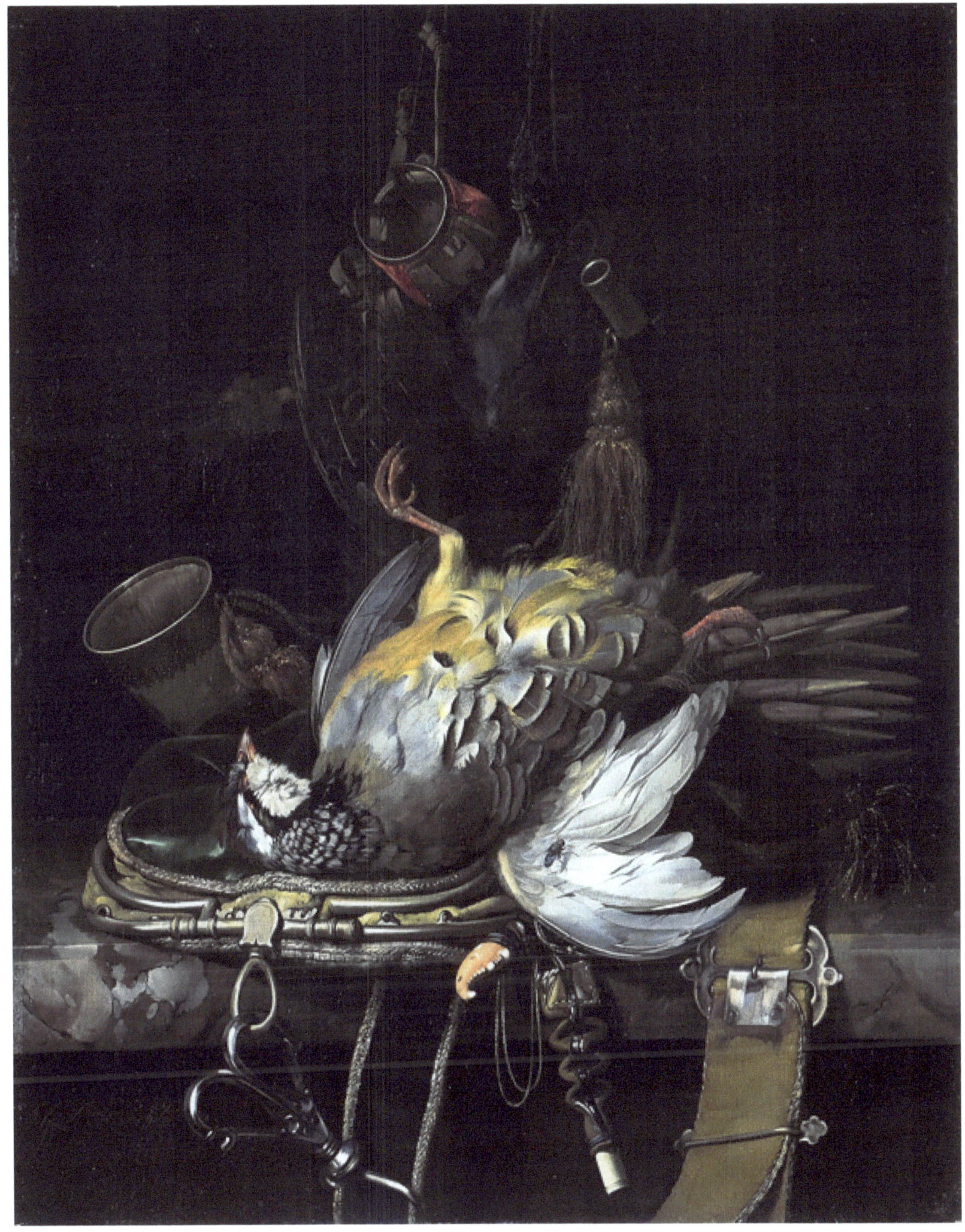

Hunting Still Life, 1671

58.8 x 47.8 cm

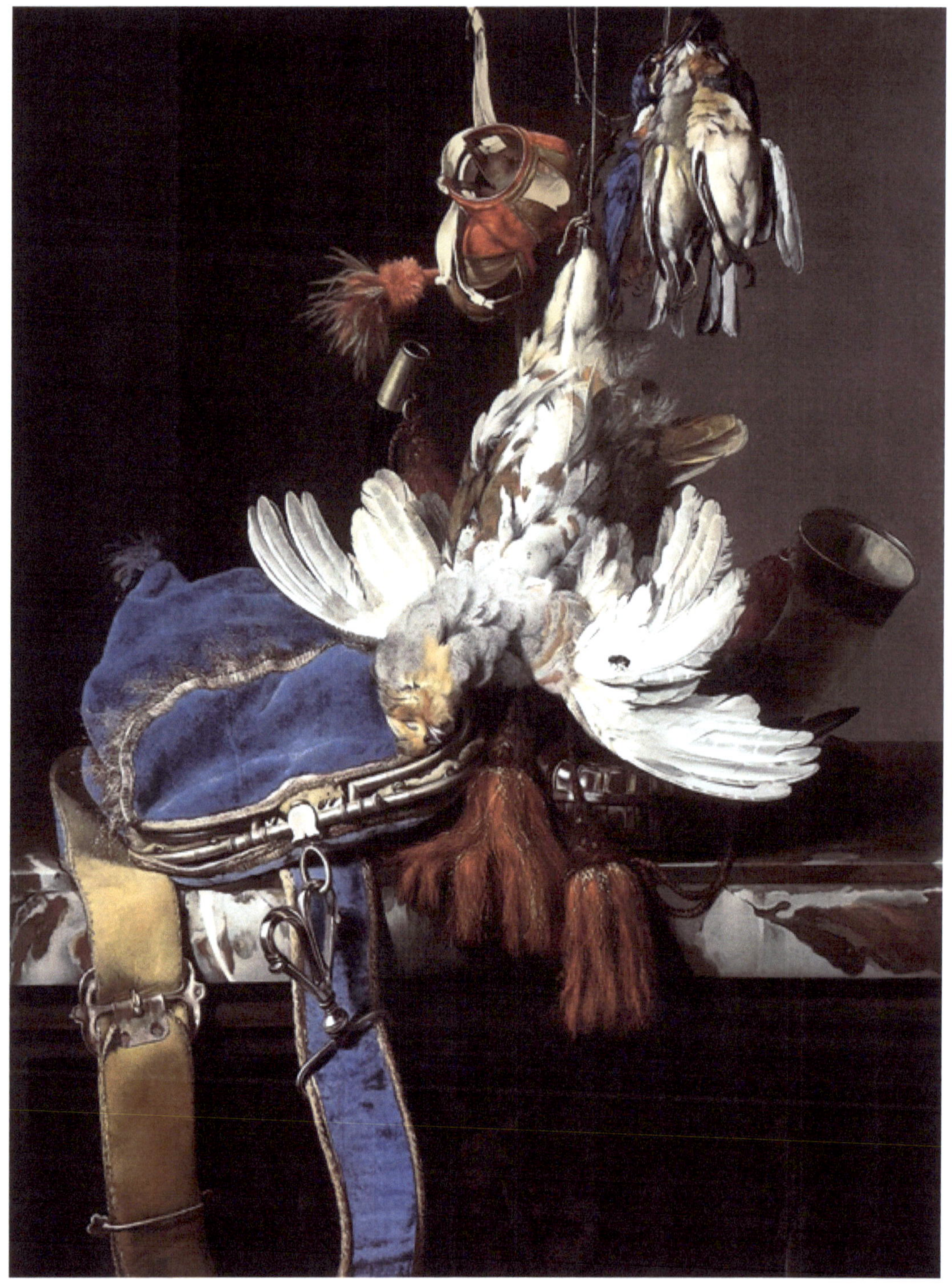

Hunting Still Life-1

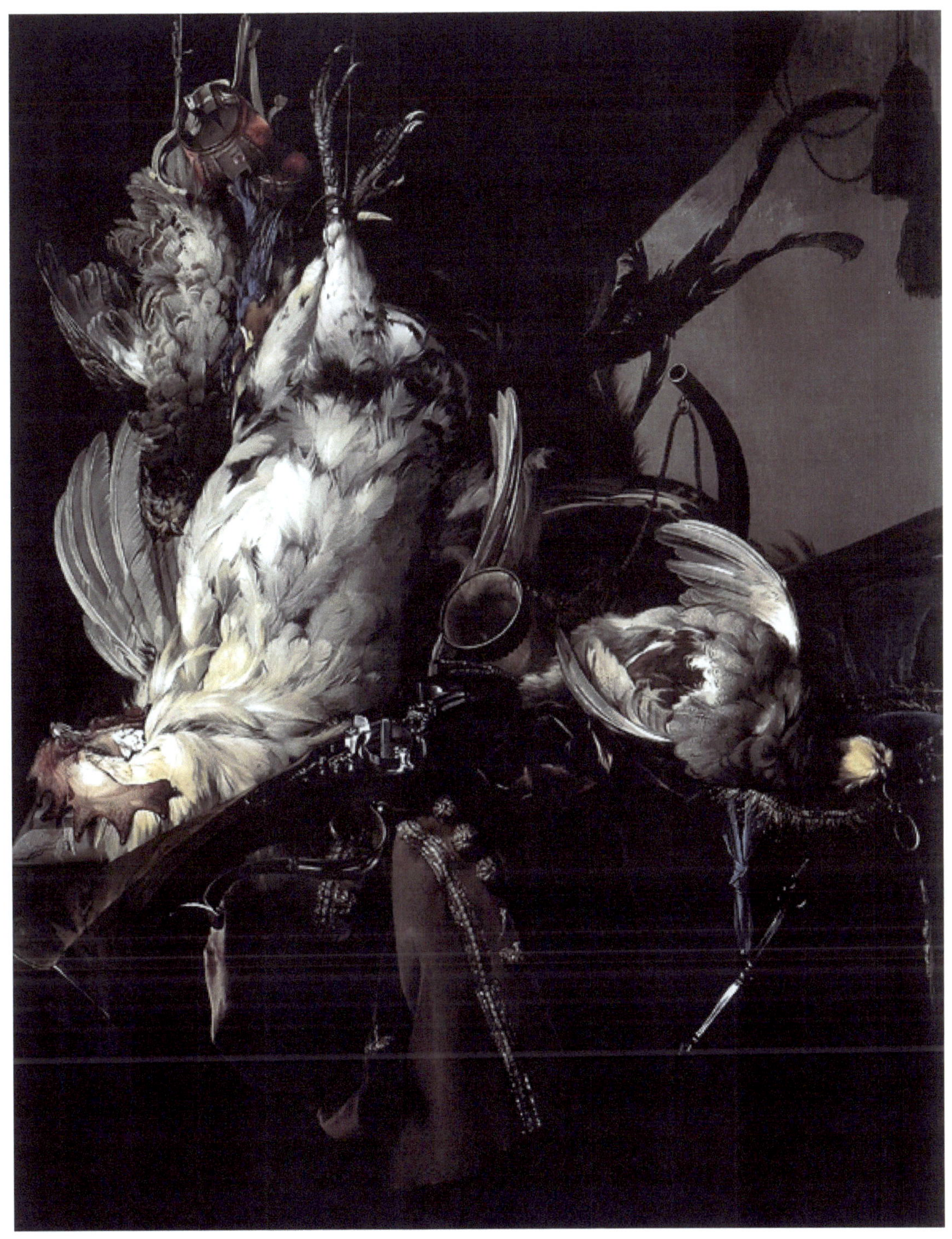

Hunting Still Life-2

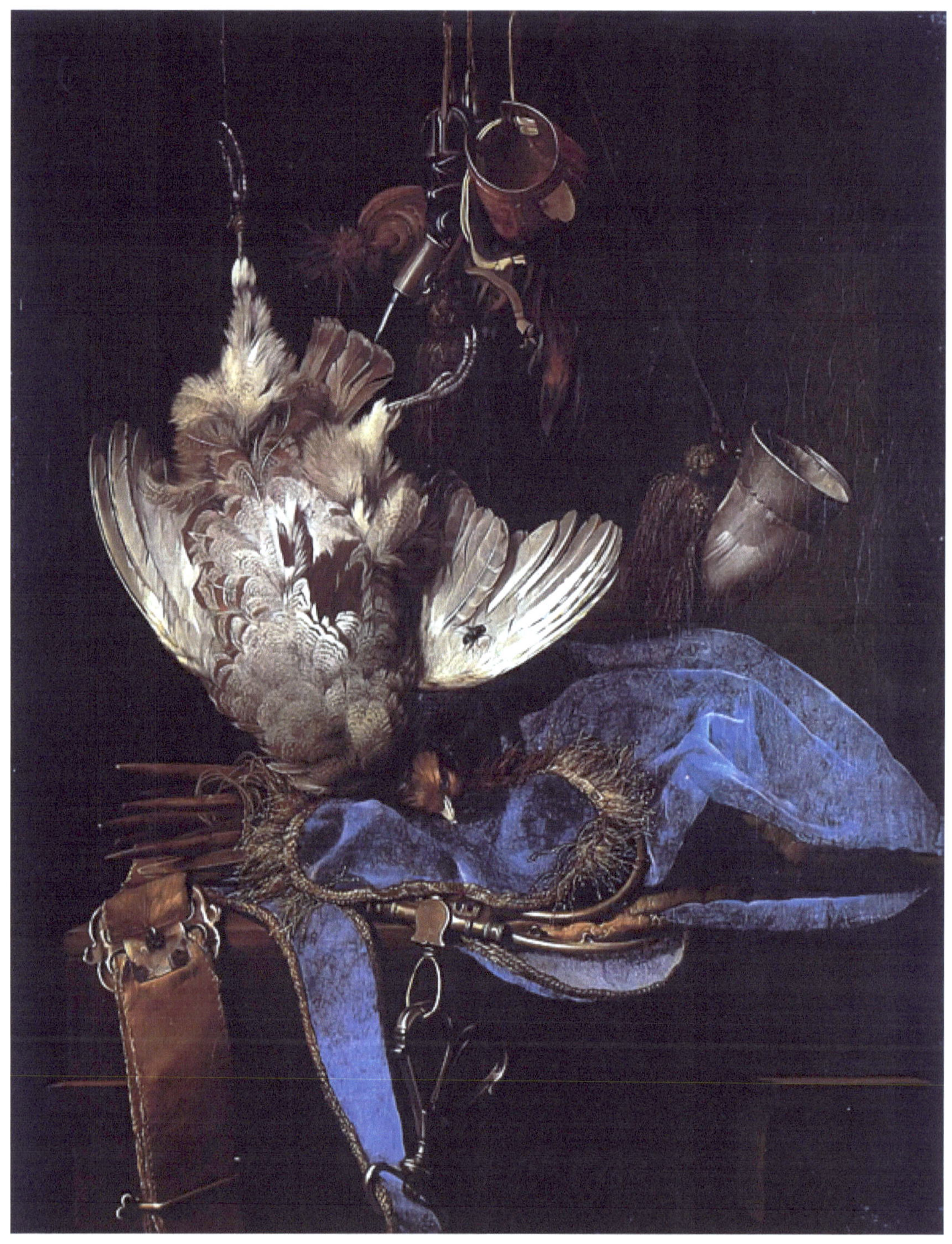

Hunting Still Life-3

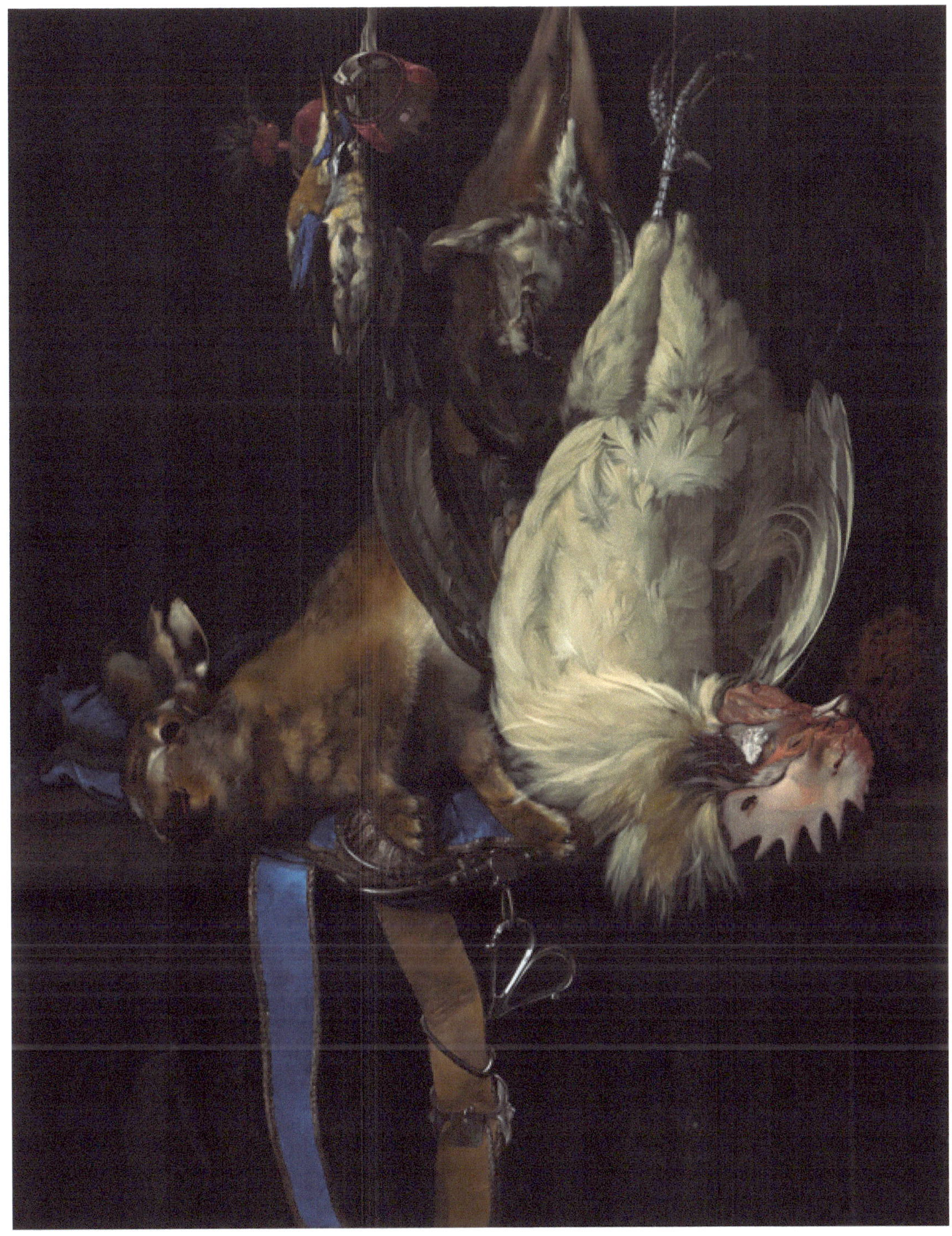

Still life with bird, 1661   84.7 x 67.3 cm

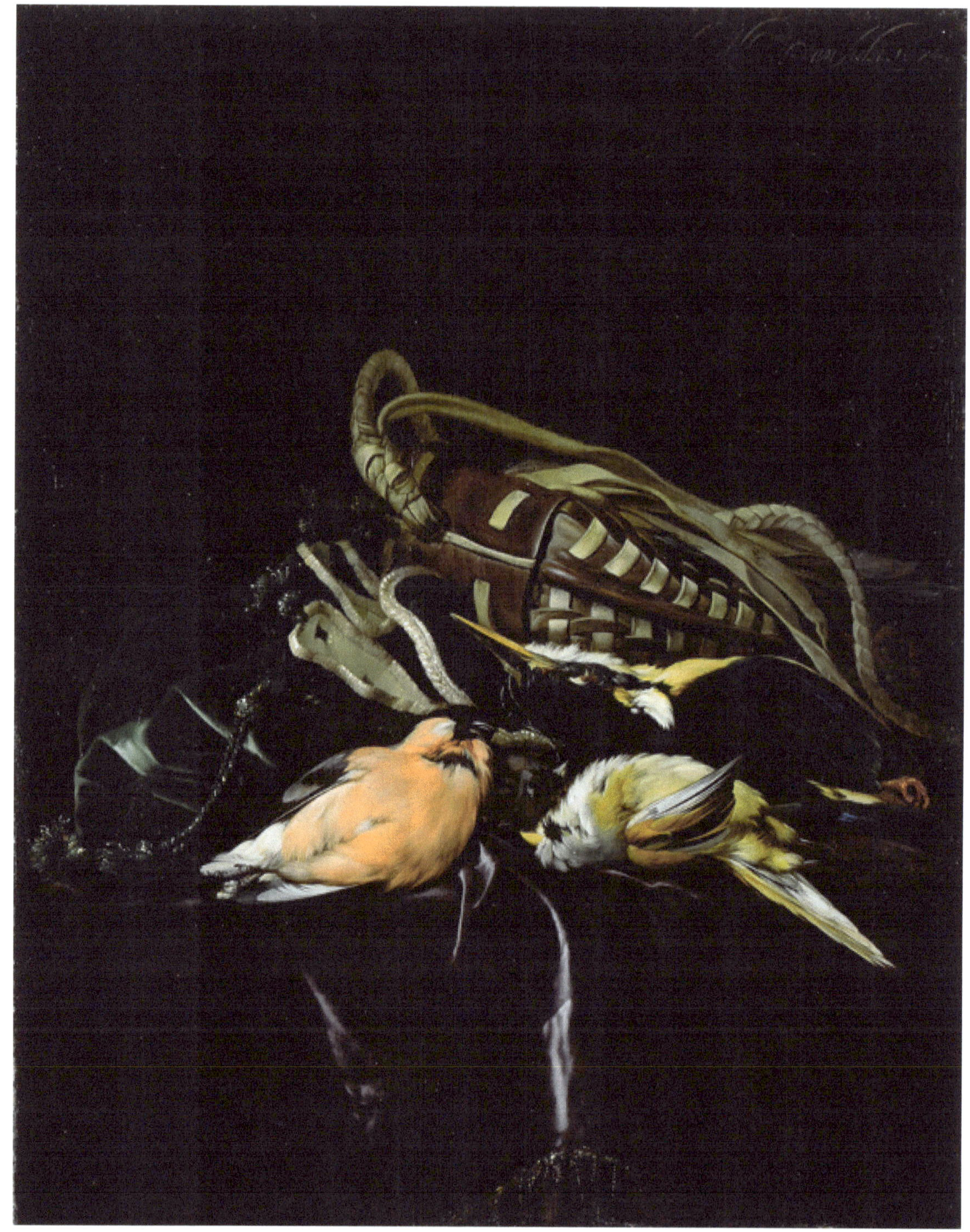

Still life with bird, 1674

45 x 37 cm

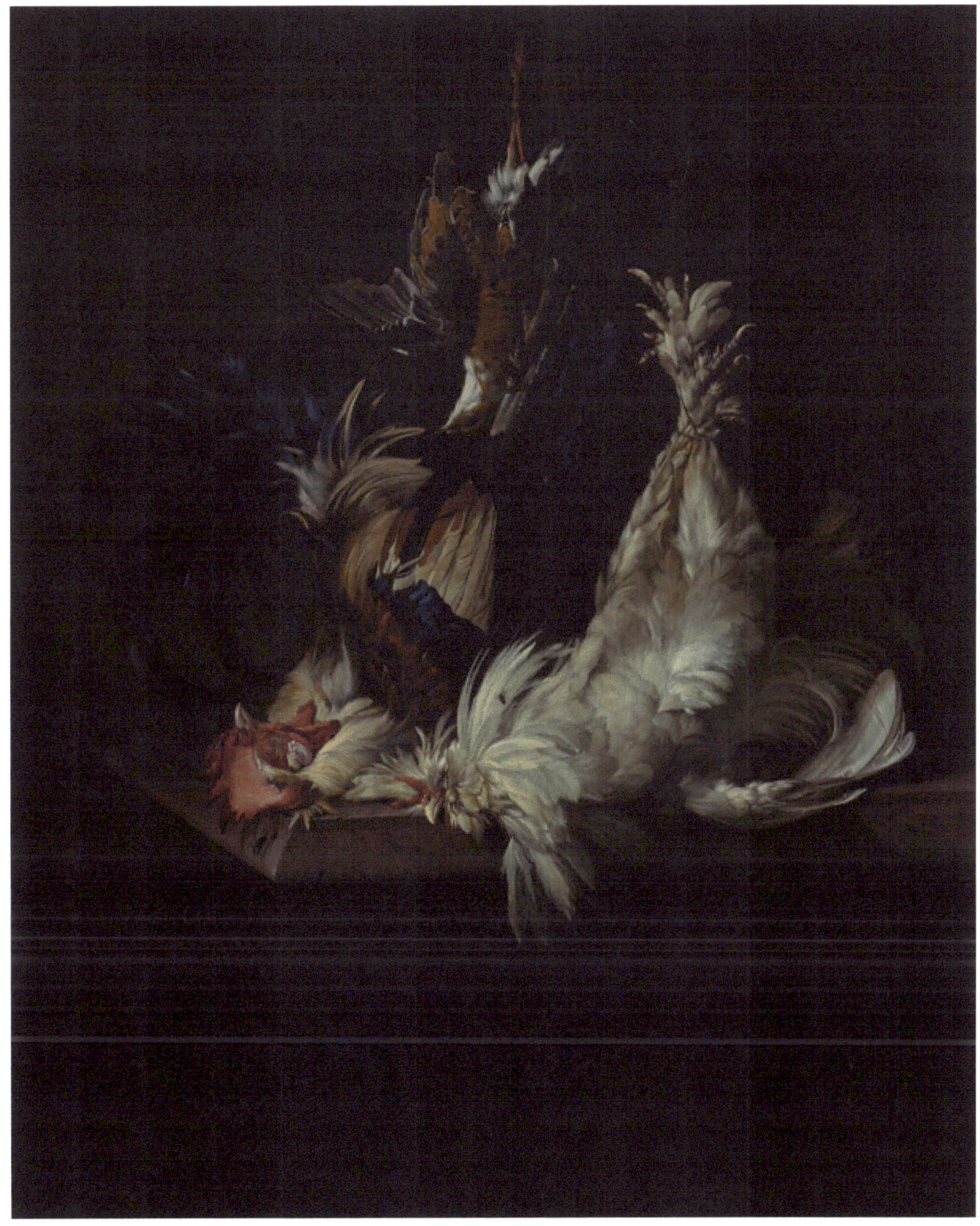

Still life with domestic birds, 1658 95 x 78.5 cm

Jan Weenix
c.1641/49 – 1719

Jan Weenix is a prominent artist of the Dutch golden age who showed excellent talents to paint landscapes, animals, still life, and hunting scenes.
Weenix was from a family of artists and his father Jan Baptist Weenx was a famous painter. He took arts education from his father at the beginning and later became an apprentice of the landscape painter Nicolaes Moeyaert. Weenix's artistic ability has developed rapidly and has been recognized for his excellent techniques and attention to meticulous detail.

In addition to landscape paintings, Weenix was also famous for its excellent ability to draw animals and hunting scenes. His paintings were loved due to the accurate expression and realistic quality of objects such as animals for hunting, hunting dogs, and other animals. He was excellent at capturing the texture of the hair and feathers and the expression of the animal subject. Weenix's work conveys a colorful and luxurious feeling by expressing carefully arranged animals, colorful still life elements, and delicate leaves in elaborate compositions.

His painting was popular among wealthy elites and received numerous commissions from prominent sponsors, including European aristocrats. Weenix's style has developed through various approaches throughout his career. In the second half of his life, he was influenced by the works of Italian art and contemporary artists, showing a change to a more classic and formal style.

Jan Weenix's works can be found in famous collections and museums around the world, including the National Museum of the Netherlands in Amsterdam, the Louvre in Paris, and the Hermitage Museum in St. Petersburg.

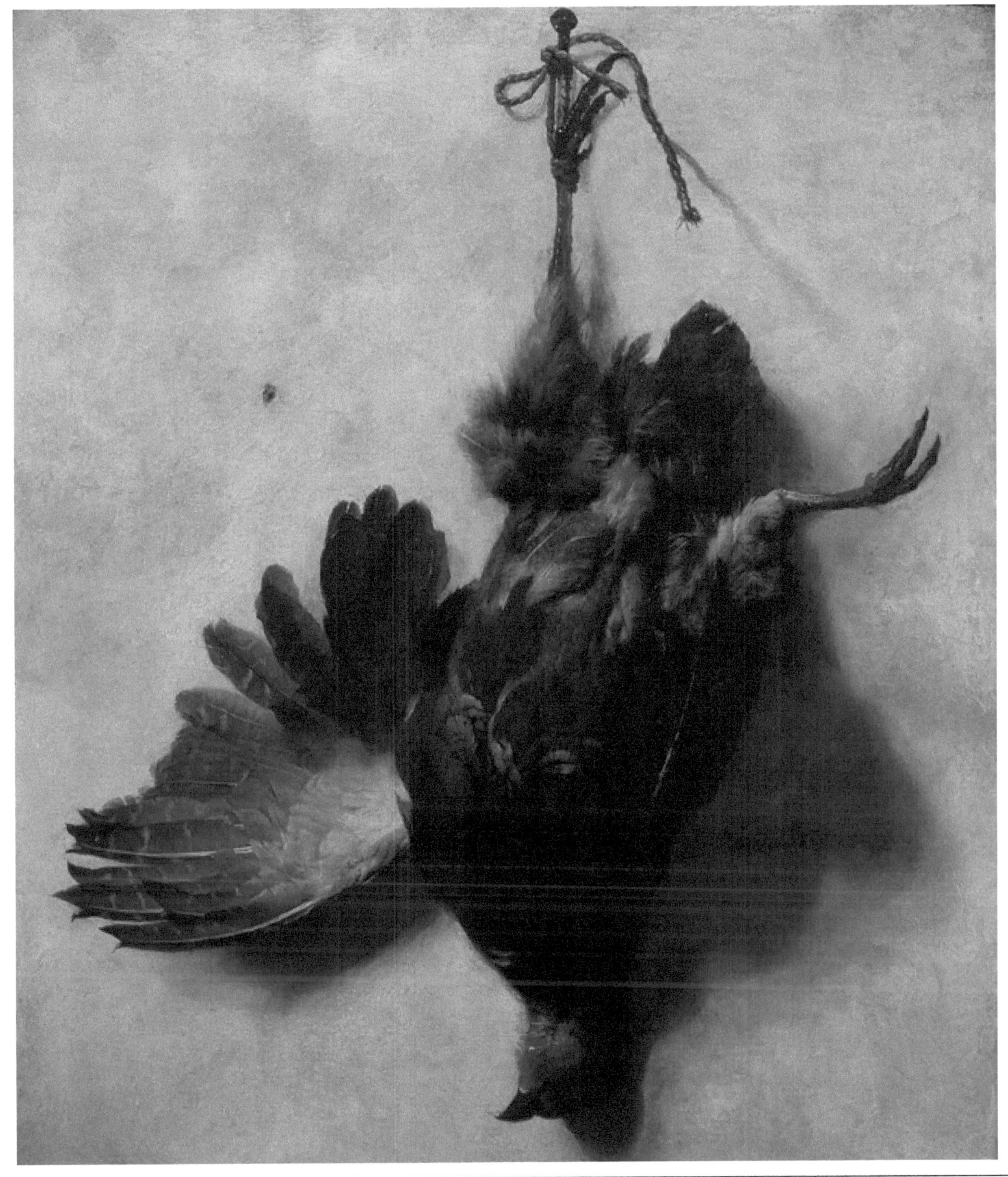

Dead Bird, 1656-60   50.6 x 43.5 cm

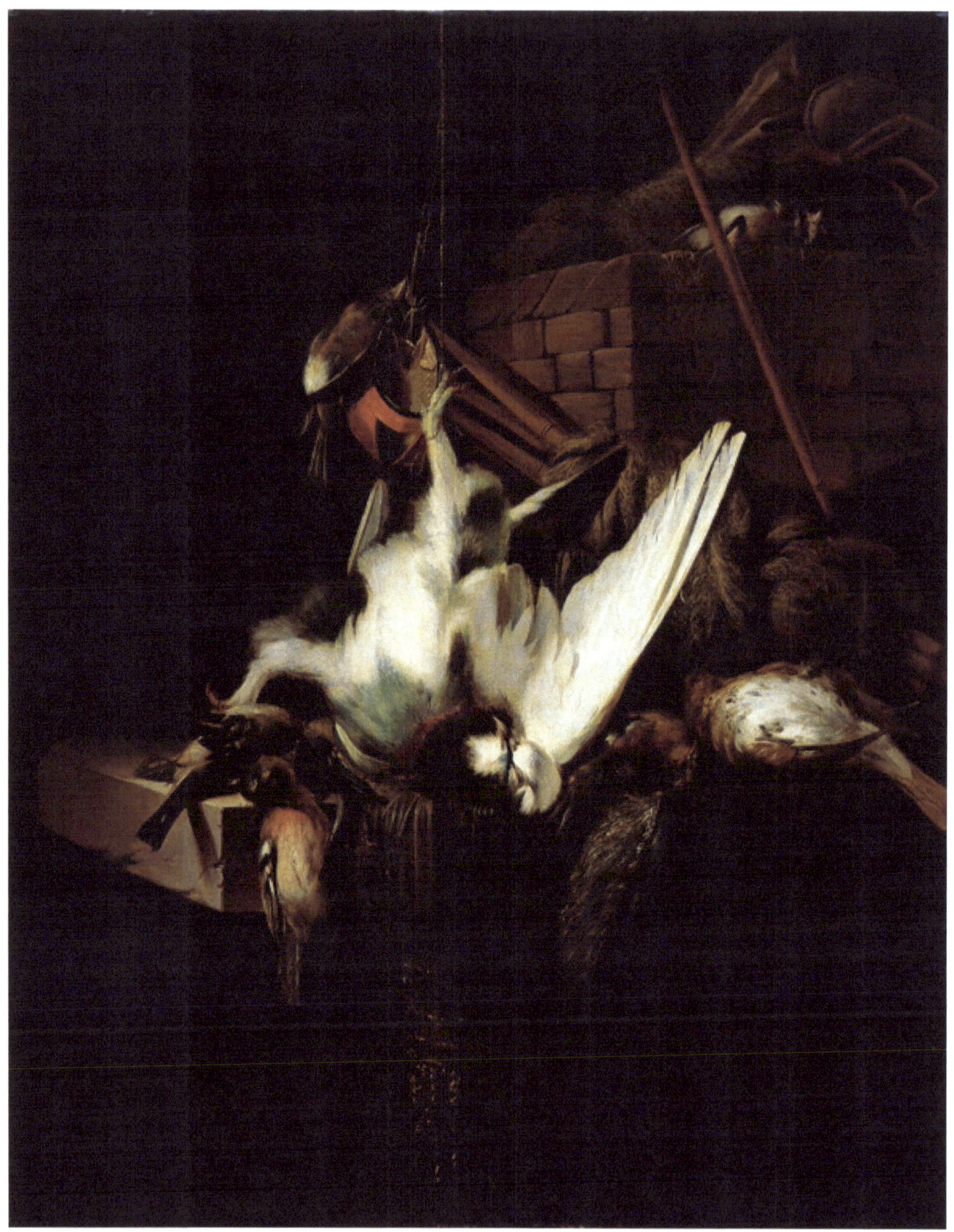

Still life with bird, 17th century 70 x 56 cm

Into the details

The Appearance of Dead Animals_Hunting Still Life

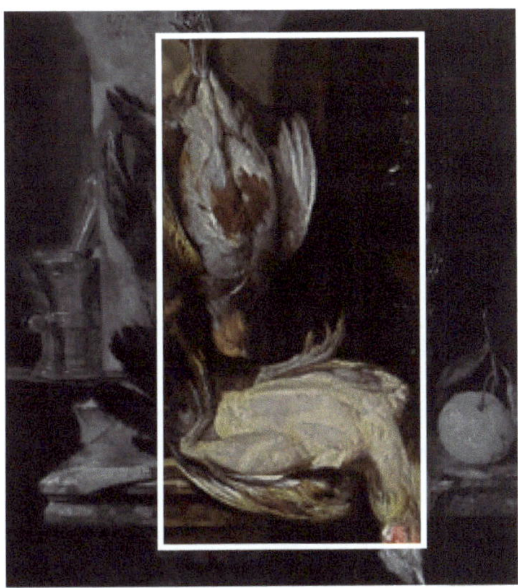

Still life with birds p.79

Abraham Hendrickz. van Beyeren

Hunting Still Life refers to a certain sub-genre of still life that appeared in the 17th-century Dutch golden age. Drawing the body of hunting animals was a common theme in 17th-century art, especially in Dutch paintings. Through hunting still life, many were able to experience the grandeur of the hunting tradition that only the elites could enjoy. Depicting dead animals, such as poultry, animals for hunting, fish, or other animals, had a variety of meanings and purposes.

Symbol of Wealth

It was to show the wealth and prosperity of the 17th-century Dutch Republic called the Dutch golden age. Animals depicted in the paintings, such as birds, rabbits, and fish, were considered luxurious and expensive. By appearing these animals in the paintings, it could be known that there are abundant food and resources in Dutch society.

To show the artist's skills and abilities

It was a challenge for artists to show their skills to describe the texture and details of the dead animal feathers, hair or scales. Through this, it was possible to show mastery of light, shadow, and texture, which enhanced artistic reputation.

Use as a tool of record

At a time when interest in the discovery of nature and new species increased, these paintings played a role in recording the diversity and complexity of the natural world.

Frans Snyders

1579 - 1657

Frans Snyders is a painter of Fanders, who has an excellent talent in still life, animals, and hunting scenes. He was born in Antwerp, Belgium in the late 16th century and he became one of Baroque's representative painters.

Snyders was educated under the guidance of the famous painter of the time, Pieter Brueghel the Younger, and Hendrick van Balen at the beginning. Afterward, he moved to Italy and studied the works of the Italian Renaissance masters and absorbed their techniques and artistic impact. Snyders returned to Antwerp has become a popular painter with the sponsorship of the wealthy elites. He became especially famous for his skills in the description of animals, creating a vivid and dynamic composition that captures the beauty and energy of various species of nature. Snyders' artistic focus was mainly on animal descriptions, hunting scenes, and still life composition. He was especially famous for his ability to draw animals surprisingly accurately and precisely by capturing the texture, hair, and expressions of animals. In his paintings, various animals used to appear as dynamic compositions from tamed pets to wild creatures. Snyders's work was very popular with prominent sponsors, including royalty, nobles, and collectors across Europe. He became one of the most famous animal painters of his time thanks to his talent for depicting animals and skillfully expressing the textures and colors of animals.

In addition, Frans Snyders has included elements that can sometimes be interpreted as a symbol of Vanitas in detailed and lively still life. In addition to animals and still life, Snyders also painted religious and mythical scenes and animals also appeared often in these works. He showed a keen understanding of the natural world and brought lively and energy to his works. He frequently collaborated with Peter Paul Rubens on important collaboration or various projects. Snyders professionally painted animals and still life elements in the masterpiece with him contributing to the overall visual effects of the work. He also collaborated with other prominent artists of the time aside from Peter Paul Rubens.

Frans Snyders's legacy leads to an impressive work, captivating the inspiration and heart of art lovers. He became an Fimportant figure in the 17th-century art world due to his ability to paint lifelike animals and still life, his technical mastery, and his humorous temperament.

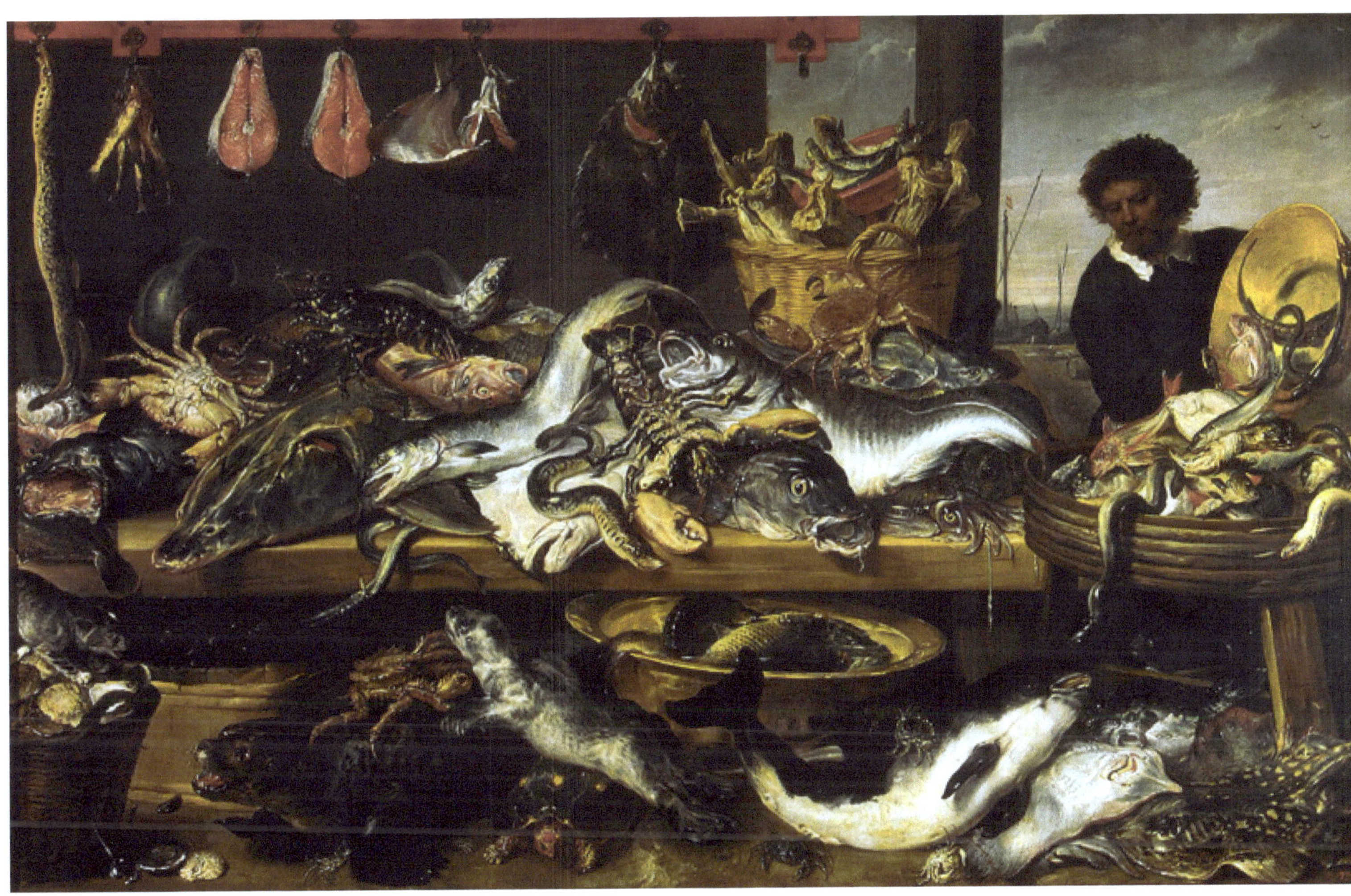

Fish Shop, 1620s 209.5 x 341 cm

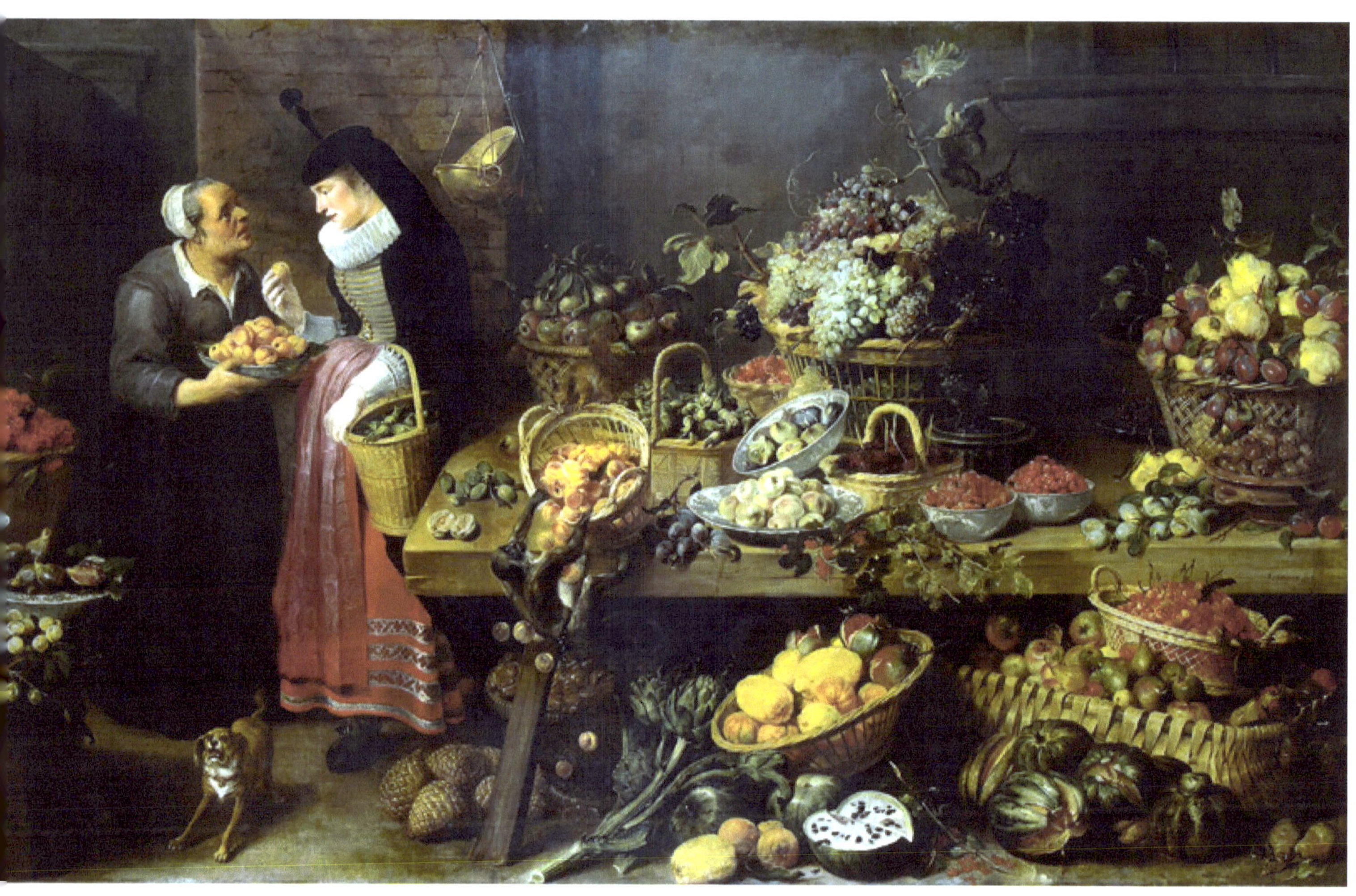

Fruit Shop, c.1618-21   206 x 342 cm

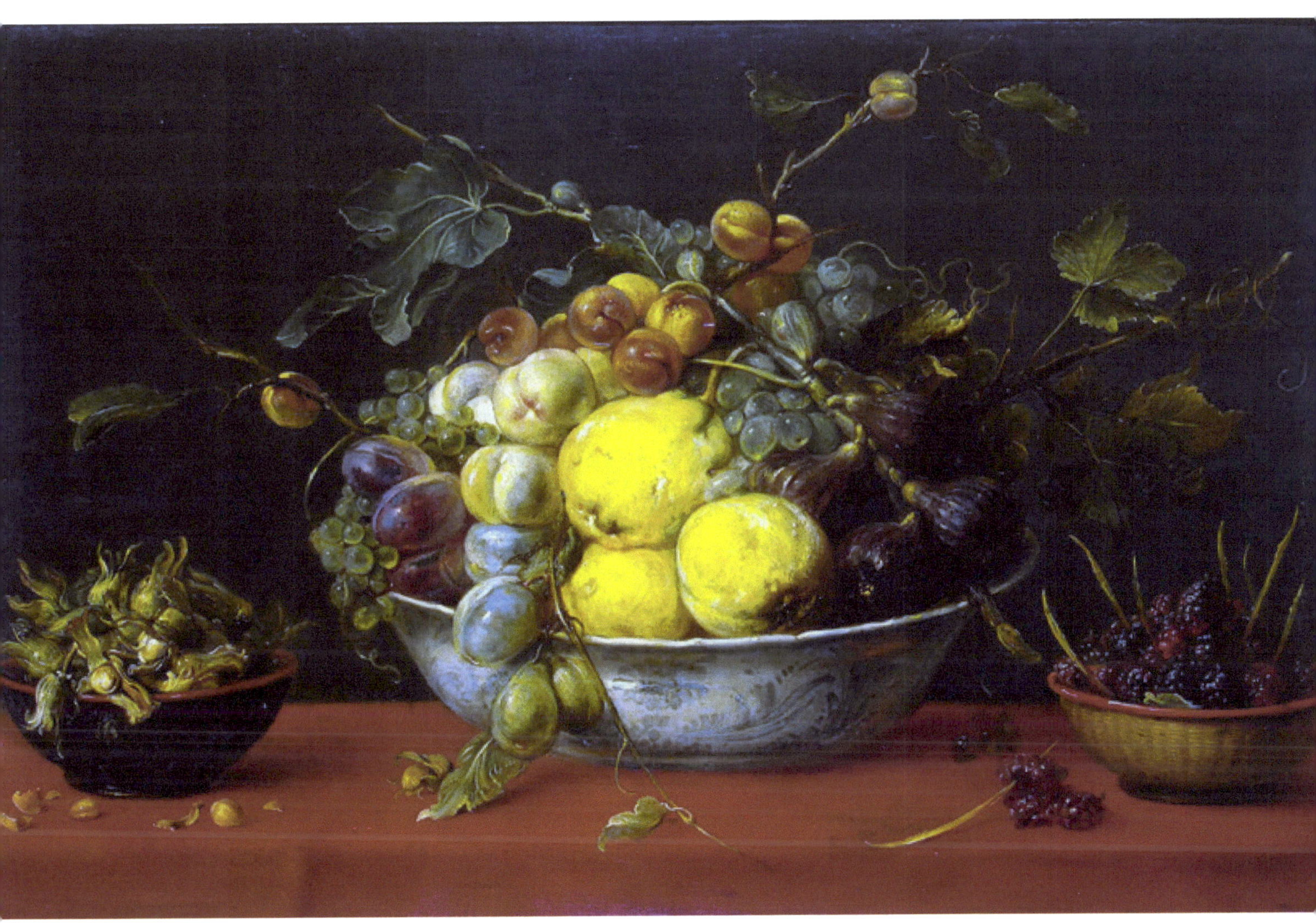

Fruits in a bowl on red tablecloth, 1640   59.8 x 90.8 cm

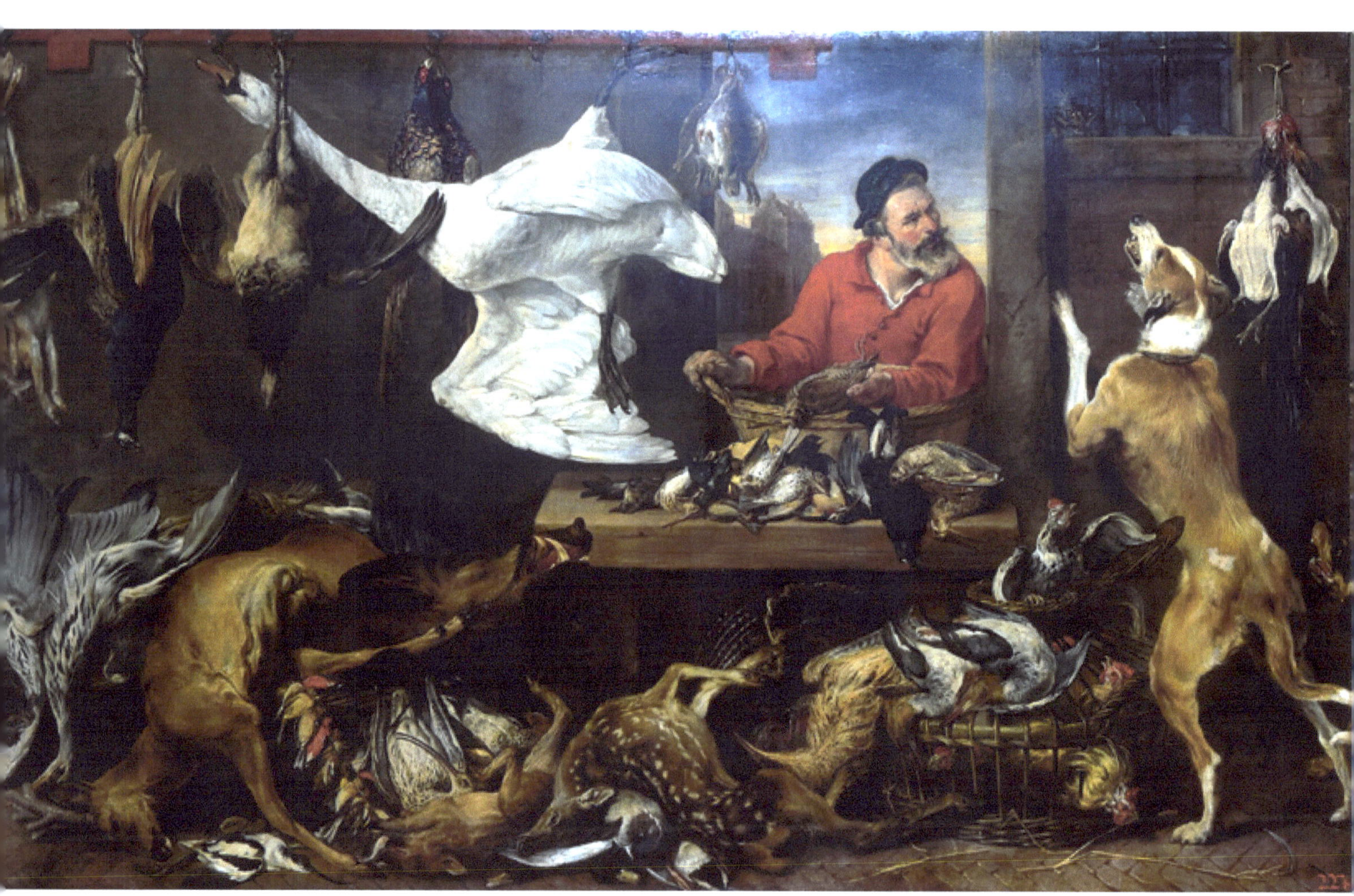

Game Shop (together with Jan Wildens), c.1618-21   207 x 341 cm

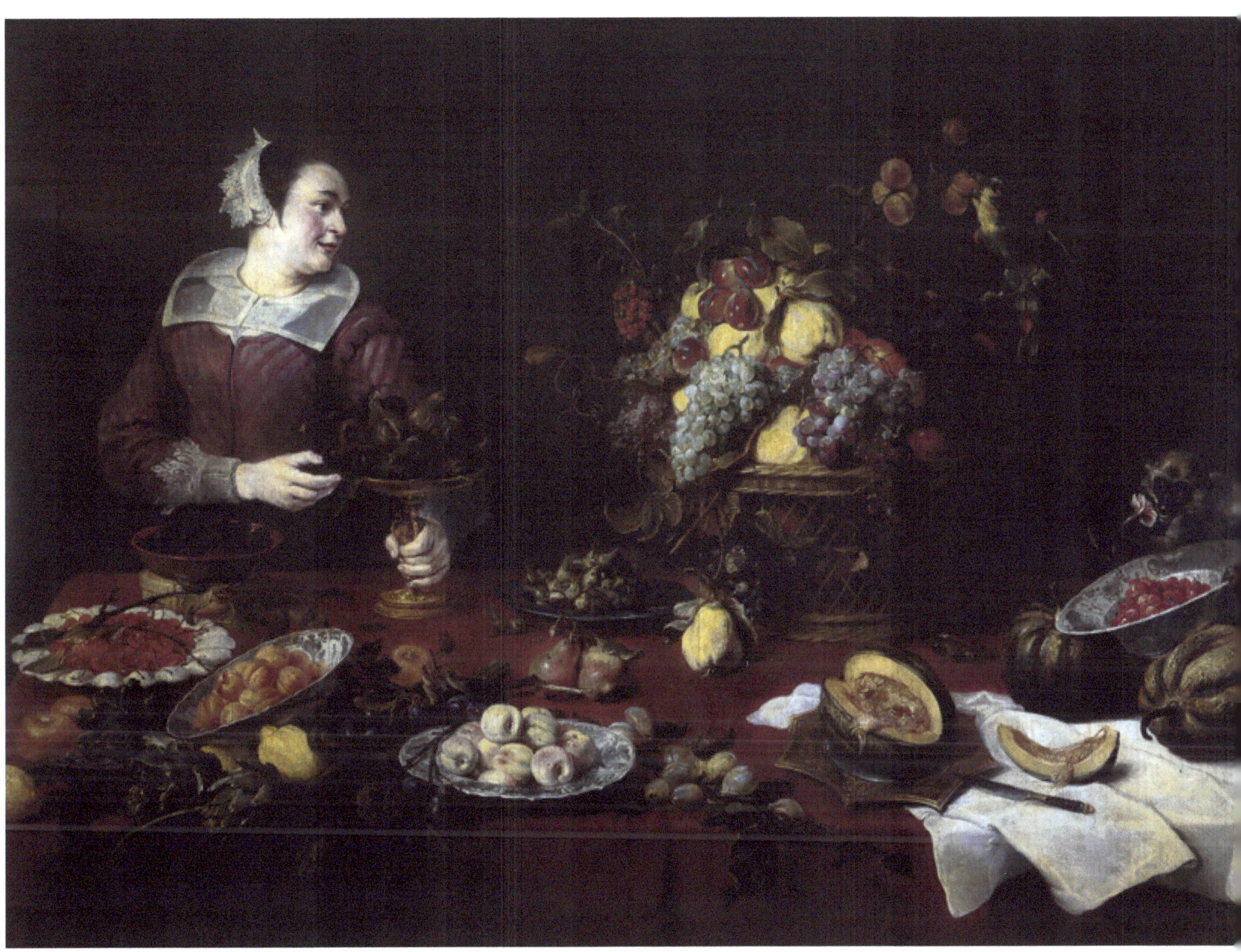

Girl with fruit, c.1633 153 x 214 cm

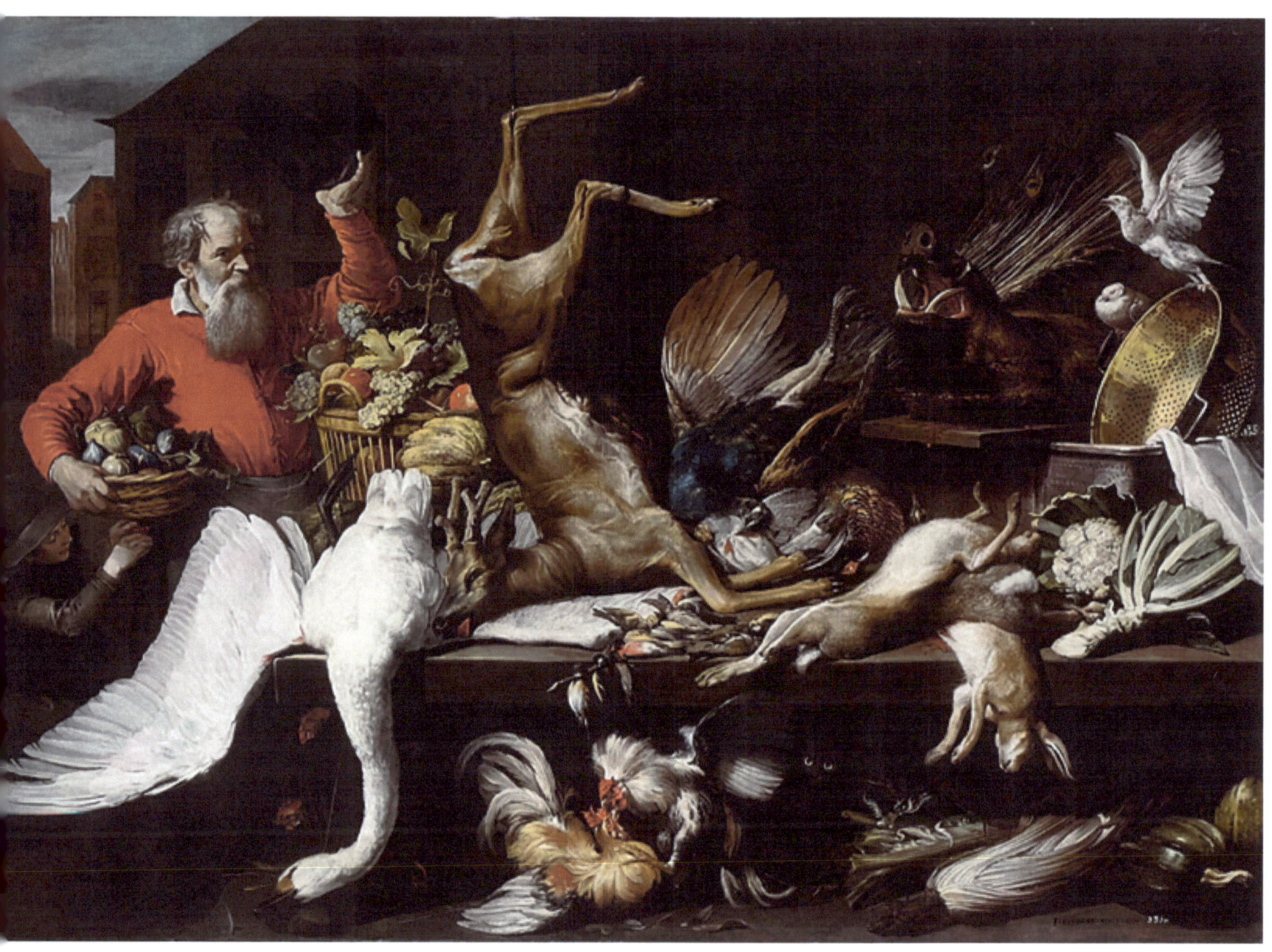

Grocery shop, 1614   212 x 308 cm

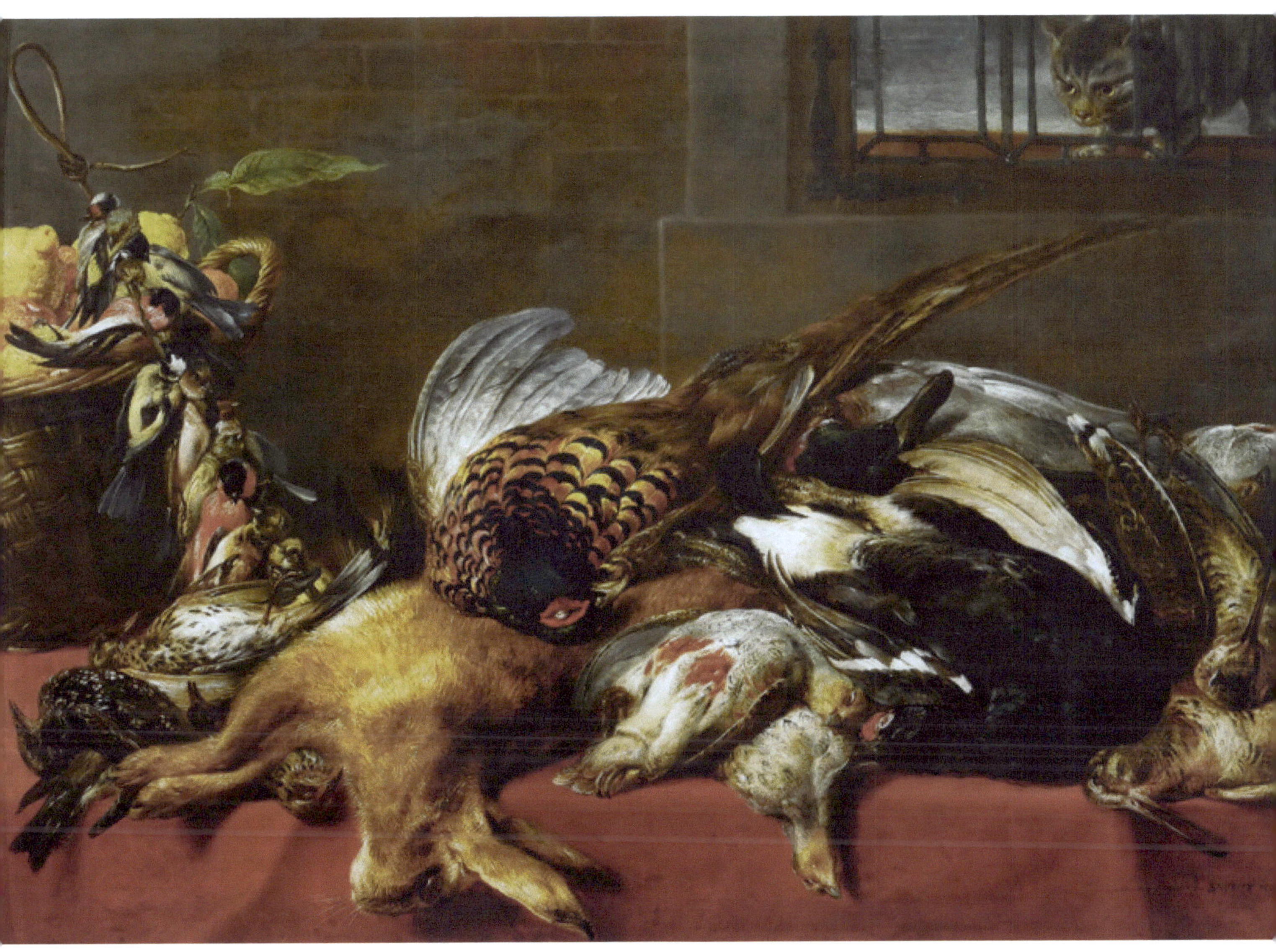

Hunting Still Life, 1640s

75 x 107 cm

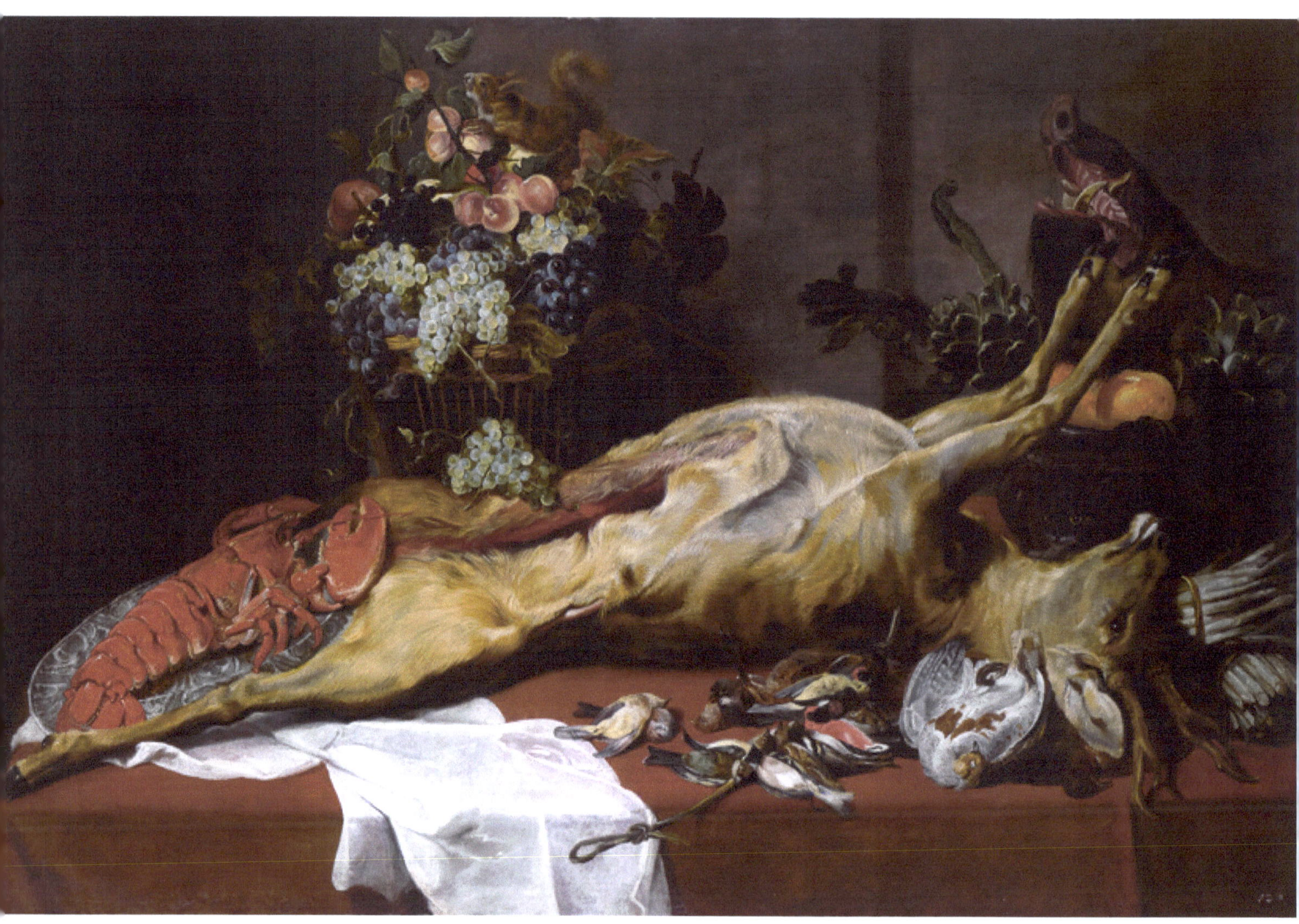

Still life with roe and lobster

117 x 179 cm

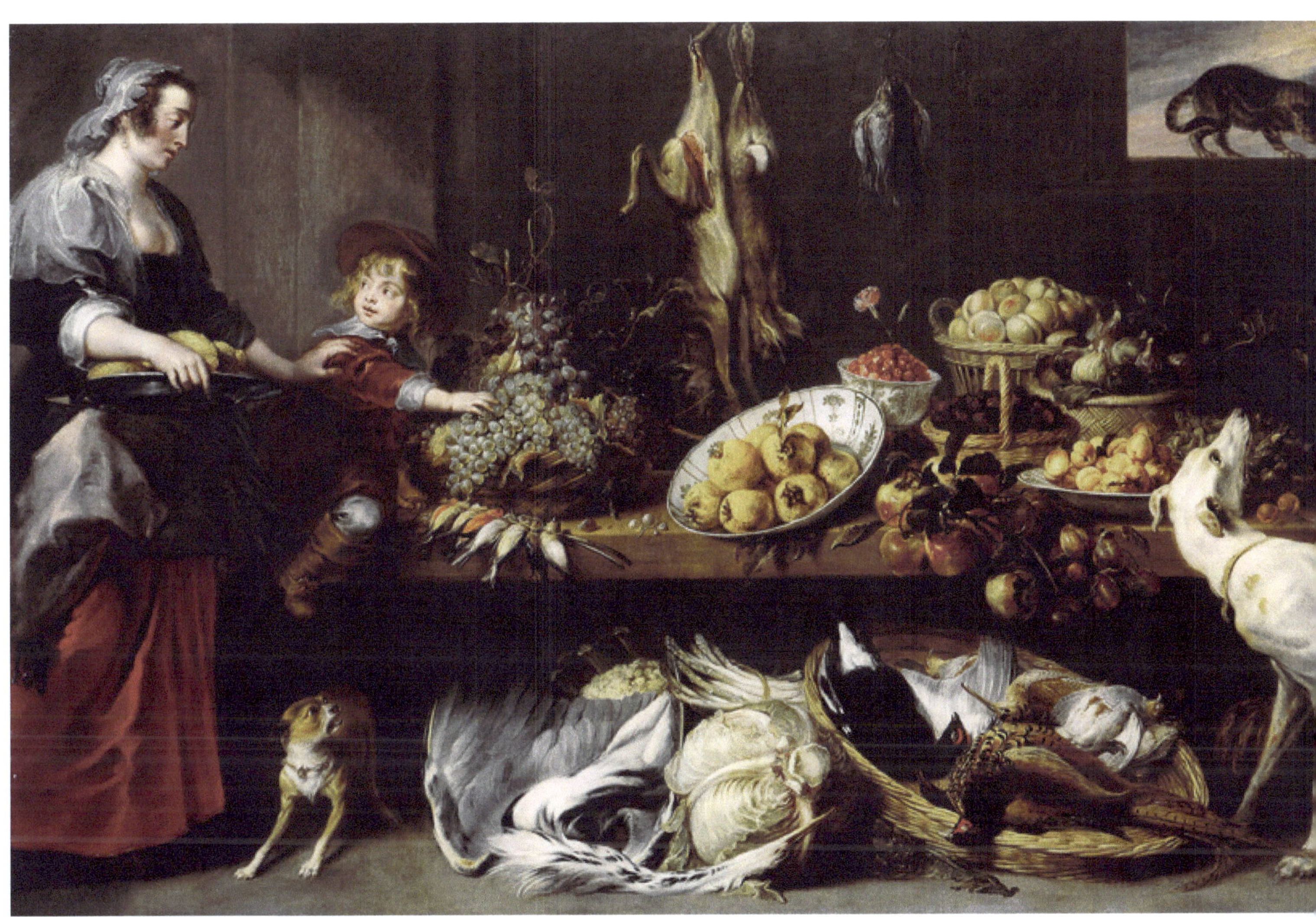

Still life with a maid and a boy   152 x 240 cm

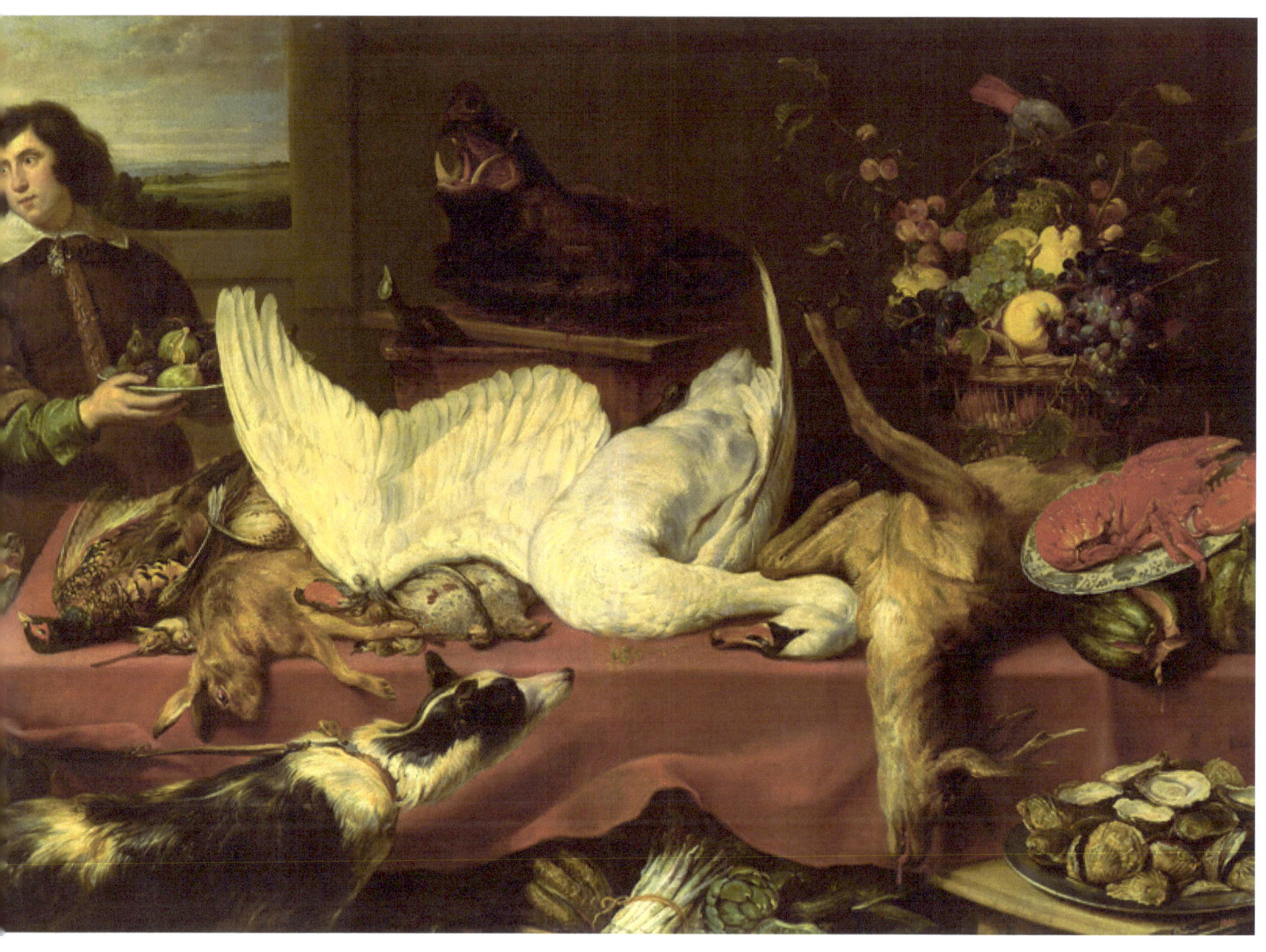

162.5 x 235 cm

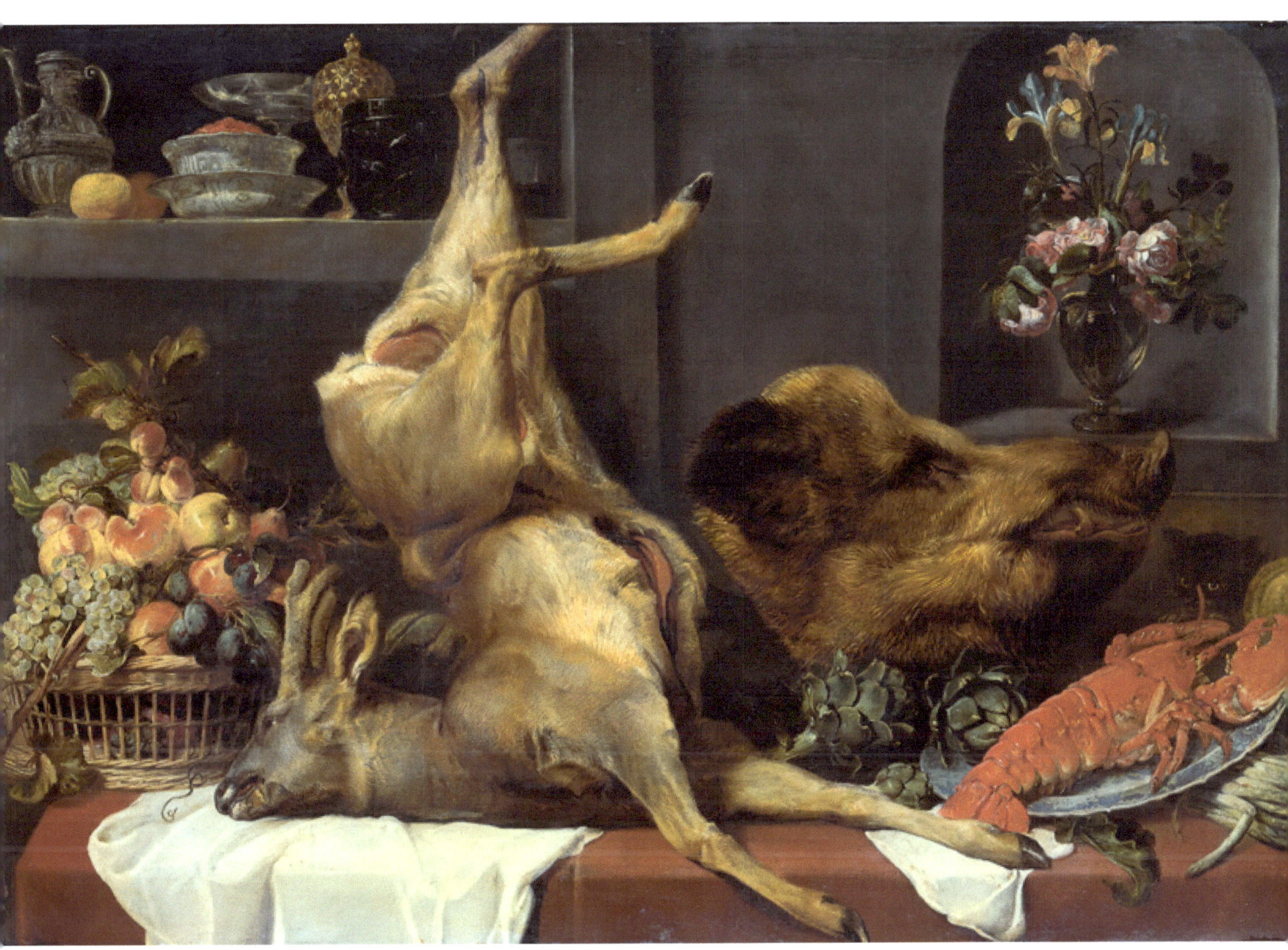

Still life with deer and wild boar head, lobster and fruit, c.1657

120.5 x 176.5 cm

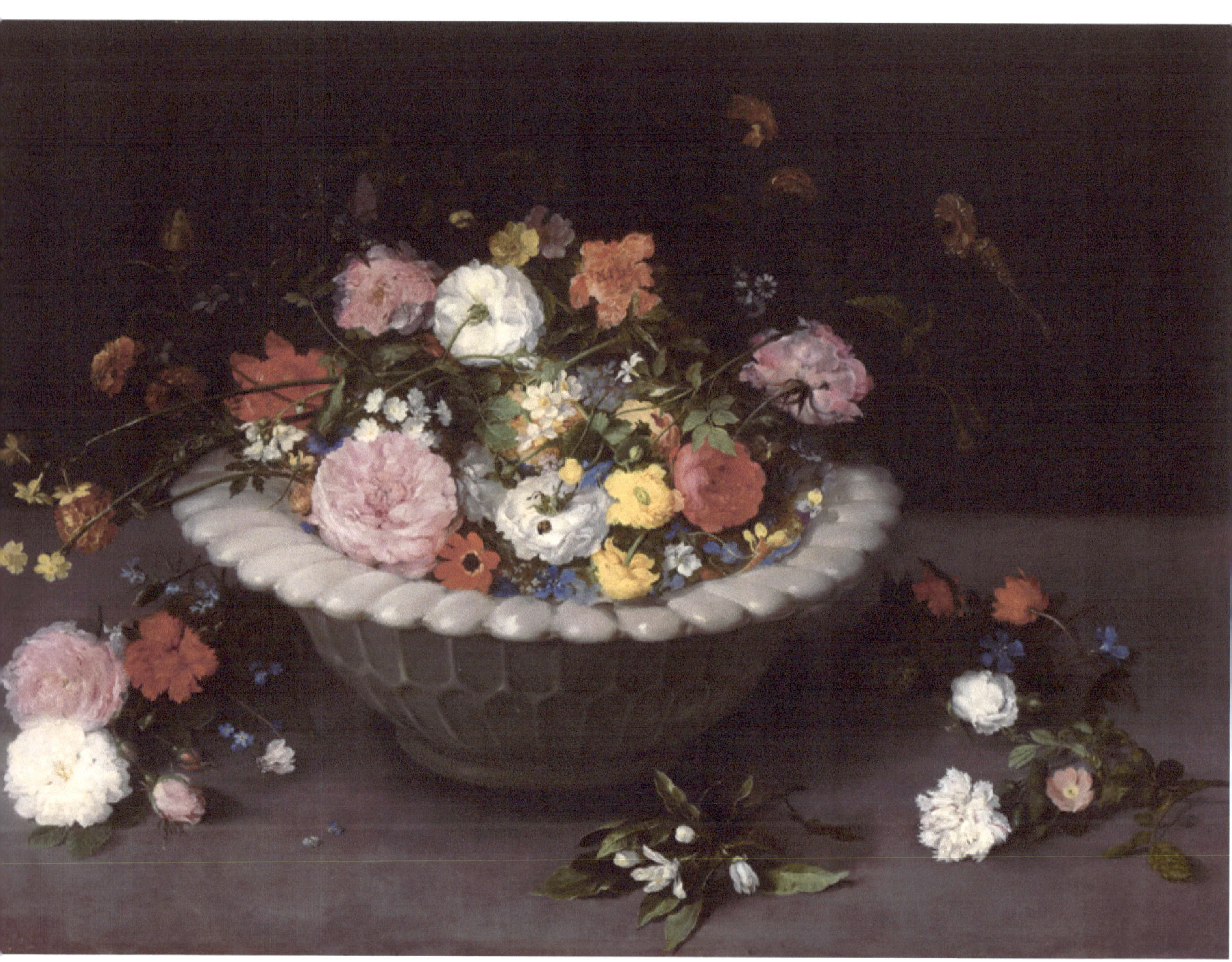

Still life with Flowers, 1615 44 x 66 cm

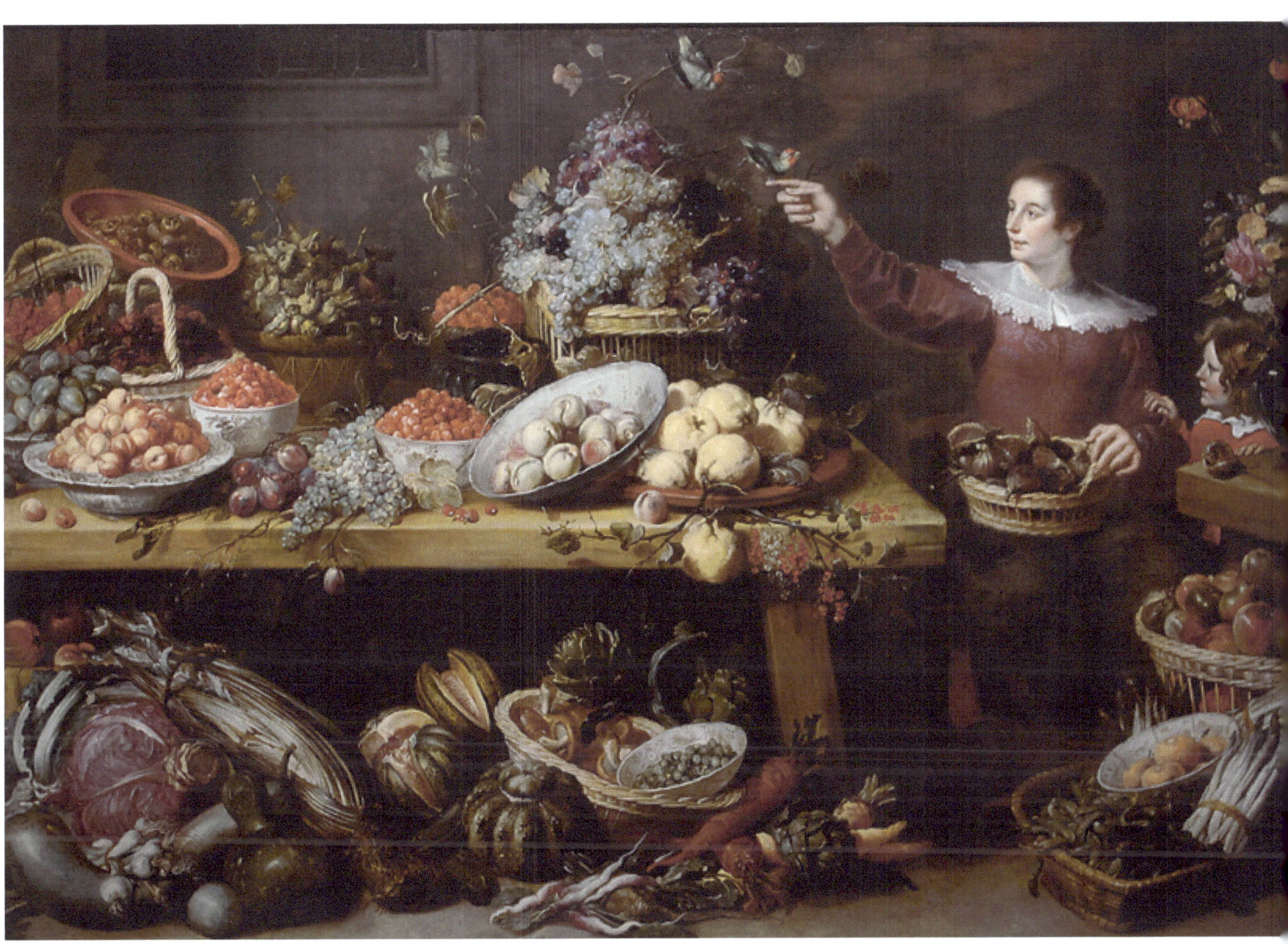

Still life with Fruit and vegetables, c.1600-50

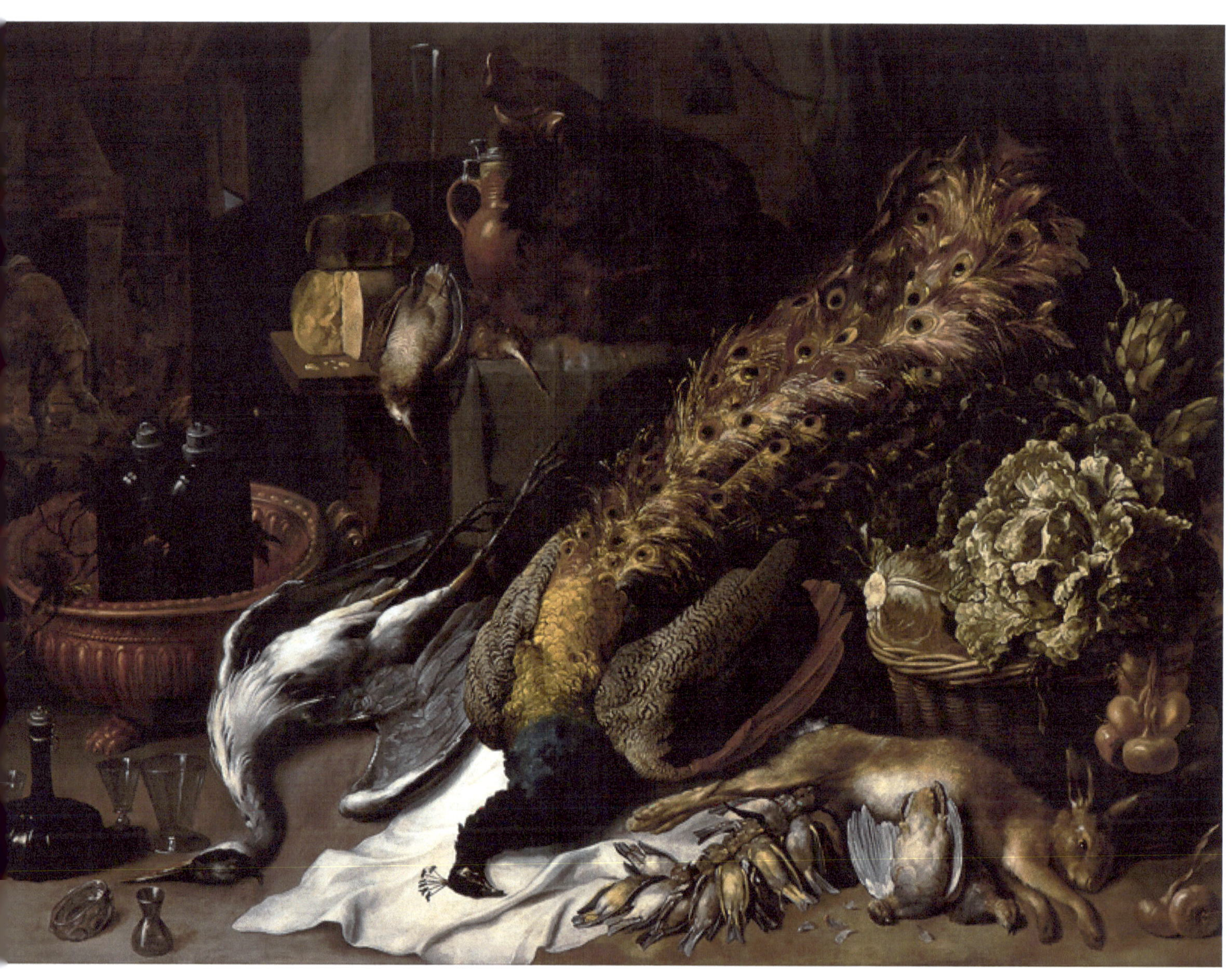

Still life with Game, 1610-20

165 x 230 cm

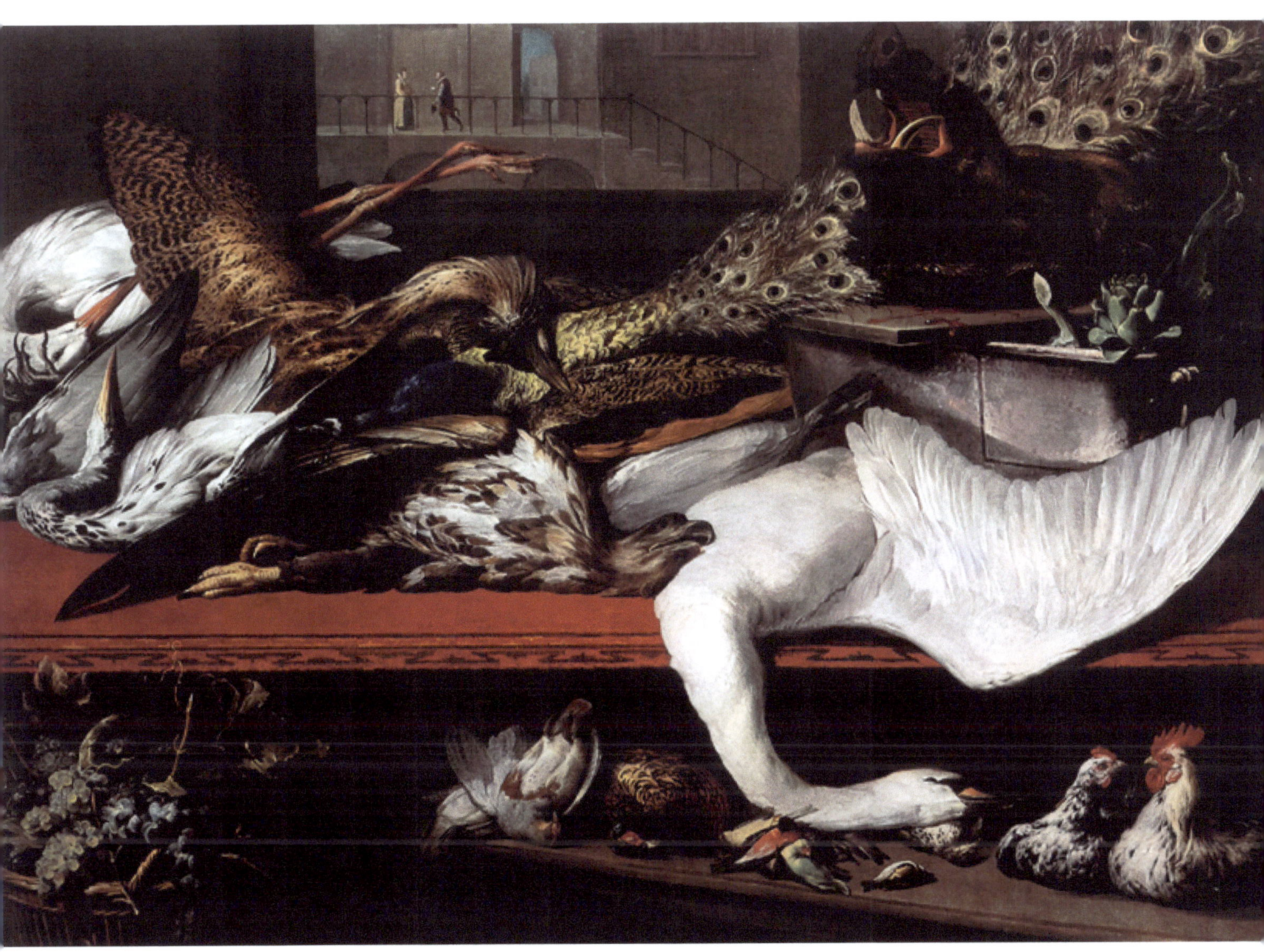

Still life with Game, 1614

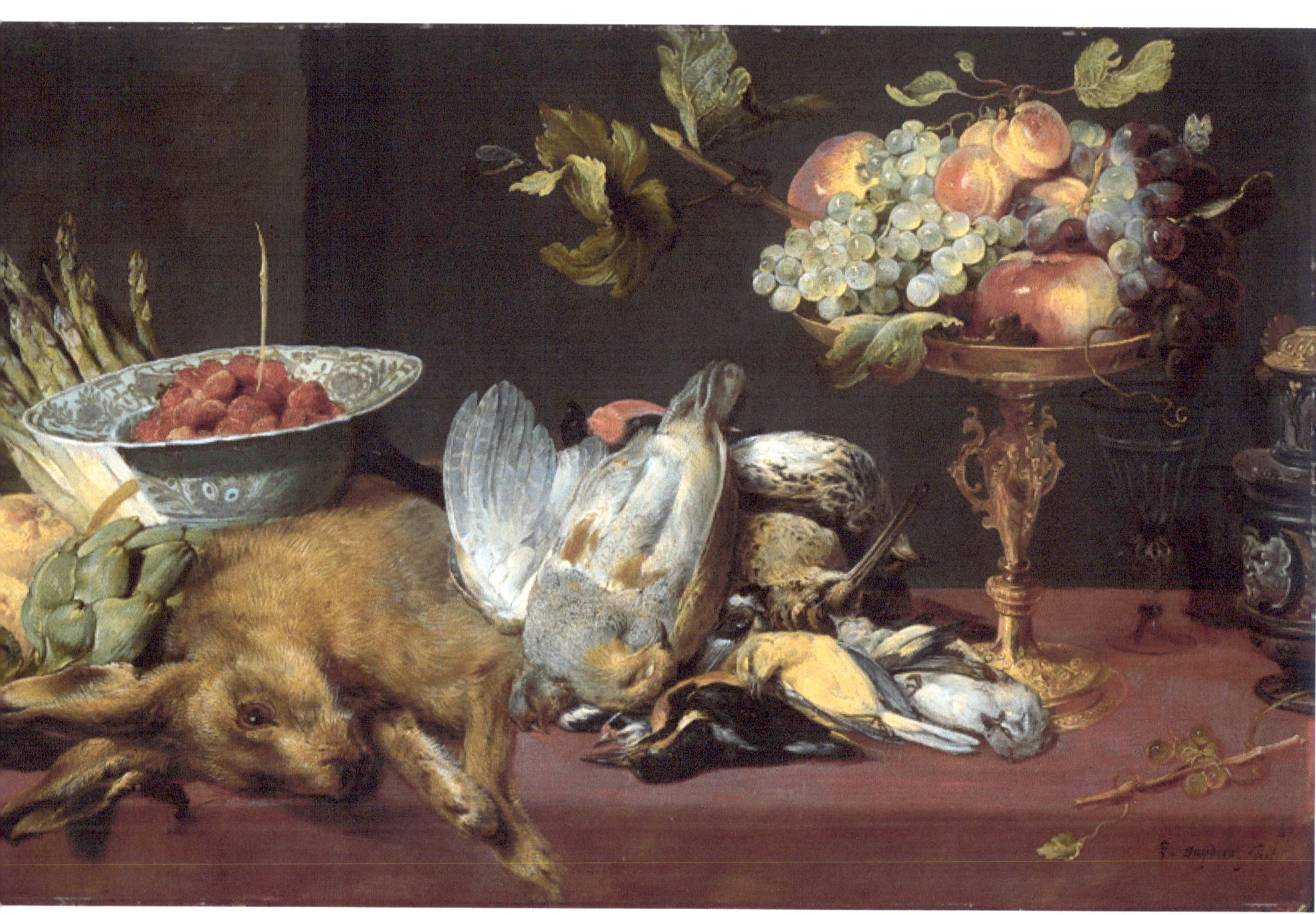

Still life with Game and Fruit, 1600-57

57 x 88 cm

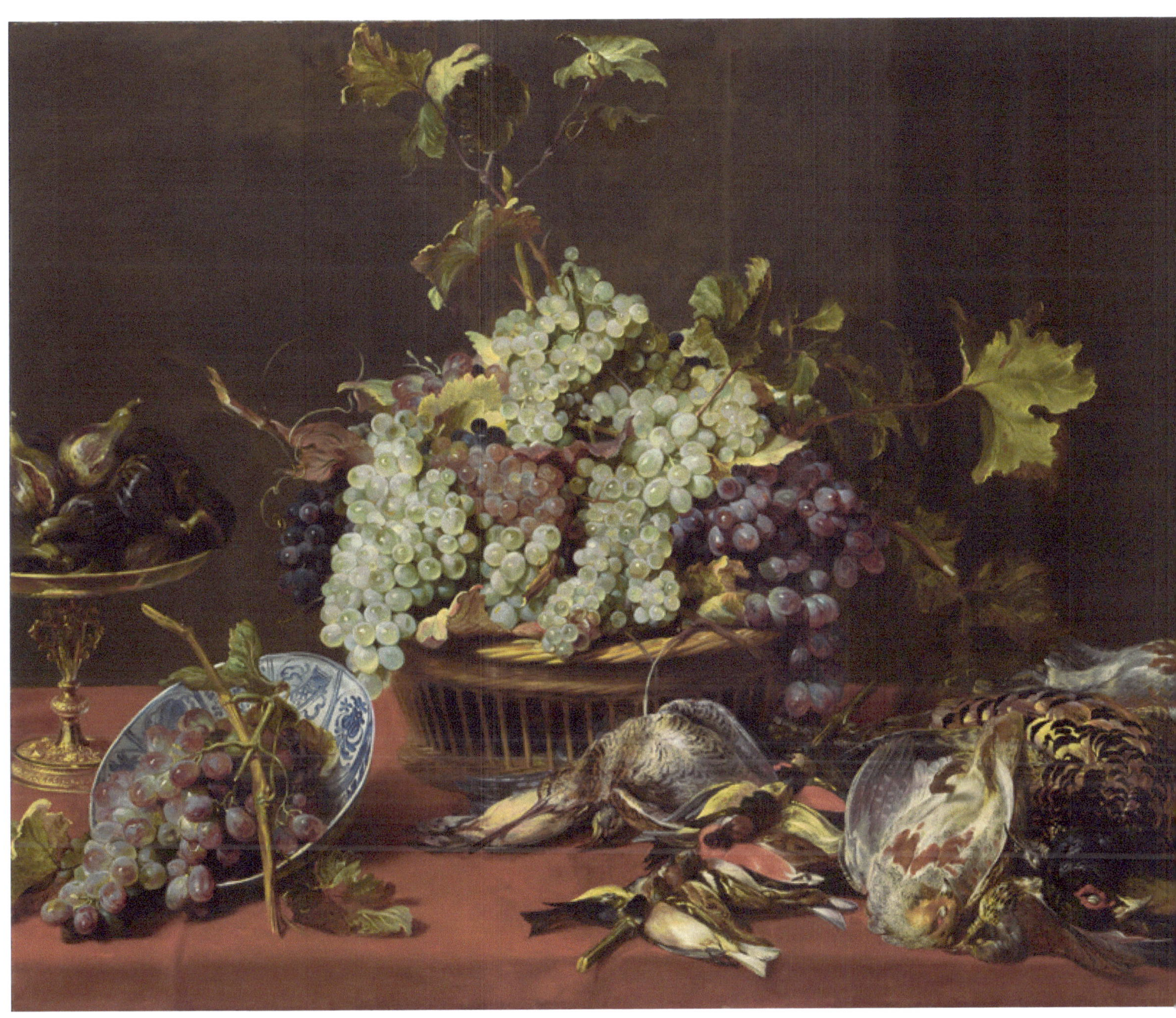

Still life with grapes and production, c.1630

90.2 x 112.1 cm

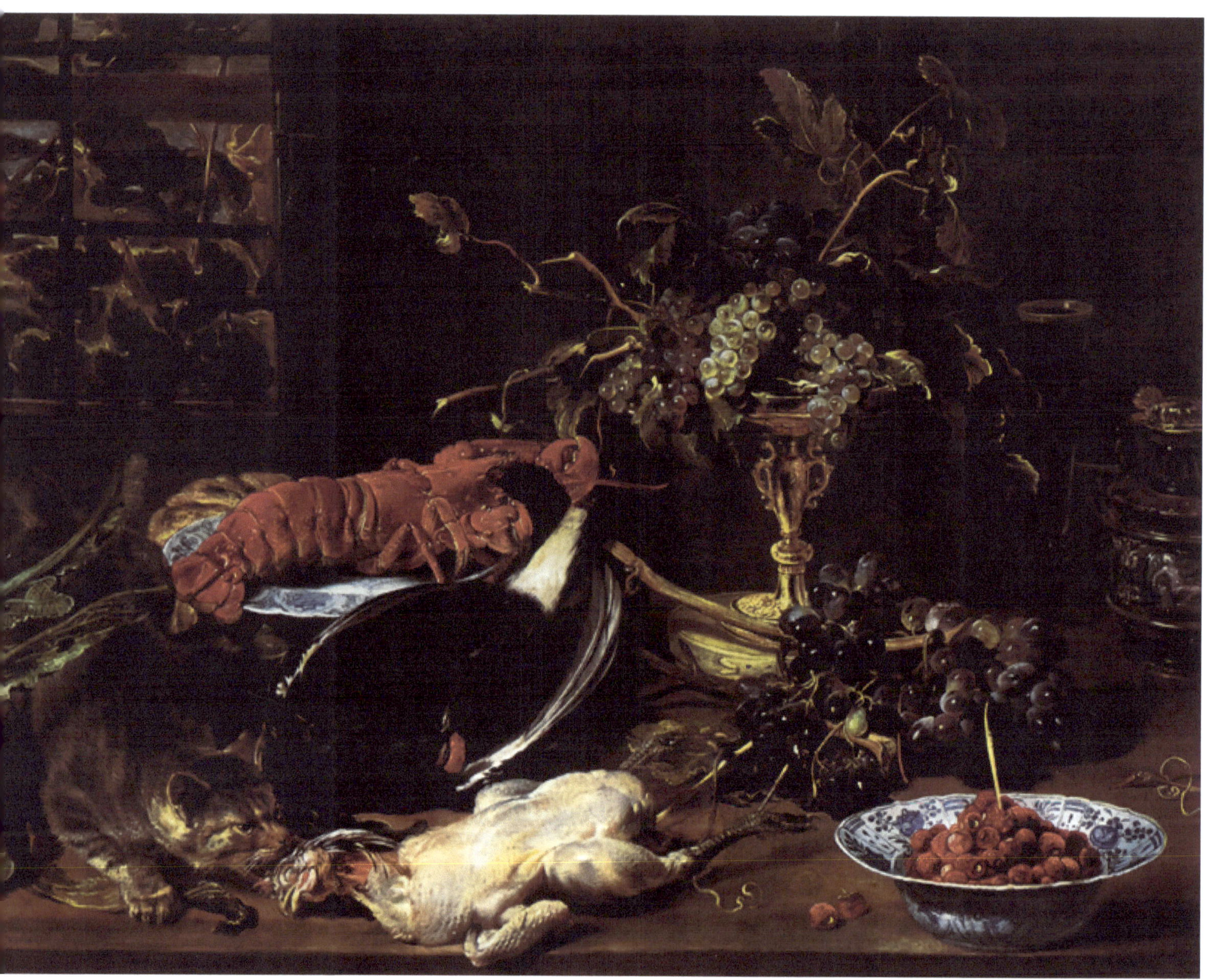

Still life with Lobster, c.1615-20

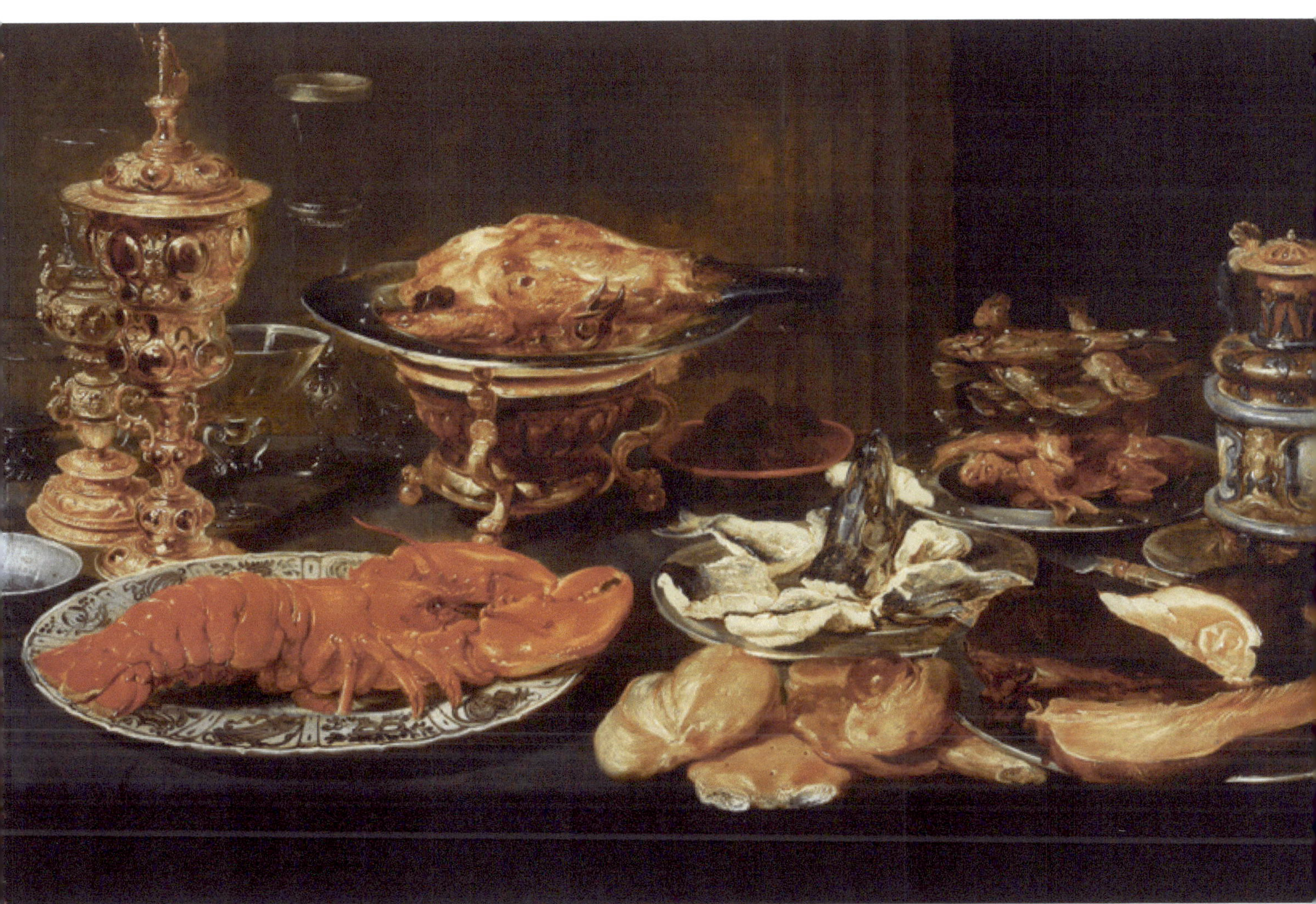

Still life with Lobster

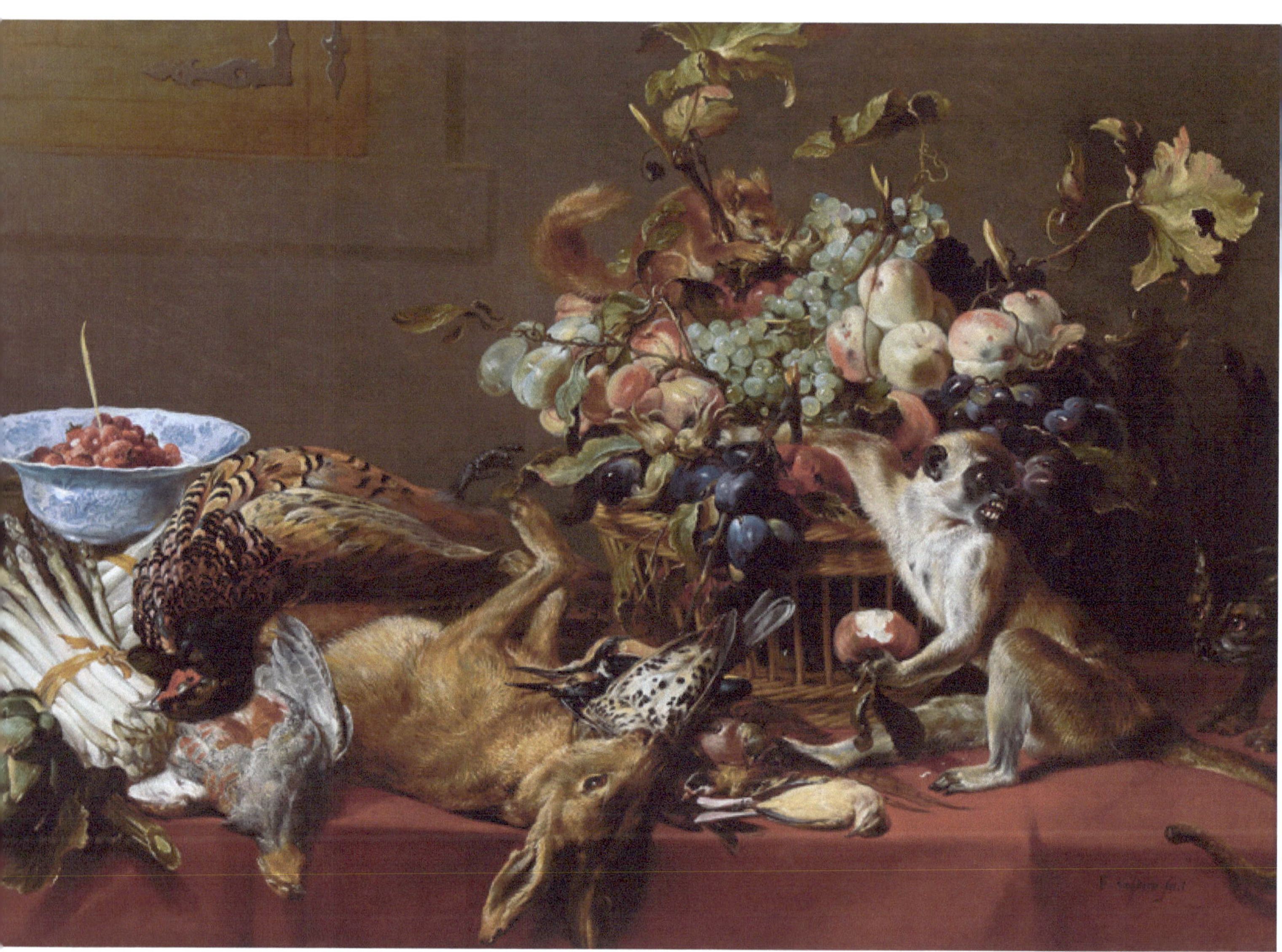

Still life with marmoset, cat and squirrel

81 x 118 cm

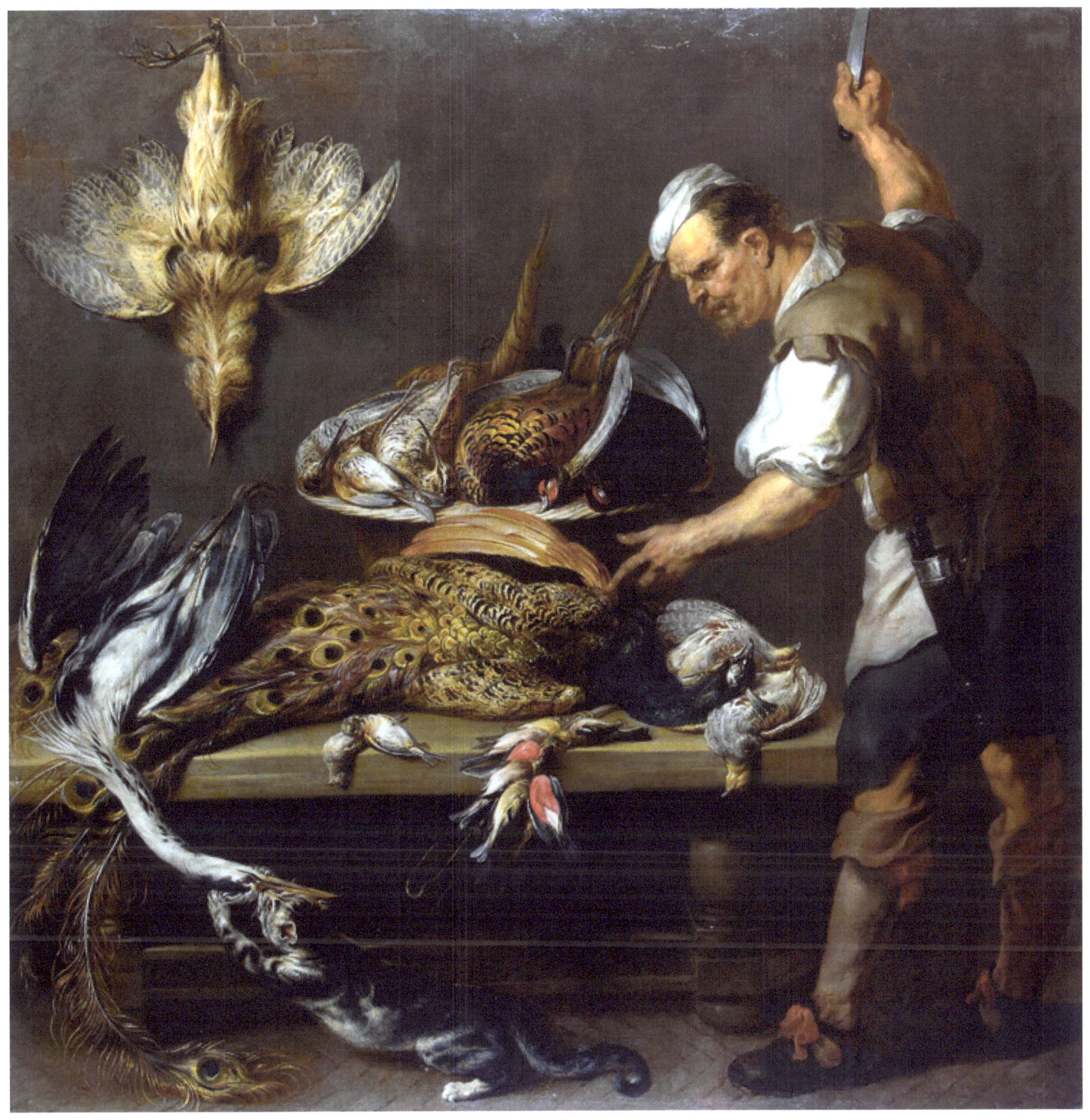

The chef at the table with game, 1634-37   171 x 173 cm

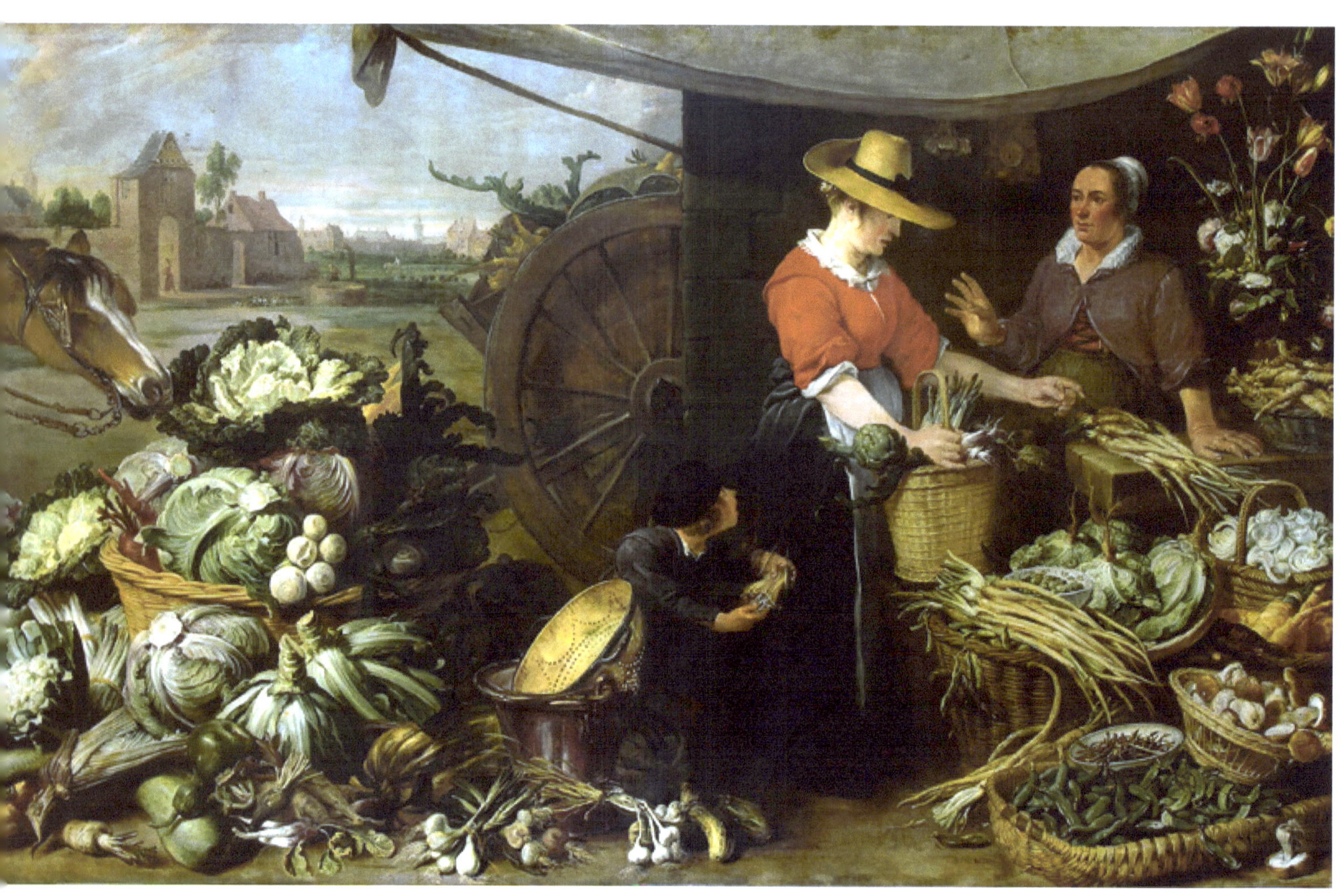

Floris Gerritsz van Schooten

c.1585/88 – 1656

Floris Gerritsz van Schooten is a Dutch painter famous for still life.

Van Schooten worked in the Dutch golden age when art and culture flourished in the Netherlands. He became famous for his artistic tendency at the time and for describing still life, especially banquet and kitchen scenes. His paintings often featured a variety of foods, tableware, and other things arranged in attentive and visually attractive ways. Van Schooten had an excellent eye for capturing texture, light, and shadows, so his work was full of realism and depth. He mainly painted still lifes but sometimes painted landscapes, the daily life of Dutch society, and scenes in that cultural nuances could be seen.

The exact date and place of the death of Floris Gerritsz van Schooten is not recorded, but it is estimated that he passed away in the Netherlands in 1656. Today, his works can be found in various museums and personal collections and you can see the artistic achievements of the Dutch golden age in his work.

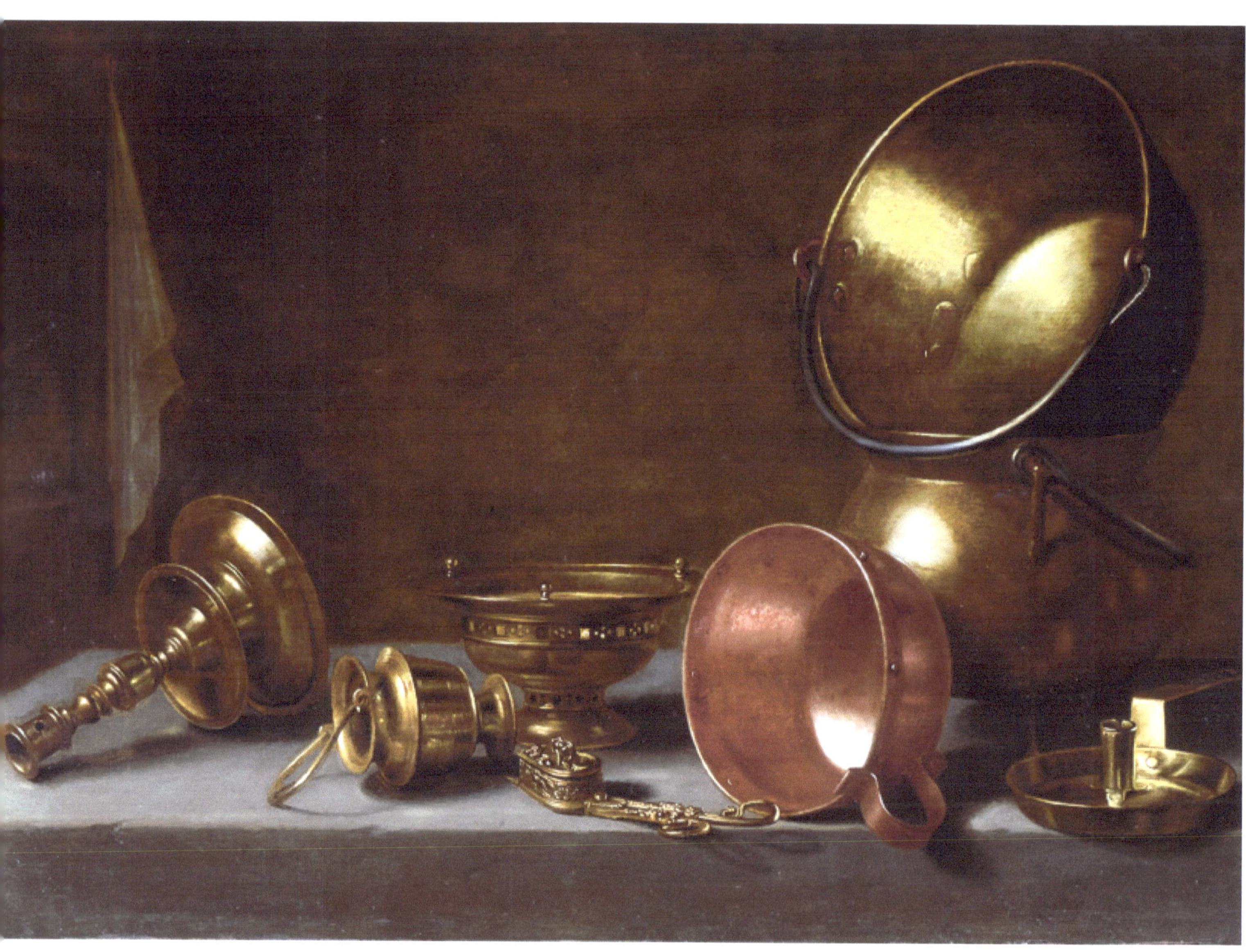

Still life with copper tableware, c.1655

51.7 x 74.5 cm

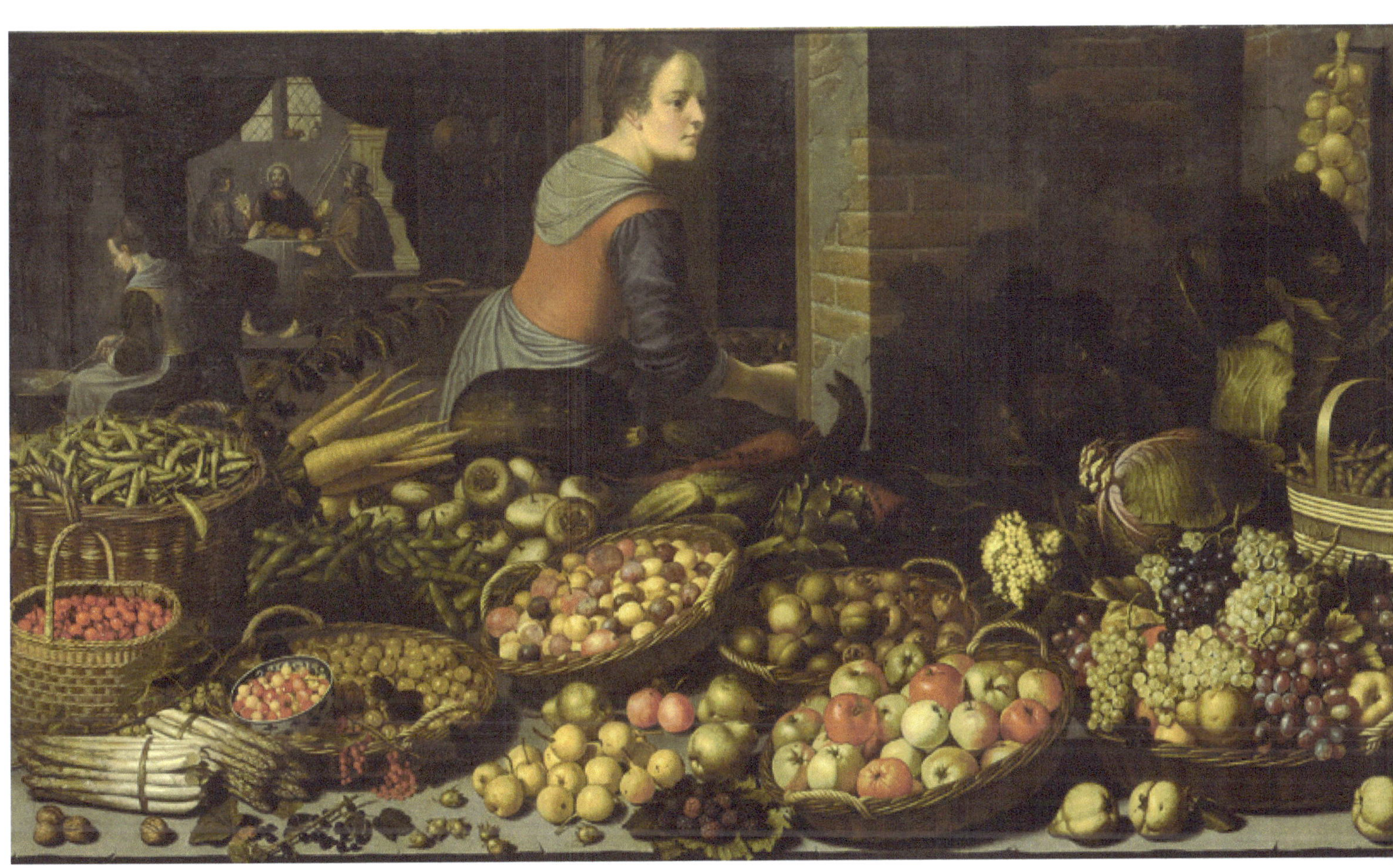

Still life with fruits, vegetables and dinner, 1651   113 x 200 cm

Into the details

Harmony of Animate and Inanimate Subjects_Genre Still Life

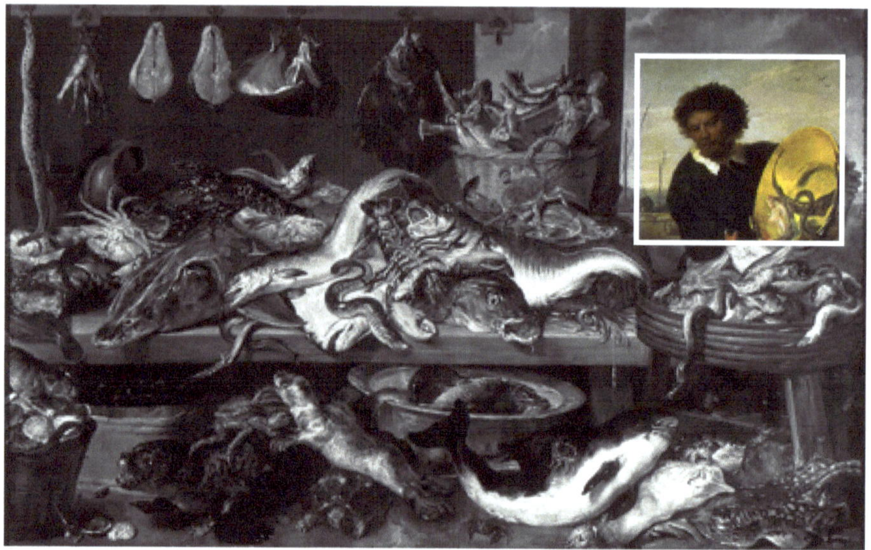

Fish Shop p.99
Frans Snyders

Still life is generally a painting that focuses on fruits, flowers, bowls, and other inani-mate objects placed in compositions. 'Fish Shop' by Frans Snyders with animated people is generally not considered to be traditional still life. However, there may be exceptions and transformations within the still life genre. In some cases, the artist can include animated people or animals in still life to add narratives or contextual elements. This composition is called "animation still life" or "genre still life" because it contains animated subjects. This transformation expands the traditional boundaries of still life and creates a dynamic and attractive work of art that combines the elements of still life and genre painting.